MW00580845

WITH OUR LABOR AND SWEAT

With Our Labor and Sweat

*Indigenous Women and the
Formation of Colonial Society
in Peru, 1550–1700*

KAREN B. GRAUBART

STANFORD UNIVERSITY PRESS

STANFORD, CALIFORNIA

Stanford University Press
Stanford, California

Printed in the United States of America on acid-free, archival-quality paper

Library of Congress Cataloging-in-Publication Data

Graubart, Karen B.
 With our labor and sweat : indigenous women and the formation of colonial
society in Peru, 1550–1700 / Karen B. Graubart.
    p. cm.
 Includes bibliographical references and index.
  ISBN-13: 978-0-8047-5355-5 (cloth : alk. paper)
  1. Inca women--Economic conditions. 2. Indian women—Peru—Economic con-
ditions. 3. Women—Peru—History. 4. Peru—Economic conditions. 5. Peru—
History—1548–1820. I. Title.
F3429.3.W65G73 2007
985'.02--dc22

                                                                    2007008797

Typeset by Thompson Type in 10/12.5 Palatino

Published with the assistance of the Hull Memorial Publication Fund of
Cornell University.

For Mateo

Contents

Map, Tables, and Figures

Acknowledgments

I have incurred many debts, personal and intellectual, large and small, during the process of writing this book. First, I must thank Carmen Diana Deere and Karen Spalding, who nurtured me and my work during many years of graduate school and since. Not only have they been exemplary intellectual inspirations, but also terrific models for being a humane and engaged scholar and teacher.

My institutional debts include the wonderful staff at the Archivo General de la Nación in Lima, particularly Yolanda Auqui Chávez and Alex Escobedo Hinostroza; Laura Gutiérrez Arbulú and the staff of the Archivo Arzobispal de Lima; Srta. Imelda Solano Galavetta of the Archivo Arzobispal de Trujillo; and most especially Director Napoleón Cieza Burga, Martha Chandavi Céspedes, Silvia Romero Benites, and the deeply missed Walter Arteaga Liñan, of the Archivo Regional de La Libertad in Trujillo. I was warmly welcomed at the Instituto Riva-Agüero and supported by my friends and colleagues Carlos Gálvez Peña, Ada Arrieto, and Renzo Honores. I was fortunate to receive the assistance of the late Dr. Franklin Pease G.Y. and Dr. José de la Puente Cándamo, both at the Pontificia Universidad Católica; and María Rostworowski and Carlos Contreras, of the Instituto de Estudios Peruanos, were generous with their time and resources.

In the United States, I found a lovely temporary home at the John Carter Brown Library in Providence, where I held a Ruth and Lincoln Ekstrom Fellowship in 1997. Not only did this provide me with a gorgeous setting and spectacular resources, but one of the most intriguing and provocative groups of colleagues imaginable. Many conversations with Susan Niles, David Murray, Rich Rath, and others colored the writing of this book.

I have received financial assistance for this project from many generous sources: the Fulbright Program funded my initial dissertation research in Peru (1995–96); the American Association of University Women funded much of the writing-up process through their American Fellowships (1996–97); later research trips were supported by a trio of Cornell University's academic resources: the President's Council on Cornell Women, the Society for the Humanities, and the History Department; as well as an Albert J. Beveridge Grant from the American Historical Association.

Many other friends and colleagues, in Peru and in the United States, have provided invaluable assistance through their friendship and scholarly conversations. Juan Castañeda Murga made Trujillo a fascinating and lively place for me, through his apparently boundless historical knowledge and wonderful outings to visit archaeological sites. In Trujillo, Rosalía and María Kemper and the Castro-Obando family all provided me with comfortable homes and ad hoc extended families. Béatrice Raboud González was an engaging housemate and friend, and I must give special thanks to the Távara family, particularly Pepe and Charo, for being my family abroad. A short list of those who vitally contributed to my intellectual development as this book was written includes Susana Aldana, Carollee Bengelsdorf, Michelle Bigenho, James K. Boyce, S. Charusheela, Colin Danby, Monisha Das Gupta, Dora Dumont, Tamara Loos, Teodoro Hampe Martínez, Jane Mangan, Susie Minchin, Karoline Noack, Rachel O'Toole, Susanne Pohl, Ana María Presta, Karen Powers, Rich Rath, and Nancy van Deusen. Stanford University Press chose two exceptional readers for my manuscript: Susan Ramírez and Kymm Gauderman provided constructive, informed, and supportive comments that helped me move toward the final stage. The manuscript also benefited from careful readings by Derek Chang, Marikay McCabe, and Kathryn Burns (multiple times!). I feel particularly fortunate in my affiliation with Stanford University Press. Norris Pope has been a model editor: efficient, straightforward, and just delightful to deal with.

Finally, I offer heartfelt thanks to my friends and family for putting up with my belated trip to graduate school and my constant to-and-fro across continents. My mother Sylvia and brother Barry have contributed material as well as emotional support. I am sorry that my father Hyman did not live to see this work, but his sense of humor certainly kept me sane through its writing. And most important of all, thanks to Mateo for showing me what really matters in life: cats, fans, water fountains. I am grateful that you will be able to accompany me on the adventures still to come.

WITH OUR LABOR AND SWEAT

Introduction

IN APRIL 1653 FRANCISCA RAMÍREZ, an indigenous resident of Trujillo, Peru, received a notary in her home on what she thought might be her deathbed. The notary, a Spaniard named Antonio Álvarez, took down the careful instructions for her funeral services and burial in the convent church of San Francisco: she should be dressed in the brown habit of the Franciscan order and laid to rest in the chapel of San Antonio de Padua, where she had already made financial arrangements with the prelates. Álvarez filled more of the six double-sided pages of the document with the names of her debtors and creditors, a list of bequests, and a detailed inventory of her worldly possessions: her houses, jewelry, religious images, furniture, bedclothes, and a substantial assortment of clothing. The document describes the provenance of many of these luxurious items: Chinese damask, a small green shawl of Castillian *bayeta* cloth with three rows of gold trim and purple taffeta edging, an embroidered altar cloth from Quito, and two small wooden chests from Belgium. Despite her position as a non-European woman in a small city in colonized South America, the vast majority of her personal effects were items either imported from Europe or those that had been fashioned by local tailors and artisans from imported materials.[1]

While Ramírez's inventory of goods encompassed her significant personal wealth, it also represented items for sale in her store. In addition to imported silks and pearl and gold necklaces, she also sold large quantities of the corn beer of indigenous origin, *chicha*, as evidenced by a debt for thirty pesos' worth of corn owed to the royal treasurer don Diego Quirós. The clothing for sale in her store appears to be all after the European fashion—shawls, skirts, bodices, blouses—and only one item was referred to with indigenous-language terminology, a velvet *lliclla* or rectangular shawl, "still to be made." An earlier will, dated 1633, makes it clear that she had originally had an indigenous clientele, who purchased from her moveable stall (not yet a store) chicha and Andean women's dresses called *anacos*, worn with the lliclla, though these were made in fabrics other than the more traditional hand-loomed cotton and wool of the Andes. And by the time of what appears to be her fourth and final will, 1686, her entire inventory could not be distinguished from that of a Spanish woman of moderate income.[2] This might indicate that her clientele had shifted toward Spaniards and mestizos, or it might mean that tastes among urban elites of all ethnicities were converging in these styles.

Francisca Ramírez is provocative for those of us who study gender and ethnicity under Spanish colonial rule. First, she left at least four wills and a number of other documents bearing her name, allowing us to compose at least a partial picture of an Indian woman building a career and a fortune in a moderate-sized urban center over the better part of a long lifetime. Although most indigenous women (or men for that matter) did not leave such extensive paper trails, it is frankly difficult to peruse colonial records without coming across contracts and wills in their names, giving us at least some new perspective on their lives. Ramírez's case offers, through her many interactions with the notary, unusual insight into the experience of urban indigenous women in seventeenth century Peru.

Second, Ramírez maneuvered through ethnic identifications and social classes in a way that suggests that these categories were fluid and contestatory. In early wills, she appeared as "Francisca Ramírez *yndia*"; in later ones, she was simply "Francisca Ramírez," with no ethnic marker at all, and at the end of her life she was "doña Francisca Ramírez *yndia*," acquiring the Spanish marker of hereditary nobility while returning to her juridical status of "Indian." She exercised her profession in her own name with little apparent difficulty, despite legal restrictions on married women's economic activities. She served a clientele that encompassed caciques (the indigenous nobility) and elite Spaniards as well as servants, artisans, plebeian Indians, and free and enslaved Africans, according to her accounts. Thus her story enables us to question the longstanding notion that there were meaningful, stable ethnic identities in early colonial Peru and clear-cut social divisions between genders, ethnicities, and classes, in at least some settings.

Third, although Ramírez was married twice, to men apparently of Spanish descent, she was adamant that all her wealth came from her own exertion and entrepreneurship. In testamentary language common to many men and women of the period, indigenous and Spaniard alike, she calculated what had come from her own "labor and sweat" in clear acknowledgment that colonial law protected her dowry and her half of the couple's earnings during marriage. We should not take her at her word, of course: her first husband, a carpenter who "brought nothing whatsoever" to her in marriage, did operate what might have been her (or their) first store in his name between 1637 and 1641, and this could represent the expansion of her business from selling from a *cajón* or portable trunk in the plaza of Trujillo to a more permanent establishment with a better clientele.[3] But Ramírez appears to have flourished on her own, and was quick to use legal means to defend her interests, including a demand for an ecclesiastical divorce from her second husband and lawsuits against a tenant for arrears.[4]

Francisca Ramírez was certainly an uncommon individual in her time. Her successes, however, suggest that she was particularly good at taking advantage of factors that existed for others as well. The new cash and credit economy; a legal system offering redress to indigenous as well as African and Spanish complainants; Catholic community organizations that provided capital as well as moral support for their memberships; multiple identity and status codes including European, indigenous, and transculturated dress and hair styles—all these were factors that allowed Peru's colonial inhabitants to move, however slightly and sometimes dramatically, up and down the social scale.

Because of their structural position within the new political economy of colonial Peru, indigenous women (among other subordinate groups) were largely excluded from top-down political processes, such as the writing of legal codes; the administration of the bureaucracy; and the enforcement of ecclesiastical, civil, and criminal laws. However, none of these legal, economic or social systems were perfectly imposed upon the subaltern colonial populations. They were negotiated, contested, and ignored, often in surprising ways. The traces of how these systems came to function within colonial society produce a history of the actions of those excluded from the highest levels; in this case, of indigenous women.

Studying Gender in the Andes

This study follows in the footsteps of many scholars, who have participated in a long and sometimes contentious dialogue about gender in the Andean regions. The pioneer in Peruvian gender studies is indisputably

María Rostworowski, whose attention to the histories of women in social organization virtually created the field (and identified many of the
major and more obscure sources). Rostworowski has tirelessly located
(mainly elite) women in the historical record and worked to identify the
social structures affecting gender relations in prehispanic and colonial
Peru. For example, and important for the context of this study, her 1961
analysis of litigation documents from the north coast of Peru demonstrated that, at least in some isolated cases, indigenous women held
political office, with prehispanic precedent.[5] Her attention to the ethno-
histories—histories that do not start with the colonial period but reach
back into prehispanic times as well—of the less-studied coast as well as
the Inca highlands has provided a refreshing and sometimes unexpected
perspective, one that has not always been taken up by subsequent historians of gender.[6]

Although Peruvian gender studies began with Rostworowski's
work on the coast, the biggest single splash came from the highlands,
with Irene Silverblatt's provocative and polemical *Moon, Sun, and
Witches*, published in 1987. Silverblatt's theses—that gender was a key
component of prehispanic social organization and an important tool in
the series of conquests (both Inca and Hispanic) that transformed Andean relations, and that women's political roles, once nearly equal to
men's in their own parallel sphere, grew increasingly more restricted
and exploitative with each wave of gendered conquest—place gender
at the center of understanding communities, states, and empire. Her
work concludes, somewhat controversially, that indigenous women
suffered disproportionately under Spanish rule, especially the poor, as
sexual and economic victims. The heroes of her story are rural women,
who were said to have fled to the puna or high scrublands of the Andes
in active resistance of colonial rule. Some of Silverblatt's more colorful
arguments have now been revisited and challenged, but her recognition of the relationship between social organization and gender has
been key in setting the tone for gender studies in the Andes and Latin
America more generally.[7]

A contrasting position has been put forth by Elinor Burkett, whose
studies of notarial records in the coastal city of Arequipa argue that
not only did indigenous women experience the conquest differently
than their male counterparts, but they acculturated relatively better
than men and in many cases prospered, due at least in part to their
proximity to Spanish households, as servants and marketeers.[8] These
findings must, however, be modulated: Burkett's sample came from

wills and other notarial instruments that heavily favored more successful women. Those who did not acculturate as well left few records, with important exceptions such as the seventeenth-century census of household servants analyzed by Luis Miguel Glave, who argues that household servants were among the most miserable members of colonial society, lacking ties to their birth communities and forced to participate in petty manufacturing in addition to their domestic service.[9] Glave's contention that the failure to maintain ties to natal communities indicates social dislocation is, to my mind, unsubstantiated, but there is no doubt that his investigation properly complicates Burkett's rosier picture.

Works like those of Burkett and Silverblatt, among the first scholars to pay critical attention to women in the Andes, were more than occasionally polemical and tended to utilize universal categories like "women" while speaking of members of particular classes, ethnicities, and locations. They also tended to calculate women's lives in terms of singular categories of "progress" or "loss," treating gender history as a zero-sum game with winners and losers. As Karen Powers has argued, these are part of a larger trend of studies of women in colonial Latin America that have seen women solely in terms of victimhood, be it economic or sexual exploitation.[10] But as social historians have more generally shifted to smaller regional settings and more restricted prognoses, historians of gender have also looked at specific populations and circumstances, offering the possibility of more nuanced and less dichotomous analyses.

Most important, historians place the intersections of gender, class, and ethnicity at the center of their studies, allowing our stories to take complex trajectories that suggest both larger patterns for social groups as well as the possibility that individuals might have various options within society. Ann Zulawski, for example, has studied urban indigenous women in colonial Bolivia, paying attention to "the ways in which gender, class, and ethnicity interacted to foster considerable diversity in women's activities and at the same time limit their economic possibilities."[11] Such an approach has now become more commonplace, with a number of studies that attest to the relative success or failure of women of various strata of colonial societies. In particular, the social mobility of urban entrepreneurial women has received a great deal of attention, since this phenomenon flies in the face of so much older ideology about women and work in patriarchal society, as well as the supposed stagnation of colonial society.[12]

Other scholars, however, continue to concentrate upon indigenous women as a marginal community, which they surely were, despite the gains of some. These authors now often utilize Gramscian or Foucauldean theory to show that, although marginalized in the formal sectors, Indian women deployed power in informal yet sometimes potent ways. Such studies have been more common outside of the Andes, yet they must have important reverberations for colonial Peru. Laura Lewis, for example, proposes an "unsanctioned domain" where Indian women sold witchcraft and healing services that undermined the sanctioned power of Spaniards, while reinforcing the hegemonic caste and gender structure of colonial New Spain.[13] And Martha Few uses Spanish Inquisition and extirpation of idolatry records to bring to light indigenous women's participation in the social relations of power in colonial Guatemala, again arguing that it was through spell casting and healing that they found agency.[14]

These tales of men convinced that their impotence derived from the malefic actions of their Indian or black servants, or of priests visited in humiliating nightmares by sorcerer-witches, are rich and fascinating entrees into the psychology of gender and power in early modern times. Yet the use of religion and sorcery by a (mainly but not always) female underclass to terrorize the bodies and minds of their superiors, or the tendency—more likely—of these superiors to imagine danger in the bodies of those they were exploiting, is by now a truism, illustrated from medieval Europe to colonial Guatemala.[15] Although these studies illuminate the multiethnic and cross-class social networks of colonial society, analyses of power deployed mainly in a psychological realm (albeit occasionally with material benefits) also reinforce the notion that colonial society was clearly drawn into discrete socioeconomic–racial categories, that those of European descent always commanded, while those of indigenous and African heritage were always and only the exploited, who could only wield power through limited informal mechanisms like witchcraft.[16]

In contrast are studies—like this one—of the ways that those who theory (and law) tells us were marginalized from political–economic power nonetheless found agency in that material realm. Most stunning, perhaps, has been Kathryn Burns's superb study of the political and economic machinations of the nuns—mostly of Spanish heritage, but including a small number of mestizas—of Cuzco's convents, who directly and indirectly controlled the major source of financial capital

in that city.[17] Jane Mangan's and Kimberly Gauderman's urban marketwomen of Quito and Potosí were less dramatic in their interventions into law and economy, but nonetheless could be spectacularly
successful. In fact, indigenous women and men sat on both sides of the
table in colonial Latin America. Many indigenous women, to be sure,
were too poor even to appear in the notarial record, but more left their
mark than one might think.

The following study, then, enters into this ongoing debate over gender, power, and ethnicity in the Andes, but it proposes to do so in a
novel way. First, and unlike nearly all other gender histories of the
Americas, it begins within a few decades of the conquest of Peru, asking how gender relations affected and were affected by early contact
with Europeans. In particular, this study highlights the enormous economic changes, positive and negative, that took place within a generation or two of conquest and traces how these relations of production,
consumption, and distribution changed the lives of men and women
in the Andes. Its perspective is predominantly urban—that, of course,
is where the richest documentation exists—but it also investigates rural
women's economic production (for the urban market) as well as their
ongoing ties to their urban kin, as part of the larger context in which
urban lives were constructed. By pushing back the starting point
for examining colonial history to the 1560s, we can glimpse the reac-
tions of men and women who could still recall life before the arrival
of Spaniards as well as study the choices of those born into a colonial
system.

We will also consider the lives of women at different ends of the economic scale: members of prehispanic ruling classes who learned to use
not only the Spanish legal system but also European preconceptions
about gender and politics to their advantage; struggling new converts
to Catholicism who scraped together a few coins and personal possessions to pay for funeral rites; and women who rose from domestic
service to become entrepreneurs, property owners, and even slave
owners. And unlike most previous studies of indigenous women in
the colonial economy, this one looks at them in the context of men and
women of all ethnic groups. Tracing the trajectories of small groups of
indigenous women, as so many have done before, is a useful practice,
but it is only by putting them fully within their social context that it is
possible to identify the roles played by gender and ethnicity. By using
gender as a prism through which we examine the changes brought on

under Spanish colonialism, we can also identify the construction of distinctive ethnic identities as well as a shared colonial world.

Places and Ethnicity: The Formation of Colonial Cities

It has been the thesis of some recent studies that colonial society was far more mobile, more ambiguous, and more contentious than was once thought. As Douglas Cope has argued, for example, seventeenth-century Mexico City was a rather fluid urban center, divided more clearly along class lines than ethnic or racial ones. Ethnic designation was, in fact, not conceptualized in a biologically determinist way, but rather culturally.[18] What we will here call ethnicity, or the perceived belonging to the colonial legal categories of "Spaniard" and "Indian," did matter.[19] But the acquisition of a set of social and cultural skills (including religion, dress style, and language) was fundamental to access to economic mobility and social position, even among plebeians.

The studies that have come to this conclusion have, for good reason, made very cautious assertions about the societies that produced such ethnic ambiguity and social mobility. They have argued, for example, that this was a late-seventeenth-century phenomenon, caused by a commercial revolution that developed after the 1650s. They have been careful to note the uniqueness of their cases, suggesting, for example, that while Quito might have been integrated, it was unusual in this sense.[20] And they have tended to locate integration, mobility, and ambiguity only in the physical spaces of the less elite, taking for granted that the "Spanish" centers remained homogeneous and "pure" while the Indian neighborhoods became multiethnic with the influx of poorer Spaniards, freed slaves, and peoples of mixed descent.

This study, on the other hand, places such integration at the very beginning of colonial relations—in Peru, by the 1560s—and even at the very centers of power, the plazas of colonial cities. While Trujillo and Lima may have been exceptional cases for historical reasons, the notion that a small, often warring group of Spanish elites was able to draw together to create segregated living and working spaces is no longer tenable. Many, and probably most, urban centers became somewhat multiethnic and ethnically interdependent, in their elite as well as plebeian neighborhoods, within a generation or two of the conquest.

In great part, this occurred because the commercial revolution that other authors have placed firmly in the late seventeenth century really began in the sixteenth, almost contemporary with the arrival of

Spaniards in the New World.[21] Merchants rapidly circulated goods between Europe and the Americas; then between American cities; and eventually between even small, mainly indigenous towns. The small population of Spaniards was hardly adequate to sustain trade by itself. Markets became ubiquitous, from urban real estate markets feeding upon the shifting fortunes of falling conquistadors and rising indigenous elites, to the second-hand clothes auctions that took place after the death of even the poorest residents.

It therefore seems likely, if ironic, that it was the earliest period of colonial rule that offered the most flexibility and opportunity to those who were not members of the conquering classes. Most historical studies, however, have tended to place the greatest weight upon later years, when processes of centralization were taking form and economic transactions increased. Not coincidentally, the volume of documentation also increased over the seventeenth century, and those materials are more likely to have survived to the present. Thus this study begins at the earliest period when notarial records are available, the mid-sixteenth century, taking us through the next 150 years.

Through an analysis of documents from Lima and Trujillo, Peru, I argue, then, that the sixteenth and early seventeenth centuries provided ambiguous spaces where ethnic and gendered identities were being hammered out, and the ethnically dichotomous class domination that European colonists hoped to impose was still in the process of formation. This reading of colonial life suggests that, despite our knowledge of the outcome for Latin America—where to this day indigenous communities are often marginalized and impoverished— inhabitants of early colonial Peru did not necessarily see their options in such stark terms and used multiple and malleable categories of identity in the circumstances of their lives.

Two Republics? Colonial Settlement in Peru

Despite its intention to create a unified Christian society in the New World, the Spanish Crown utilized a dualistic model of governance, adapted from its experience exacting tribute from newly conquered Muslim and Jewish populations in an increasingly Christian Iberia.[22] The European and indigenous populations were theoretically to be maintained apart in spheres known as *repúblicas*, each with its own legal and religious apparatus, though they were not autonomous and at top were governed by the same (Spanish) individuals. Although these were not territorial designations, the "Republic of Indians" was assumed to have jurisdiction over the scattered rural populations as well as those prehispanic towns not taken over by Spaniards for their own use. The "Republic of Spaniards" (which included all peoples other than Indians, including free and enslaved Africans and the ethnically mixed groups known as *castas*) would have its seat in the new cities, founded by European settlers who evicted local populations and often built over their structures. In an early moment the Spanish Crown theorized that some Indians would profit so quickly from the European encounter that they would become excellent Christians and be able to govern themselves freely and equally with Spaniards, but this optimistic phase ended before South American settlement was underway in the early sixteenth century.[23] The two republics were expected to be interdependent (Spaniards needing Indian labor, Indians needing Spanish religious guidance) yet segregated.

Each "republic" had its own hierarchy, representing the power dynamics of contact society. Although the Spaniards lacked a significant titled nobility, they included a small elite made up of conquistadors given grants of Indian labor (called *encomenderos*), high-ranking bureaucratic officials (often on temporary assignments), and international merchants. The indigenous nobility fought to retain their access to privilege, including exemption from tribute payments and access to Indian labor and the ears of the colonial government. Both contained middling groups, including artisans and traders who were dependent upon these elite retainers for access to wealth and laborers, and a large plebeian sector, including the entire Indian peasant population as well as the lower segment of Spanish society. The lower classes also included African slaves, first brought to Peru by Francisco Pizarro to help in the expeditions and explorations of South America. Free and enslaved Africans were not an enormous presence in the first century of colonization, but they probably equaled the Spanish population in number and were, like the Europeans, concentrated in coastal cities.[24] In fact, a very small group of conquistador/encomenderos extracted tribute from a vast indigenous population, until the Spanish Crown reined them in and slowly substituted a decentralized bureaucratic apparatus. Vigorous, often illegal, competition for access to both the producing masses and the elites who collected and lived off tribute characterized the colony's early economy.

It is obvious that any scheme to maintain these republics physically separate was bound to fail, given that the productivity of Indians was to be the sole basis for Spanish wealth. The failures of this project have been related in numerous studies, and need not be rehearsed here except to note that colonization refashioned the activities, values, and tastes of all concerned.[25] Indigenous populations were shuffled to new locations, reorganized according to the whims of lesser and higher officials, and forced to produce commodities that they themselves had little use for, most notably silver. Indigenous elites quickly learned to use the legal system and other instruments of colonial power to their own personal, and less often communal, benefit. Early rule was, for most, an economic disaster, characterized by a dismal mortality rate, political and social fragmentation and reorganization, and general impoverishment. The Spanish Crown and its viceregal representatives found themselves faced with constant crises, proposing and implementing reforms intended to increase the flow of silver and gold to European coffers, to fund not only Spain's wars in Europe, but also growing administrative and military expenses in its colonies.[26]

Not only did European colonization encroach upon these "Indian towns," through priests, bureaucrats, and overseers who observed their subjects' progress in memorizing Christian catechism and learning the proper work ethic, but central to policy in the Andes, as in Mexico, a forced labor draft was instituted that moved large segments of the rural indigenous population in and out of cities on a regular basis. Peru's *mita*, a term borrowed from Quechua that once described the annual labor service ceremonially "requested" by the Inca and coordinated by local *kurakas* or lords, now brought large groups of indigenous men, women, and children into mining centers and other urban sites to work for Spaniards.[27] There they mined for ores and mercury, refined precious metals, constructed innumerable Catholic churches, built and maintained irrigation systems and roads, and carried out other monumental projects. But another effect of all these forced labor projects was to bring Indians into close relation with Spanish society, markets, and labor specializations and expectations.

The fact that so much of the indigenous population of Peru remained in rural towns belies the scope of the changes that took place after Spanish conquest. While some institutions and aspects of culture remained under local control, European values and demands entered rural society in numerous and often indirect ways, via the crops now required for tribute, new kinds of markets and monetary exchange, and the institution of private property and the legal system designed to support it.[28] Temporary and permanent migration also increased the connections between cities and rural areas, further breaking down the notion that Indian towns might be segregated from Spanish urban centers. As we shall see below, many migrants joined new urban communities and appear to have left behind their old kin and ways, yet others continued to hold and manage property in rural areas, and some purchased lands in agricultural communities closer to their new urban homes. City and town were not fully integrated, but both experienced colonial transformations.

And although cities were meant to be reserved for a European elite, they too rapidly followed their own logics. In Peru, conquistadors who had impressed Francisco Pizarro with their service received *encomiendas*, grants usually entailing political control over a native cacique or over-lord who was then responsible for supplying the labor of his subjects. In exchange for this minor lordship, encomenderos agreed not only to care for native souls, but also to settle and defend the new district. They would build their houses around the *plaza de armas*, the symbolic center of the new cities. That this residential requirement was of primary importance to the Spanish Crown and of lesser appeal to the encomenderos (who preferred to live in more cosmopolitan capitals) is evident from the many royal provisions of the 1530s and 1540s ordering, for example, "that the encomenderos keep their houses populated and that they live in the city of the district of their encomiendas." This requirement came concomitant with repeated, but not always well-enforced, orders that encomenderos marry or bring their wives over from Spain.[29]

The question of residence was more than simply about stability of settlement; as Valerie Fraser notes, most early cities were built atop existing Indian towns and included large Indian populations that could only be displaced by the constant incursion of European colonists. For a city like Trujillo, where even in 1575 only one in four residents was of direct Spanish extraction, a constant and armed occupation of its center was a necessity.[30]

These new leading citizens had to be housed in conditions befitting their status, in sites around a gridded plaza, with its central church and municipal buildings. The public plaza would become integral to the performance of power relations and hierarchy throughout the baroque colonial period. City dwellers also needed central access to markets and ports. These gridded "Spanish cities" had little relation to anything extant in Spain, and really represented an idealization of European values deployed as a part of the process of colonization. Indian populations—the dispossessed inhabitants, but also those who migrated to and from the cities with the cycles of the mita—were intended to be corralled into walled communities, like Lima's Cercado, or at least kept outside the city walls, as in Trujillo's plan.[31]

The Royal Orders on settlements of 1573 asserted that no Indians should even be allowed to enter a Spanish city until it is entirely built, "so that when the Indians do see it they are amazed . . . and they will fear [the Spaniards] and will not dare offend them, and they will respect them and wish to have their friendship." Yet, as Fraser also reminds us, this was impossible given that no Spaniard would perform the labor of building a city when there were subjected Indian populations nearby to exploit.[32] And although there were attempts to gather Indian laborers into segregated neighborhoods, the need for artisans, laborers, domestic servants, and vendors meant that even residences and households were quickly multiethnic.

Thus neither the Spanish nor the Indian "republic" could be, or was even truly meant to be, entirely segregated. The Indian labor force was the basis for most economic life in the colonies, and the religious and social mission of the conquest necessitated European Christian overseers for their new flocks. Although formal interrelationships like cross-ethnic marriages were unusual, and sometimes officially frowned upon by the Spanish Crown, quotidian interactions were the rule rather than the exception. Even Polo de Ondegardo, a legal and economic advisor to the viceroy, admitted in 1571 that "there are not two republics but only one."[33]

Two Colonial Cities: Lima and Trujillo

Lima and Trujillo were two of these early Spanish cities, built on the lands of coastal indigenous groups to the demands of the new *vecinos* or propertied citizens (see Map 1). Lima had been a southern valley settlement of some 200,000 people under the jurisdiction of the kuraka or lord of Lima, probably a religious center as well as a town, and was not far from the important temple and ceremonial center of Pachacamac. It was founded in January 1535 by Francisco Pizarro as a settlement from which the Spaniards might control their new conquests. Trujillo, in the Moche Valley, along the north coast near where Pizarro had first made his approach to the Inca in Cajamarca, was less densely settled and was probably the site of ancient *huacas* or mountainlike shrines in the Chimú realm, not far from its massive political seat, Chan Chan. Trujillo came into legal existence in late 1534, founded by Diego

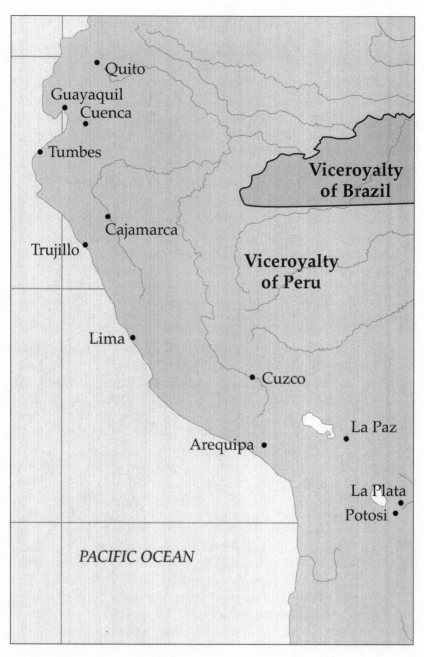

Viceroyalty of Peru and environs.

de Almagro in order to establish Spanish domination over local indigenous lords, who had recently murdered some Spaniards.[34]

Both quickly became important colonial settlements, organized for access to maritime trade as well as local labor and resources like water and wood. Lima would rapidly grow to become a major hub of movement, of peoples as well as commodities. Trujillo never achieved quite this economic or social scale, but was prosperous enough due to the encomiendas, haciendas, and sugar plantations organized by the early settlers.[35]

The cities were laid out on irregular gridded plans, with central plazas where first a church, and then a cathedral, as well as *Cabildo* (municipal government) offices would be rapidly constructed. From these plazas radiated the *solares*, quarter-block plots that would be offered to the conquistadors who found favor with the Crown. Other Spaniards would soon join the first *vecinos*—clergy, merchants, artisans, and unskilled laborers who hoped to siphon off some of Peru's celebrated silver for themselves.

The conquistadors rapidly dispossessed and removed the original indigenous inhabitants of the Lima Valley. In the 1560s, the cacique don Gonzalo argued that his Indians should be exempt from tribute payment because their lands were in the hands of Spaniards, and "we are very scattered and very few."[36] I have found no parallel information about the natives of the Moche valley, though we can imagine that they too were slowly displaced to the margins of Trujillo as their lands were redistributed. As these left, indigenous immigrants from the rural areas around the city began to move in, alongside African men and women freed from slavery.

Thus migration was an important factor for the establishment of populations in both cities; in the early years, nearly all their inhabitants were (by definition) immigrants and subsequently there were always large influxes of new immigrants of all backgrounds, particularly from outlying rural communities where demographic collapse and the encroachment on community lands led to increasing tribute burdens and made the cities attractive for short-term labor contracts or long-term stays.[37] By the beginning of the seventeenth century—the first period for which there are even marginally reliable population studies of both cities—each city had a substantial and economically important indigenous minority. Lima, with a population counted by one contemporary source as 25,447 in 1614, had some 2,000 Indians registered as living and working within it (the real figure is certainly higher than this, not to mention the regular groups of mita workers that came through the city). Trujillo, a much smaller city of less than 3,500 residents in 1604, was 36 percent indigenous, with another 32 percent roughly categorized as "black or mulatto." The final 32 percent was recorded as a mixture of Spaniards and mestizos, suggesting that the actual population who could trace all of their ancestry back to Europe was a minority, perhaps just a few hundred men and women.[38] Given the ethnic fluidity we have mentioned, these census numbers are hardly unchallengeable, but they do suggest the multiethnic makeup of both supposed "Spanish" centers.

Not only were the cities multiethnic, but everyday life was similarly integrated. Indigenous men and women lived in close contact with Spaniards, blacks, and people of various ethnic mixes (castas), as apprentices, servants, tenants, and neighbors. Even the most concentrated Indian neighborhoods included non-Indian inhabitants as well as Indians of various socioeconomic classes: Lima's Cercado, purportedly closed to non-Indians by its Jesuit founders, included Spanish, mestizo, and African tenants, and some Indian households even owned African slaves.[39]

The culture of daily life even more insistently demanded integration, since Indian men and women held crucial jobs as marketeers, artisans, domestic servants, and construction workers. All manner of people were dependent upon indigenous and casta vendors and store owners for staple goods; middle- and upper-income homes (of all ethnicities) had African slaves and indigenous, African, and European domestic servants; people of all classes and ethnicities sought out indigenous and casta healers. Indians also apprenticed to and served (legally or not) as shoemakers, tailors, silversmiths, painters, construction workers, ceramicists, and makers of hats and hosiery and even musical instruments. It would have been a sheltered Spaniard indeed whose path did not cross with other ethnicities regularly (and even those Spaniards most notable for being sheltered—cloistered nuns— lived among Indians, mestizos, and Africans in their convents).[40]

Although Trujillo had a smaller population overall, it may have been less stratified in some ways than was Lima. For example, the Cabildo of Trujillo sold solares within the city to Indians who "lived like Spaniards" and even made one Indian, Rodrigo Suarez, a vecino in 1553, so ordering because "he speaks Spanish and is married and has the occupation of tailor and has children and so that he may [raise] them as Christians and in the law of reason and that others may take him as an example and do the same as he."[41] Trujillo's *cofradías*—religious sodalities so important to the construction of community life in the cities—were likewise not segregated by ethnicity, as they sometimes were in Lima. Trujillo was hardly egalitarian, of course, and the original encomendero elite was so entrenched in local government that a number of its merchants, artisans, and farmers, long excluded from power, became the founding citizens of an autonomous new town, Santiago de Miraflores de Saña, in the nearby Saña Valley.[42] Trujillo's cultural identity would shift drastically in later periods, when African slaves were imported in growing numbers to work the sugar plantations that became the region's economic mainstay, while the indigenous population suffered high mortality and migration rates. But during the late sixteenth and early seventeenth centuries, the focus of this study, Trujillo was profoundly multiethnic.

Who were these urban immigrants? According to Lynn Lowry's analysis of an incomplete 1613 census of Lima's Indians, more than 60 percent of the indigenous population it enumerated had been in Lima fewer than five years, and only 22 percent had lived there between six and ten years. Only a total of twenty-five Indians, or 3 percent of the surveyed population, had lived in that city for more than twenty years. In terms of how and why people immigrated, Lowry calculates that the great majority of Indian males arrived in Lima before they were twenty years old, suggesting that many came as servants or as laborers rather than established in an occupation. No equivalent data exist for women, but they probably arrived as youthful (even preadolescent) domestic servants, as wives of migrating laborers, or—as historians have culled from the records of idolatry proceedings—fleeing miserable home lives and abusive husbands.[43] Many of these single men and women would live in the households of wealthy families or would rent rooms from landlords.

Unfortunately there is no early residential survey of Trujillo comparable to the 1613 Lima census, with its remarkable wealth of ethnographic detail. A fragmentary census from 1604 and archival records do, however, offer some interesting parallels as well as compelling images of the city in its own right. According to the census, at the turn of the seventeenth century Trujillo boasted some 166 houses, "inhabited by the *Justicia* and *Regimiento* [the colonial judicial and bureaucratic officials], ecclesiastics, vecinos [here specifically property-owning citizens], encomenderos, *ciudadanos* [residents of less property and standing], merchants, businesspeople, artisans, young unmarried women, widows and single women." Approximately one half of the total Indian population was resident in the houses of the vecinos; the rest lived in their own homes or rented houses and solares, working as artisans or farmers. The majority of the vecinos of Trujillo were encomenderos, whose insecure wealth was produced by the rapidly dwindling rural indigenous communities of the province.[44]

Trujillo, like Lima, was not separated into ethnic neighborhoods until nearly a century after its foundation. In fact, within a few decades of the contentious division of the solares of its plaza among the leading Spanish conquerors of the region, Indians, mestizos, plebeian Spaniards, and even Africans had taken ownership of many of them. In the face of constantly changing economic fortunes, many conquistadores found themselves selling or abandoning prime solares, and they were bought out by those who had prospered. Some of these previously excluded residents even found themselves able to become citizens, a designation often thought to have been reserved for Spaniards.[45] In 1603, Viceroy Velasco ordered a zone called San Esteban created outside the city limits to accommodate the indigenous immigrants who "in order to enjoy liberty come here from their towns."[46] But a large population remained living among the Spaniards, and a significant number owned or rented solares within the city limits.

Households were integrated as well as neighborhoods. All wealthy Spanish households included some combination of Indian, mestizo, and/or Spanish servants as well as enslaved men and women of African descent. Living arrangements also included rentals of apartments or chambers that also crossed ethnic and other social boundaries. It was, for example, common for indigenous artisans to rent office and living spaces in larger compounds. The proceedings of a criminal action in 1606 recount how an Indian named Agostina was knifed in her Spanish mistress's kitchen by Agustín Colquemango, an Indian tailor who rented a chamber in that house. Other household members who gave testimony included two indigenous *yanaconas* or retainers, a black woman, and two young Spanish women, apparently all servants.[47]

Lima's housing was similarly mixed, as artisans employed Indian workers and apprentices, and landlords rented rooms or shacks (called *aposentos*) to anyone who would pay. For example, the 1613 Lima census described "the house of Juan de Lemos, surgeon; in his corral there lived some Indians in rented aposentos" including a fisherman from coastal Ica, another from highland Chachapoyas, a married couple from Trujillo, and a married woman from Chancay whose husband was away in

Cuzco. The very next house belonged to a free black or mulatto woman, who rented her *aposento* to an Indian tailor from Chachapoyas.[48]

The living arrangements in both cities complemented working relations: the indigenous residents provided foodstuffs for all, selling in the central plazas as well as through shops and informal arrangements. Lima's streets were originally named after the trades located there, including *Mantas* (shawls), *Botoneros* (buttonmakers), *Escribanos* (notaries and scribes), *Espaderos* (swordmakers), *Plateros* (silversmiths), and *Bodegones* (general merchandise stores).[49] These blocks housed stores selling goods that came to the cities from overseas via tradeships, overland from the highlands, or from surrounding farms and haciendas.

In summary, the two urban centers we have compared here are notable for their mutability and transculturation, which were key characteristics from the earliest years of colonial settlement rather than the effects of opening commercial markets in the late seventeenth century. Over the sixteenth and seventeenth centuries, thousands of men and women arrived in Lima and Trujillo, some coming from the Iberian peninsula and African coasts, but many were migrants from rural indigenous communities within the viceroyalty of Peru and elsewhere in the Spanish colonies. Together they constructed colonial life and, as a byproduct, produced their own identities as members of corporate groups such as "Indians," but also as individuals on the ever-shifting margins.

Methods and Sources

A final aspect of the present study that bears discussion is its consideration of aspects of material culture as well as economic and political analysis. That is, it seeks to learn how indigenous women experienced their lives, in some limited way, by investigating how they used their access to new material possessions brought by contact with Europe. This chapter began with a glimpse of a woman's life through the reading of a series of wills she left across the seventeenth century. It is my contention that Francisca Ramírez made choices about her self-presentation and her clientele, mirrored in her changing stock of fashionable clothing. As her fortunes increased, she was able to utilize different sets of cultural codes, drawn indirectly or directly from Europe, Africa, and the Americas, that were concurrently available to her. My analysis of archival evidence shows that this was a common practice, that men and women used fashion and other possessions to signify their relationship to a changing social order, and the state often saw this as a threat. More broadly, certain colonial residents—mainly urban and/or elite—drew upon a hybrid or transculturated set of social structures as part of their attempts to accommodate or simply survive colonial rule. These social structures reflected predecessors in the Americas as well as Spain and Africa, yet were newly configured to respond to the new environment.

Hybridity, as used here, is not a contextless menu of choices spread before subalterns, nor is it something experienced as a traumatic break from norms.[50] The term encompasses both the actions of accommodation to the demands of colonial society and also the material effects of those actions, and thus hybridity was an organic response by groups and individuals to their changing environment. But a careful analysis of circulating commodities as well as shifting legal and social strategies indicates that at least certain groups of colonial subjects not only experienced this transculturation but recognized the novelty of their situations and were conscious of the repercussions of their choices for their presence as part of new social groups.

The process of adapting aspects of a conquering culture is well documented around the colonial world. Fernando Ortíz, in his seminal study of tobacco and sugar in Cuba, coined the term *transculturation* to emphasize that this was not simply a matter of colonized subjects adapting to the culture of their masters—his critique of a literature describing colonial "acculturation"—but one of jointly forging a dynamic culture that is (often violently) transformed by colonizer as well as colonized.[51] Ortíz's insights are foundational to this study, which investigates the transculturation of colonial institutions in early Peru and firmly rejects any notion that the use of Spanish law or clothing, for two pointed examples, by indigenous subjects represented a loss of agency in the colonial world.

Cultural theorists have tinkered endlessly with this language, often out of concern that certain terms privilege one group of actors over another or imply a particular trajectory of change. Although this theoretical hairsplitting reflects a well-intentioned desire for exactitude as well as respect for our subjects, it has also led to a morass of academic jargon that takes us far from the historical moment.[52] On the other hand, colonial subjects created their own cultural languages to demarcate their positions, one that would do us well to investigate.

Residents of colonized towns and cities did see much of the world as a menu of cultural codes containing ethnic allegiances and political ramifications. When Francisca Ramírez stocked her *cajón* or trunk with llicllas and anacos, she was participating in an economy that signified the subordinate status of tributary Indians, who produced, bought, and wore such garments. When her income and status allowed, she dressed in silks from the Far East, worn according to the fashion of a European woman, signifying her decision to participate in a more elite political economy that was not "natural" to her as it was to women of Spanish origin. The fact that, as we shall see below, class and regional factors overwhelmingly correlated with these sartorial decisions (and options), as well as the existence of laws and commentaries that attempted to discipline bodies that dressed "inappropriately," indicate that colonial residents well understood the significance of their clothes to the social order. It is these significations that require a new vocabulary from us, to mark the ways in which people self-consciously were agents of change.

One way to describe these cultural changes is *creolization*, a term used more by historians of colonial North America than of Latin America, to refer to cultural and especially linguistic shifts that occurred with the migration of new populations to the New World.[53] The etymology of the word *criollo* is still a bit murky: it seems to be related to the Portuguese word *crioulo*, itself derivative of *criar*, to grow.[54] It was certainly used to describe people of African descent born in the New World, as opposed to the *bozal*, or person born in Africa.[55] (This may have been its original use; in Brazil *crioulo* still only refers to "blackness.") From there, the term appears to have been taken over by other groups, including (and most famously) by people of Spanish descent born in the Americas, thus acquiring another patina of temperament and social expectations: creoles as "authentic" Americans capable of self-determination, or as spoiled and deformed Spaniards, inept to rule themselves, depending upon the speaker's prejudice. Latin American historians tend to gloss creole as simply meaning "born in." But a straightforward geographic identification is misleading: individual African men and women can be traced through a process of moving, in the documentary record, from *bozales* to *criollos* over a lifetime, suggesting that the acquisition of the Spanish language, conversion to Christianity, and other cultural features were at stake more than one's birthplace.[56]

But most interesting, perhaps, is the use of this term by indigenous men and women beginning at the turn of the seventeenth century, to describe those Indians born in or associated with urban centers rather than in rural indigenous communities as *indios criollos*. Here Indians saw their own creolization not simply as a matter of birthplace (since

Indians by definition were born in the New World) but as an association with a particular urban colonial culture and an alienation from *ayllu* or community life and tributary status. As we will see, this particular (and largely uncommented) Spanish American usage indicates a self-consciousness about changes in place and culture at this early juncture in the colonial period. While they may not have theorized themselves as "hybrid," clearly indigenous men and women wanted to mark off difference in ways that mattered to them in the context of competing cultural codes.[57]

Thus this study intends not only to describe the various ways that indigenous women accommodated the increasingly creolized colonial world that faced them in the sixteenth and seventeenth centuries, but also to imagine, through the documentary record, how they might have experienced these changes. Wills, then, become the most enticing documents left from the colonial world, since they offer this entry point into daily life and, to a degree, consciousness, albeit at moments of great crisis and under deeply mediated conditions. A substantial database of indigenous women's wills, 55 from Trujillo and 147 from Lima, covering the period 1565–1698, forms the core of this study. These testaments have been culled from the hundreds of notarial registers in the central archives of those cities, and while they do not constitute all the wills still extant, they represent a fair cross section of classes, social statuses, neighborhoods, and occupations. These wills have been supplemented by a number of other sources, including records of economic (especially real estate and labor market) transactions from notarial registers; transcripts of civil and criminal trials; ecclesiastical records; censuses and *visitas* (administrative inspections); legal commentaries; and chronicles left by colonial adventurers and authors. And importantly, a large and diverse set of supplementary wills left by indigenous men as well as men and women of other ethnicities, from former slaves to elite Spaniards, has also been compiled in order to provide contrast and context for deciding what actions and issues could be considered a function of gender and ethnicity as opposed to part of a more common social structure. As a result, this study offers a truly rich portrait of colonial society, with a broad sweep focused by attention to a series of questions about social and economic relations in women's lives.

Wills were written by people who typically fell into one or both of two categories: those with property they sought to protect or assign after death (which could be small or substantial) and the Catholic faithful, who worried that their progress out of purgatory would be slowed without the proper masses and funereal rites. Because the culture of colonial Latin America, like that of early modern Spain, was obsessed with record keeping, vast numbers of men and women called upon notaries on their deathbeds or at other moments when mortality was a concern, including prior to childbirth and long voyages. Many of these were relatively well-off, with property, furnishings, and cash income to be protected and distributed. But a surprising number were truly poor, some only possessing a couple of used garments that might be sold for a few coins to pay for a keenly desired burial and mass. In fact, the hospitals, known as dumping grounds for the dying poor, were patrolled by notaries and priests who were encouraged by hospital officials to extract wills from patients, so that their bills could be settled. As a result, the wills surveyed here do not only present the upper strata of colonial society, but a diverse group of individuals who chose, for different reasons, to use a notary's services at times of crisis.

The role of the notary (and the legal system more generally) cannot be underestimated in the writing of a will or any other legal document from the period.[58] Testaments followed accepted formats, though deviations were possible, and they included personal information that could reflect statements made by the testator or simply the opinion of the notary, for example, the marginal notes that often recorded the ethnicity of the testator. Wills almost invariably recited formulaic invocations of the Holy Trinity and saints in the Catholic pantheon, as well as provided for religious services after death. Yet they often included detailed lists of personal belongings, sometimes described by the notary as he literally opened chests and boxes in the testator's home, and they do offer personal information in idiosyncratic forms. Thus while we must make allowances for the mediations of the state and its agent, the notary, wills and other notarial documents can give us access to parts of the social structure not otherwise open to view.

Conclusion: The Formation of a Colonial Society

The project undertaken in these chapters, then, is to investigate colonial institutions in their process of formation, to understand both the expectations and demands of colonizers, on the one hand, and the ways that indigenous peoples, especially women, contested and changed these. But I also highlight here the lived experience of daily life under colonial rule, from the integration of native populations into the market and world economy, to the forms of self- and other-identification utilized by colonial subjects, not reducible to "Indians" and "Spaniards." Thus I will examine aspects of the lives of some of the poorest and most marginalized as well as the most privileged and thus most threatened and intrigued by colonial integration.

Chapter 1 will take us to rural communities, where Indians held in encomienda faced the earliest challenges of colonization. Required to produce masses of commodities for tribute, from food products to cloth to mineral wealth, they had to reorganize themselves to maintain their own levels of subsistence and to make up for the loss of community members from early death and migration. The example of tributary cloth production, perceived as an enormous burden by many communities, demonstrates not only this process of reorganization but also the specific effects of this new political economy on the gender division of labor, where women became the major producers of cloth for tribute as well as for the market. As a result, indigenous women moved rapidly into wage labor relations and the colonial market and learned to utilize the viceregal legal system to seek redress when cheated by the encomenderos, priests and merchants who loosely employed them.

Chapter 2 follows some of these women as they emigrated to urban centers, where they, like indigenous men, had to make a new place for themselves. For many, the route began with domestic service, but often encompassed multiple income-earning strategies over a lifetime, including producing food and beverages for market, selling assorted commodities, purchasing and renting out real estate, and owning small businesses and enslaved laborers. We will follow a somewhat exceptional group of these women, who left wills documenting their estates and their religious beliefs, to examine how new communities were formed out of diverse migrant populations in these multiethnic centers.

Wills also provide us a glimpse into the frustrations of these colonial lives; they are instruments that seek to protect assets from usurpers, they attempt to recover property that has been taken away, and they try to restore honor at the end of life. In Chapter 3, we look at these various strategies to see what they tell us about the trials faced by urban indigenous women and how these might be similar to and different from the concerns of indigenous men.

Chapter 4 moves from the external relations of property and occupation to ask how indigenous men and women differentiated themselves in a multiethnic urban world. Through an analysis of changing clothing styles, we see a conversation about identity developing, fostered by the availability of new status products from Europe, broader access to high status products from Inca Peru, and the flooding of markets with regional tributed cloth. As well, indigenous men and women found other ways to identify themselves, as property owners, as members of an artisan class, and by place of birth.

Finally, with Chapter 5 we return to rural Peru, this time to examine the political careers of a group of elite women. These noblewomen were able to take advantage of certain aspects of Iberian inheritance law as it transferred to the colonies and what was at least a mythology about preconquest female lords to promote their candidacy for *cacica*, or female chiefs. The success of a few isolated cases quickly led to an expansion across the viceroyalty, although this came concomitant with a decline in the status of the *cacicazgo* (chieftanship).

The following chapters examine, then, the lives of indigenous women in two coastal cities, Lima and Trujillo, and their rural environs in the early years of Spanish colonization. As more than half of the indigenous population after its precipitous sixteenth-century decline, and a far larger presence in the colony than Spaniards of either gender, indigenous women were assuredly ubiquitous in the social, economic, and political lives of their towns and cities.[59] They produced and sold much of the food and clothing consumed in the colony, they raised children and cleaned houses for the upper and middle classes, they provided midwifery and healing services, they owned real estate and even slaves and, on occasion, held political office. As a result we can see them as indispensable to the construction of the incipient colonial society, but we can also watch colonial society develop through them.

La ropa de la tierra:
Indigenous Women and the
Tributary Economy of Early Colonial Peru

Introduction

In 1567, some thirty-five years after the first Spaniards arrived in Peru, the colonial inspector Garci Díez de San Miguel traveled to the southern highland province of Chucuito to investigate tribute payment and economic relations in the communities of the Lupaqa Indians. One of his informants, the judge Bernaldino Fasato, spoke about the current system for producing handwoven wool cloth for the market. He recounted how a group of "elderly Indian women" had come to him in his official capacity, complaining that "[their caciques] ordered them to spin wool for cloth and had not paid them anything for that." Upon further investigation Fasato learned that the caciques, who were commissioned for this purpose by merchants and other colonists, had fed the women while they worked, but had indeed failed to pay them any wages; in fact, the Lupaqa caciques had customarily kept, on behalf of the community, all the cash paid them by Spanish officials for all such enterprises, which must have totaled thousands of pesos annually.[1]

In the summary of his findings, Díez exclaimed that "[the caciques] have collected the money and have not given a thing to the Indians, they have spent it all on works for the church and ornaments and having seen the works as sumptuous as they have made them, it seems to me that they have pretty much spent it all, although I have enough suspicion that they have kept some money for themselves."[2]

Spanish officials heading up the investigation, called a *visita*, fixated upon the potential scandal of caciques commandeering the income from this putting-out system. But the records from the visita offer us much more than insight into early colonial corruption. Through pages of testimony taken from local notables over a ten-month period, including Spanish officials like Fasato, as well as scribes and merchants and the caciques themselves, the Chucuito visita presents a variety of perspectives on the local experience of colonization in a small, rural community in the highlands.

From the perspective of examining a gendered history, what stands out from Fasato's testimony is that a group of "elderly Indian women" had approached that colonial official to complain that their cacique withheld their pay. This suggests a transformation of Andean social relations: not only were Indian women participating in what they believed to be a wage-labor relationship, but they now considered the colonial authorities either parallel to, or more effective than, their caciques in questions of local governance.

In fact, the system set up by the caciques was on its face consonant with prehispanic practice in the highlands. Caciques commonly "requested" labor from their subjects, including tasks such as spinning and weaving, and gave the workers food and drink during their period of employment. This cloth was then "spent" in religious and political practices, including ritual burning and clothing the Inca elites and the army.[3] But in the thirty-odd years since the Spaniards had replaced the Incas as the imperial power in the southern highlands, expectations about proper norms for production, distribution, and consumption had been radically altered. Rather than expecting food and drink as part of a system of reciprocity, workers demanded wages from caciques as compensation for their labor. And when they could not resolve disputes within the community, they took their complaints to the colonial authorities. The fact that this particular complaint was made by a group of elderly women indicates that it was not only men, but also women who were being challenged by migration patterns, access to paid labor, and the predations of the consumer economy that Spain hoped to impress upon its new subjects.

Although the extraction of precious metals and minerals was the most immediate economic goal of the colonization of the New World, the reality of economic relations was more far-reaching and complex.[4] Spanish conquistadors initially collected all the booty they could find, and many did return to Spain wealthy. But many more stayed, influential in the creation of a flexible and dynamic economic sector, not only of encomiendas—grants of indigenous labor to produce commodities according to practices overseen by native chiefs—but also of artisans, agriculture, and markets, both regional and international.

The colony's domestic economy in the early years involved, in areas without direct access to gold and silver mines, the redistribution of commodities produced by indigenous communities, now for the profit of these colonists. Of these local products, produced by skilled artisans as well as the general population for their own use, the most important and ubiquitous commodities by far—both to the Spaniards and to native peoples—were rectangular blocks of woven cloth made of cotton and wool, known as *la ropa de la tierra*, "native clothing," by the Spaniards who eagerly bought and sold it. That the trade in indigenous cloth was extensive and lucrative is well known to historians of Peru: Jorge Zevallos Quiñones wrote in 1973 of the "prize" of *la ropa tributo*, the tribute in clothing, awarded by Pizarro to his colleagues at the founding of Trujillo.[5] But what should be emphasized in a retelling of economic relations in the early colonial period is the extent to which handwoven cloth production created direct links between rural and urban centers; enriched merchants who realized that there would be a market for rural production in the new urban and mining centers; and changed productive relations, including gendered relations, in the rural communities that produced this homespun clothing.

Studies of the colonial Andes have long debated the extent to which native communities were "destructurated," in Wachtel's polarizing term, or resisted or accommodated the demands of Spanish colonialism.[6] Regional studies like those of Spalding, Ramírez, and Powers, among others, have demonstrated the extent to which native elites, pulled in so many directions by the contradictory demands of colonial officials as well as their own subjects, adapted their practices such that the most successful became important power brokers in the colonial political economy.[7] Using these studies as context, I take the analysis to a "micro" level to historicize how households, individuals, and in particular, women, might have experienced what Stern has termed the "challenge of colonialism" just a few generations after the first contact. And, to move us beyond the urban-rural dichotomy and into the content of the chapters to follow, I will explore rural productive relations as part of the context for the exodus to the cities by indigenous women and men, and as a catalyst for urban market relations.

This chapter, then, looks at some of the ways that rural (and by implication, urban) society was being transformed by colonial economic and social relations by examining testimony in a series of visitas. The gender transformations we will see are evidence of just how deep some of these changes were: the fabric of community life for men, women, and children was affected by colonial economic relations, though it was clearly not destroyed, nor did these changes augur ill for everyone concerned or occur evenly across regions. The gendered reorganization of labor in the colonial period had a profound effect upon social relations in rural areas. Without falling into the trap of assuming that a total, cataclysmic break took place in 1532, we do need to question the effects of not only the tributary economy but also mercantile pressures upon relations at the level of the community and the family.

Rural communities in the middle of the sixteenth century were involved in all sorts of businesses. While the Lupaqa, because of their proximity to the mining center of Potosí, may have developed their economic networks more rapidly than remoter communities, their activities may serve as an overview of the *tratos y granjerías* available: farming; hunting; cattle raising (including European species as well as llamas); coca production; weaving and spinning; hauling merchandise (coca, cattle, woven goods) to the mines of Potosí and to the cities of Arequipa and Cuzco; and artisanry, such as silversmithing, ceramics, and construction. These activities were sometimes organized by individuals or local groups, who "exchanged" cattle, *charqui* (freeze-dried meat) and wool for corn in various high- and lowland cities, and sometimes through Spaniards, who hired them for money and in-kind wages to haul commodities long distances or, as we have seen, to weave large quantities of clothing.

We cannot tell from the numerous short testimonies of the visita exactly the nature of the social order in which all these exchanges and activities were embedded, nor the degree to which any of them represented a serious break with prehispanic practices, except for the obvious introduction of European commodities, plants, and animals, and especially the introduction of large-scale credit, which concerned the authorities greatly.[8] But the testimony, especially about the weaving operations, made it clear that social relations were changing even in rural regions, and plebeians as well as caciques had new expectations about their work roles as well as the appropriate forms remuneration would take.

Rural indigenous women and men were incorporated into the colonial economy with what could be described as both "pushes" and "pulls." Merchants, bureaucrats, and church officials, as well as their own caciques, encouraged or required them to produce food, cloth, and other commodities for market as well as for tribute. But Indian laborers themselves were learning of alternative arrangements, either through their own experiences or from relatives who had moved to the new urban centers. Communities shifted to meet the new demands of caciqués as well as Europeans, and learned to deal with the demographic crisis and patterns of migration that left many communities with a significantly larger female than male population toward the end of the sixteenth century.[9] This chapter investigates the transformation of rural society, particularly the ways in which indigenous women engaged with and shaped the colonial economy at its very birth.

Colonial Dislocations and the Gender of Weavers

Peru's colonial economy was constructed in contestation: the relations of production and consumption that developed were the result of ongoing small and large conflicts between social and ethnic groups and not the simple triumph of one system over another. One arena for contestation was the gender division of labor, the social order that normalizes men's and women's productive roles. In the Andes, the division of labor was deeply transformed by demographic crisis and by the organization of the encomienda and market economies. The normalization of these new relations meant that rural Andean women, identified by the state mainly as weavers, mothers, and agricultural workers, became invisible historical actors, while rural men, assumed to be the tributaries, *mitayos* and wage workers, were taken to be the main agents of colonial economic relations.[10]

More recently, historians have sought to complicate this picture by including gender in their analyses, though their interventions have most often come in studies of urban economies.[11] As Ann Zulawski has argued, it is "artificial" to study Indian women apart from Indian men, and likewise rural society without attention to the family economy.[12] And attention to gender as a central constituent of the economy reveals the dynamism of cultural contact in this period, as it also recognizes the complexity of women's economic contributions and responses to colonization. As colonial economic demands indeed brought more indigenous men out of rural communities to mining regions, large agricultural enterprises, and urban centers, indigenous women were sometimes compelled and other times found it advantageous to produce cloth and other market commodities for a rising class of Spanish middlemen and -women.

Spanish chroniclers—often conquistadors or otherwise participants in the conquest—went to great lengths to document the work habits of the peoples who were to become their labor force. Some were particularly taken by the strange propensities for men to perform "female" labor, or vice-versa. Although men in early modern Spain, as in much of Europe, wove textiles, they were usually high-status artisans, often members of a guild, and had the possibility of becoming a master artisan or at least self-employed. European women, on the other hand, were encouraged to sew, spin, and weave within the setting of the home, either for family use or to supplement family income. Although women did perform this labor in other settings—most famously in the silk-weaving industry, whereby "the kingdom of Seville is kept rich by the women," according to a contemporary report—they were usually restricted in terms of earnings and worked in a putting-out or a workshop system where they experienced little occupational mobility or independence.[13]

Thus some Spanish chroniclers, like the Jesuit Fray Bernabé Cobo, interpreted the division of labor in conquest-era Peru as inverted, where women "do most of the work, because, besides bringing up the children, they cook, make *chicha* [corn beer] and all the clothing they, their husbands and their children wear, and they do even more work in the fields than the men."[14] Although we should not dismiss the rhetorical aspects of this description—turning indigenous males into lazy savages (or feminized sodomites) was part of a political agenda aimed at legitimating the conquest rather than producing accurate ethnographic texts—the gendered complementarity of labor in the prehispanic Andes required that women work alongside men in many tasks.[15]

In fact, many early colonial sources indicate that agriculture was indeed joint labor: informants of the 1567 visita of Chucuito stated explicitly that men and women both grew the crops for their cacique's salary, and a 1562 visita of Huánuco gives additional broad support for this view.[16] But Spanish policy insisted upon adult males as the nominal producers of the surplus they collected in the colony. Thus census rolls tended to name only adult men, and the informational questions that administrators asked during periodic visitas were directed toward the male "head of household." Although there are clear indications that informants understood and spoke to their interlocutors of the importance of female labor to most productive tasks, the documents themselves are structured so as to negate that perception.

As a result, colonial law—which emanated from Spain or from urban viceregal capitals like Lima, rather than centers of agricultural production like Chucuito or Huánuco—was drawn to support the fiction that indigenous men were the agents of production in the colonial world. But law had a limited reach in colonial Peru. The productive capacity of Indian women did not escape the notice of Spanish encomenderos, merchants, and other elites, who quickly grasped the importance of this labor force. As a result, indigenous women and men both came to occupy new social and economic roles in the early years of colonization.

The lack of alphabetic writing before Spaniards came to the Andes and the relative scarcity of relevant prehispanic iconographic materials means that we have little concrete information about the gender divisions of labor that existed prior to the European conquest. By the era of the first *visitas* containing ethnographic material on labor practices, the 1560s, practices may already have changed due to European contact and local demands, and Spanish chronicles are not always reliable on this topic. But as evidenced by the numerous surviving textiles as well as spinning implements and looms in archaeological sites, weaving and spinning were both common and socially important activities, in more ancient periods as well as under Inca domination in the fifteenth century.[17]

The Incas in particular placed a high value on the fine tapestry-woven cloth called *cumbi* produced on an upright loom.[18] According to colonial sources, garments made from cumbi could only be worn or distributed by the Inca. Thus cumbi was a common gift to ethnic lords (*kurakas*) as a nominal fulfillment of the reciprocity between these and the Inca. It was woven by groups of specialized artisans, women called *acllas* or *mamaconas* (generally the daughters of kurakas "donated" to the Inca as another part of the reciprocal imperial relationship) and men called *cumbicamayos* or "makers of cumbi," who were more or less full-time producers.[19] The acllas appear to have lived either in Inca administrative centers such as Cuzco or Huánuco, mass-producing cloth, or were given as wives to caciques. The cumbicamayos remained in their villages and produced fine textiles for tribute and probably for their own caciques as well.

That both male and female high-status workers produced cloth was probably not an eccentricity of the Incas. A pot in the British Museum from the Moche culture (AD 100–800) on the north coast of Peru depicts a cloth workshop, where a group of women and men were producing

Figure 1. Indigenous woman weaving at backstrap loom. Watercolor by workshop of Archbishop Baltasar Jaime Martinez Compañón y Bujanda, eighteenth century. (Courtesy of Patrimonio Nacional, Spain.)

ceremonial or burial cloth under the surveillance of two male over-seers.[20] Although more analysis of visual material is certainly neces-sary, it seems likely that the highest quality cloth was produced by specialized artisans, who could be male or female. Coarse cloth made on a portable backstrap loom, called *awasca* in Quechua, was woven by households for their own use and possibly for tribute (see Figure 1) Early written sources mention that men, women, and children all spun the cotton or camelid thread and wove to varying degrees, and it seems likely that domestic cloth making was considered a household task rather than one gendered male or female. Again, this seems to be a widespread tendency: Anne Paul has suggested that funerary bundles found in south coastal Paracas were the work of a family workshop, because they were woven by a small group of artisans of varying lev-els of proficiency.[21]

The visitas of Huánuco and Chucuito provide substantial evidence of this for the sixteenth-century highlands, through discussions of the labor time needed to produce the standard forms of tributed clothing. The unit of tribute was the *pieza* or set of clothing, always consisting of two large rectangles of woven cloth, either the woman's *anaco* (a dress made of a single rectangle of cloth wrapped under the arms and reach-ing to the ankles) and lliclla (a shawl pinned around the shoulders) or the man's *manta* (cloak) and *unku* or *camiseta* (sleeveless tunic) (see Fig-ure 2).[22] According to the most moderate informant in the Huánuco visita, one set of two garments required two months' weaving by the team of husband and wife if they had no other work to perform, but in the agricultural high season or when other tasks were necessary it could take up to three months.[23] In the Chucuito visita, the informant was a European cloth-buying client of the cacique who complained that production of a set took fifty days, because "they work very slowly," but when the women and children helped out the work would be done more quickly.[24] One household could not be comfortably re-sponsible for the production of more than two or three sets of garments per year, given that these were no longer the work of dedicated arti-sans, but families with other significant demands, such as agricultural labor, on their time.

We may generalize that, prior to the conquest, specialty and some tribute cloth production was carried out by male and female professional artisans, and general household clothing was produced by family mem-bers as necessary. It is clear that after the conquest the rural artisan system broke down, though some specialized weavers continued to

Figure 2. Male and female tributary clothing. From don Felipe Guaman Poma de Ayala, *El primer nueva corónica y buen gobierno*. (Courtesy of Siglo Veintiuno Editorial.)

produce cumbi for colonial clients.[25] During the colonial period, weaving on the backstrap loom came to be associated strongly with Indian women (although the introduction of the standing loom and the *obraje* or small factory would bring male labor back into the picture early in the seventeenth century). On the north coast there remained *parcialidades* or groups of Indians under a cacique apparently still devoted to making cumbi, and curiously, a 1540 visita of the Mochica village of Jayanca lists a parcialidad of female weavers (*las tejedoras*), but the later encomienda system did not encourage specialized artisans, particularly by the 1560s and 1570s when tribute was standardized into a few basic and saleable commodities.[26]

So how did weaving change from a flexibly gendered occupation to become a practice associated predominantly with Indian women? The Chucuito visita offers one possible scenario for that process. Nearly all the Indian informants in that census declared that their cumbi was made by men, with the help of women in spinning the wool, and that awasca was made by both married men and all women. The inspector, however, wrote in his final report that "only women make the said clothing [of awasca] although some men spin."[27] No Indian informant was quoted to that effect in the written record; it could have been a slip, or the bureaucrat's bias, or a reflection of what he saw during his visita rather than heard. Other Spaniards, however, were simultaneously making the same assumptions, and by the later sixteenth century merchants and middlemen were going directly to Indian women for their orders. As well, we might imagine that the European preference for female domestic servants might have added to this feminizing trend: although the caciques of Chucuito were said to have in their households both male and female Indians to make their clothes, two Spanish officials in that province were provided with only female Indian servants for this purpose.[28]

Whatever the specific evolution of these processes, by the mid-sixteenth century Spanish policy makers were discovering indigenous women's potential for commodity production.[29] Dr. Gregorio González de Cuenca, sent to review tribute practices on the north coast in 1566–67, was among the first to call for the increased commerce in indigenous cloth, though he cautioned caciques against imprisoning unmarried women in household sweatshops. He called specifically for widows and single women to make clothing, to be marketed by their caciques, and to be paid, in the presence of a priest or *corregidor* (the regional bureaucrat in charge of the Indian population), at the rather paltry rate of six *tomines* per piece, so that "the commerce in ropa de la tierra does not diminish."[30] This call was taken up again by jurists and bureaucrats such as Juan de Matienzo and Juan Polo de Ondegardo, in reports written to influence the policies of viceroys charged with reforming the colonial economy in the 1560s and 1570s.

The call to employ women in spinning and weaving succeeded. Whatever the gender of the household weaver before the Spanish conquest, female labor came to be perceived by entrepreneurs as an underexploited commodity. Administrative policy exhorted caciques, corregidores, and priests to discourage female "laziness" and "immorality" by busying Indian women with weaving for market, above and beyond their community's tributary obligations.

Textiles and the Conquest: Clothing the Wildman

To understand how this handwoven wool and cotton cloth, now made predominantly by rural indigenous women, was able to propel economic development in key regions of Peru, it will be useful to review the social meanings of cloth during the first decades of contact. For indigenous residents as well as colonizers, cloth and clothing had symbolic as well as pragmatic features: cloth marked ethnic or regional identity and socioeconomic status at the same time as it protected and ornamented the body. Contact between Europeans and Indians created contestatory dialogues about those meanings, which shifted as the political and economic effects of colonization suffused the region. In this section, I suggest some of these ambiguous meanings, as cloth—and primarily plebeian Indian women's garments—came to embody and drive the northern coastal economy.

We know from archaeological artifacts as well as colonial narratives that cloth was important to prehispanic communities. Religious rituals involved clothing: worn, wrapped around mummies, or burned as sacrifice. Miguel de Estete, among the first Europeans to see Cuzco, marveled at the mummies of Inca elites in the fortress of Sacsahuayman, embalmed and covered with "many outfits, one upon another," which he believed aided in the embalming process.[31] Many chronicles mention the ceremonial burning of cloth along with corn and other products; the Augustinian chronicle of Huamachuco in the northern Andes noted that indigenous "priests" or "witches" wore special clothing while performing rites.[32]

But dress also suggested ethnic, class, and gender identities or identifications. According to the conquistador Pedro Pizarro, "[t]he natives of this kingdom were known by their clothing, because each province wore something different from the other, and they took offense at the wearing of alien dress."[33] Most of the early chroniclers noted that groups within the Inca empire differentiated themselves by wearing typical headdresses; some believed that the Incas imposed dress codes on their subjects. Fernando Montesinos, for example, credited the (apocryphal) Inca Inti Capac with instituting a law that men and women of the empire he was building should "go about with some token by which they were distinguished . . . Some wore the hair braided; some wore it loose; others put in it certain hoops like sieves; others placed cloths upon it; others wore slings coiled in the hair; others had braids, and each province was known by its head-gear or dress."[34]

Others, like Fray Bernabé Cobo, reported that the Incas considered the wearing of another province's clothing or insignia a serious offense, since it made provincial control more problematic.[35] It is hard to know to what degree this discourse of Inca tyranny reflects the chroniclers' politically motivated desire to recall an authoritarian empire, in contrast to the imperfect integration of scattered ethnic groups into a political-economic relationship that probably existed. But the social importance of visual markers—clothing, hairstyles, headgear—that differentiated plebeian from noble, men from women, and one region from another is a common thread in Inca histories.

The prehispanic Andean nobility, and especially the Incas, indeed wore markers to distinguish themselves from commoners. In the colonial period, this costume incorporated new European as well as Andean elements, and it was adopted by those who aspired to indigenous authority as well as those descended from Incas or other elites.[36] In this heated context, Felipe Guaman Poma de Ayala, an Indian noble who had worked within the Spanish bureaucracy, drew attention to the politics of dress in his revision of Andean society—calling for the expulsion of Spaniards and the reinstatement of a (Christian) indigenous nobility under direct vassalage to the Spanish Crown. Guaman Poma argued that the contemporary aesthetic free-for-all both mirrored and caused a social chaos wherein his social class was losing its authority and privilege. In particular, he demanded that (legitimate) colonial caciques should indeed differentiate themselves from Indian commoners by their clothing, but in a way that illustrated the new hierarchies in play, via the integration of European commodities alongside Andean markers of status:

> As cacique principal and lord, he has to differentiate his clothing. He must dress like a Spaniard but with the distinction that he not cut his hair but keep it to the length of his ears. He should wear shirt, collar, doublet and breeches, boots and undershirt and cloak, hat and sword, halberd and other weapons as a lord and nobleman, and horses and mules. And he should sit in a saddle, ceremonial chair [*tiyana*] and that he should not have a beard so that he not look like a mestizo.[37]

Guaman Poma further proposed appropriate dress for the lower nobility (some European clothing) and common men (their appropriate provincial dress with no European elements); while women of all status would wear the Andean lliclla, even though elite women would otherwise wear entirely European-style garments and jewels.[38] Thus European commodities were rapidly becoming part of a social dialogue on race, ethnicity, and class in the colony.

Spanish colonizers and conquerors also approached the issue of clothing from a symbolically charged position. They marveled at the massive stores of woven cloth they found at Cajamarca and Cuzco, gathered as tribute to dress the armies of the Inca, but they arrived in the New World with certain European expectations about "Indians" and clothing, which affected both their actions there and how they wrote about what they saw.

A power-laden discourse about native clothing—or its lack—runs through much of the literature of the conquest, notably beginning with the log of Columbus's first voyage. When the Admiral first sighted what he called "Indians," he was shocked to note (as would be echoed in many chronicles to come) that they were "all as naked as when their mothers bore them"; and when he brought a female specimen on board to "honor them and make them lose their fear" through the exchange of gifts, he forced her to dress in European garments.[39] For Columbus, the nakedness of the natives was a sign of their wildness, in the face of the superiority of European civilization. As is well-known, much European literature of the contact with America took as its objective a construction and defense of European "civilization" through a commentary on American life.[40]

Thus, dressing the Indians was going to be an important component of the civilizing process, one that had some appeal for indigenous elites as well. Following upon the symbolic exchanges of European and indigenous clothing there came a growing interest on the part of elite

Indians in wearing the imported goods, for reasons of prestige as well as coercion, as illustrated by Guaman Poma's pointed commentary above. At the same time, Europeans were of many minds about sharing their own status markers with the culture they intended to dominate.

The desire for imported goods had economic repercussions, as numerous caciques and other nobles placed themselves and their communities in debt to Spanish merchants. Colonial authorities were torn over how to deal with this situation. During his inspection of the north coast in 1566, Dr. Cuenca impotently forbade the wearing of European clothing or accessories by any Indian, since these were too costly and led them to abandon their proper social place.[41] But at roughly the same time, Juan de Matienzo, Judge (*oidor*) of the *Real Audiencia* (high court) of Charcas and policy advisor to Viceroy Toledo, headed a chapter of his *Gobierno del Perú*, "How they will teach trades to the Indians of the *repartimientos* [a provincial administrative unit], and whether it is a good idea that [Indians] make gunpowder and shoot firearms, and ride horseback and wear Spanish clothing."[42] He argued that Indians should indeed be taught trades, since "there is nothing that they are taught which they do not learn well," but that they be prohibited from riding horseback, making gunpowder, and handling firearms, since some of them were better at these dangerous crafts than the Spaniards. On the other hand, he wrote,

Wearing Spanish clothing not only is not bad, but it is very beneficial for many reasons. First, because they would come to love us and our clothing; second, because they would begin to have some humanity, and I say this should be allowed for the caciques and lords; third, because being dressed as Spaniards are, they will be ashamed to seat themselves in the public plaza to eat, drink, and get drunk; and fourth, because however much money they spend, that much more silver will they take out of the earth, and that much more merchandise from Spain will be sold, all of which will increase the royal fifth. It will be, finally, a great benefit to the Spaniards, without harm to the Indians, since they have no need for either silver or gold, nor do they use it for the business they have with each other, but only that business which they conduct with Spaniards.[43]

Subsequent viceroys accepted Matienzo's market logic, but by this point it was moot: most caciques and urban Indians, and a good number of rural Indians were already purchasing European commodities with cash and credit. Even in Cuenca's Trujillo valley, the caciques found themselves thoroughly enmeshed in debt by the end of the sixteenth century. Don Pedro Anco Guaman, the cacique of Moche, owed a Spanish merchant named Rodrigo a hundred pesos "for his account" when he wrote his will in 1594, and at least two Trujillo merchants extended nearly a thousand pesos of credit to the cacique of Chicama, don Juan de Mora, for large swathes of imported silks and taffetas as well as shirts, frockcoats, and jewelry in the 1570s and 1580s.[44]

The influx of the world market and the tentacles of debt led many colonial subjects to rail against the system, from their own peculiar vantage points. Guaman Poma, the Andean noble, arguing that this "disorder" caused problems for Spaniards as well as Indians, complained that the King of Spain ought to

consider how the kinds of clothing from Castille, and from this land, and cattle from Castille and of this land, during the conquest cost very little because the Spaniards only ate their native foods and the Indians their own. And they were disgusted [at the thought] of eating the foods [of the others] and of clothing, their own [*sic*]. Nowadays all dress and eat the best and thus everything in this kingdom costs too much, Spanish goods as well as Indian. Consider.[45]

In other words, transculturation yielded higher prices for all, an economic as well as cultural misfortune. The elite mestizo chronicler Garcilaso de la Vega ironically recounted that Spaniards, attempting to promote the wearing of clothing among certain indigenous communities, found great resistance and "[t]he women refuse just as much as the men, and Spaniards often chaff them about their indecency and unwillingness to spin, and ask if they don't dress because they won't spin, or if they don't spin because they won't dress."[46] Clearly there was much more at stake here than "decency."

In summary, the Spanish elite recognized that Indian labor and purchasing power (here neatly intertwined) were at the heart of the colonial economy, which was to be their livelihood. Indigenous intellectuals, like Guaman Poma, sometimes saw this cultural access as a threat to their own privileges, though the archive reveals that their critiques did nothing to slow the process. The complicated relationship of both groups to indigenous and European clothing exposes one facet of the conflict between expectations and desires: Indians and Spaniards both had reasons to want cheap, domestically produced clothes as well as imported luxury goods. And both types of commodities were integral to the functioning of the growing regional economy, produced and distributed through the complicated interactions of encomenderos and merchants. In the remaining sections I investigate a segment of that changing economy, one which identified indigenous women as key workers and consumers whose activities helped determine the paths of the colonial economy.

La ropa de la tierra: The Tribute in Cloth (1540–1620)

As we have noted, the "prize" of the northern encomienda was the labor service and tribute of large indigenous populations, and the commodity that produced the most income by far was handloomed cotton and wool textiles, called by Spanish merchants *la ropa de la tierra*. In the initial years of conquest, tribute took the form of what Spalding has called the "plunder economy": "the expropriation of a considerable proportion of the goods produced by the members of Andean society for their own use, and for the luxury and display of the state destroyed by the conquerors."[47] Thus it would include the raiding of huacas and other shrines and burial sites for gold, silver, and other objects of value to the Europeans. But this surplus was not boundless, nor was it adequate to meet the growing stream of immigrants expecting to make their New World fortunes. In much of the new colony, labor was quickly organized to extract metals from the earth as a supplement to the tribute in food and other staples demanded of the shrinking Indian population. But the north coast had no mines and, once the major huacas had been looted, little access to those things that the Spaniards explicitly sought. By rights, the Trujillo region should have become an extremely minor player in the colonial economy. However, the fact that it did not, that its encomenderos and merchants were part of a vital and expanding economy, linked to but not determined by Lima and Potosí, indicates that other indigenous-produced commodities circulated in regional economies that also had significant effects on rural communities. The tribute in clothing was a major factor for the eighty years of its existence.[48]

Early tribute was a chaotic affair. The Viceroy Conde de Nieva later remarked sardonically that, with the death of Governor Pizarro in 1541, "the Indians contributed and paid everything that the encomendero wanted, and his mouth was their measure."[49] This included various personal services as well as any commodity—locally available or not—that struck the encomendero's imagination, and all was rationalized as both expressing continuity with the Inca past and as appropriate remuneration to the colonial overlords offering protection as well as religious instruction to their Indian subjects.[50]

Perhaps more important, under Spanish rule tribute obligations were shifted from an Inca requirement of performing a certain number of days of labor per year to one demanding specific quantities of commodities at periodic intervals, most often twice annually. In years of

floods, droughts, or earthquakes—frequent natural disasters, especially on the north coast—communities had to make up their tribute
out of their own production, leading to terrible famines and conse-
quent migrations. And the textile tribute was so feared that at least one
indigenous community, Acarí in the southern Andes, was nearly abandoned by its youths in order to escape it, according to their own statements in a 1593 visita.[51] The vast literature on the Andean tribute
system makes it clear that indigenous populations did not necessarily
see the continuity between Inca and Spanish imperial policy; in particular, this shift from labor time to quotas proved extremely onerous for
rapidly diminishing communities.[52]

Uncontrolled plunder was not a Spanish Crown policy, though, and
from as early as 1536 there were heated battles as the state tried to restrict encomendero power. As part of this battle the Crown called
for various administrative measures, especially visitas, to regulate
excesses and to maximize royal tax collection (though the administrators, corregidores, and inspectors were often encomenderos themselves). The president of the Real Audiencia or high court, Licenciado
Pedro de la Gasca, published a series of official tribute lists (*tasas*) in
1549 to curb encomenderos' demands, and in 1566, Dr. Gregorio González de Cuenca was dispatched to reform tribute practices in the north
coast, in response to growing complaints there.[53]

Cuenca's north coast visita regularized tribute into a short list of
locally available commodities, now generally coin, cloth, corn, wheat,
dried fish, and fowl, assessed according to the number of tributaries
rather than the total population. Thus, for example, a married male between the ages of seventeen and forty-seven in the community of
Collique was said to be responsible for three *fanegas* or approximately
four and a half bushels each of wheat and corn, and one and a half sets
of clothing annually. But communities still had trouble meeting the
new tasas, which in some cases were even higher than previously.[54] In
the 1570s, Viceroy Toledo further standardized tribute across the
colony, much along Cuenca's pattern, and offered the option in many
cases of commuting tribute in kind to coin, though this option was less
often taken in the mineral-poor north coast. Toledo's administrative
system also called for tribute to be collected by corregidores, but on
the north coast, perhaps because cloth played such a large role and silver such a small one, encomenderos and the merchants to whom they
were indebted continued to collect it directly in many cases, through
the turn of the century.[55]

The established tasa had the effect, at least on the surface, of regularizing the demands of the "plunder economy" toward a kind of colonial norm, which could be litigated when participants perceived abuses. Tribute was supposed to be pegged to the number of married, able-bodied men aged eighteen to fifty, and various communities attempted, with some success, to lower their tax bills as their populations steadily declined; overall though, assessed levels of tribute tended to be stagnant, and its burden on shrinking communities increased over the century.

This tributary system, which interjected the state (a growing bureaucracy that was fast becoming separate from and coming into competition with encomenderos) into the arrangement previously between encomendero and encomienda, left the encomendero with a fixed "pension" or rent—up to 60 percent of the total tribute—and distributed the rest to the royal treasury, priests, and caciques. The corregidor and his officials were supposed to offer the tributed commodities at a public auction to all interested residents of the city. There were many problems inherent in the system, however, including the fact that corruption was rampant and the inspection system was infrequent and spotty.

In the north, at any rate, it seems that the state only intervened to auction off the commodities tributed by encomiendas *vacas*, "empty" encomiendas that had reverted to the Crown's possession with the death of the encomendero (most notably the encomiendas of Jequetepeque and San Pedro de Lloco). In most other cases, encomenderos reached agreements with favored merchants to liquidate their bushels of wheat and corn and bags of clothing directly. An anonymous informant at the turn of the seventeenth century stated that encomendero rents resulted from the "clothing, silver, wheat, corn and other commodities in which the Indians of said Repartimientos are taxed by the lord Viceroys, which [are] sold by the encomenderos and other persons who have this as their charge."[56] It may be that encomenderos had in practice the option of auctioning off their tribute or selling it to a merchant independently, though this was certainly not Toledo's intention.

Into the first years of the seventeenth century the few remaining encomenderos of the north coast continued to sell off their shares of tribute in cloth, receiving large profits for their minimal effort. Frequent lawsuits over the commutation of cloth tribute illustrate both communities' dislike for this tasa and the encomenderos' desire to maintain it. In 1566 the encomendera of Cinto, doña Juana de Figueroa, went to court to have the value of cloth reevaluated for her encomienda. Her predecessor had made a fairly common "restitution" to the Indians of Cinto in his will, converting their debt in clothing to a fixed amount of silver to alleviate his conscience on his deathbed. The new encomendera argued that the cash the Indians were paying in lieu of textiles was far too little, and a number of merchants were brought in to establish the "just price" for cloth, which was subsequently set at two pesos a set.[57] In the same year, the natives of Pácora fled to Túcume and other places to avoid their own tasa of 600 sets of clothing per year, because their population had diminished to the point that they could not meet it.[58]

After a devastating epidemic of measles and smallpox, the caciques of Huamachuco sued their encomendera, doña Florencia de Mora, in 1594 for a new population count and the commutation of the tribute in cloth to additional grain, arguing that they lacked the cotton with which to weave garments. Florencia de Mora put forth a vituperative argument against the commutation, saying

that the Indians could very comfortably pay, and without work or vexation, the said tribute in clothing and not in wheat or corn and, Your Worship, because of the said recount that you ordered and the commutation of clothing to wheat and corn, there was notorious damage and vexation of the Indians because they have in their lands many hot valleys where they can sow and harvest a great quantity of cotton with which to make the said clothing as they have done, and that the clothing is spun and woven by old Indian women and widows.[59]

The community won a lower tributary count, but the value of cloth was reassessed from one peso six tomines to two pesos five tomines, probably leaving neither side pleased.

Why did encomenderos fight so bitterly to maintain their control over indigenous cloth? Although, according to notarial contracts for its sale in Lima as well as Trujillo, the market price of cloth hovered around two pesos in the 1550s and 1560s, by the 1570s it was creeping upward toward three pesos, and in the 1580s quickly began spiraling even beyond six pesos (see Table 1). Not all cloth was the same; regional differences in technique, weaving styles, dyes, and fibers (possibly a remnant of the differential costumes of the prehispanic period) brought different prices: a 1575 contract between Trujillo merchants identified at least five different regional styles, ranging up to seven pesos for a set of garments.[60] Heavier cloth, from the highlands of Cajamarca and Huamachuco, could be more expensive than the cotton cloth of the valleys; it reached six pesos first, by the early 1580s (perhaps explaining doña Florencia's anger mentioned above).

TABLE 1
Price of indigenous cloth, Valleys of Trujillo, 1561–1620

Years	Price Range	"Sets" Sold
1561–65	1p6rr–2p6t	8312.5
1566–70	1p5t–2p3t	7347.0
1571–75	1p–3p	1849.5
1576–80	3p	300.0
1581–85	3p4rr–4p4rr	1639.5
1586–95	4p4rr–7p	1313.0
1596–1600	8p	41.5
1601–05	5p4rr–6p	126.0
1606–10	6p–7p1rr	n/a
1611–15	6p–7p	350.0
1616–20	6p4rr–8p	561.0

SOURCES: AGN PN, AGN JR, and ARLL PN.

NOTE: These figures come from a less-than-random survey of archival materials in Lima and Trujillo and do not indicate the entire volume of clothing transactions for this region. Nominal prices (in pesos of eight reales) are assumed here to illustrate trends; the volume traded at these prices is an indicator of the availability of evidence for these prices as well as a general reflection of the occurrence of contracts. Some transactions are presumably resales of the same product.
p = peso; t = tomino; rr = reales

If the tribute received by an encomendero is evaluated using market prices rather than the values assessed by the Toledan scheme, it is clear that the ropa de la tierra provided the overwhelming majority of their income. For encomenderos in the Trujillo valley, where a community's tribute often included thousands of anacos and llicllas per year, this meant a steady and comfortable income.

Indigenous textiles were an extremely profitable commodity for everyone except the producers. For example, in 1565, the Indian women of the encomienda of Ferriñafe were responsible for producing 1,145 sets of anaco and lliclla as tribute, which was collected by their cacique, don Alonso, in two installments. In June he turned over the cloth to his encomendero, Melchior de Osorno, in order to receive his own salary. Osorno had already sold the entire year's production to two local merchants, Alonso Jofre and Juan de Lodueno, in February, for one peso six tomines a set. Jofre and Lodueno, anticipating receipt of their share of 572 sets of two garments, in May sold them to two more merchants, Cristóbal Marquez and Diego de Ábila, for a bit over two pesos a set.[61] Marquez and Ábila at that time also bought the cloth tribute from the encomiendas of Jequetepeque and Reque. Unfortunately the paper trail ends here, but most of the more than two thousand garments likely ended up in Lima or Potosí, and possibly some of them were sold in stores in Trujillo either to urban indigenous women who did not make their own clothing or to Spaniards fulfilling their employment contracts with Indian maids and laborers. By this point each set would cost upwards of five or six pesos, and possibly much more.

The following litigation gives a sense of the purchasing value of the year's tribute in clothing. A lawsuit was filed against Pero González de Ayala in 1569 by the merchant Alonso Carrasco, who had agreed to buy 1,500 sets of cloth garments—a year's tribute—for the price of 3,000 pesos cash. Carrasco offered, instead of the cash, some houses he owned in the plaza of Trujillo containing two *tiendas* or small stores, plus three male and three female slaves. After the fact, Carrasco thought better of the deal and sued to return to the original cash terms, and he won.[62] Indigenous cloth was clearly of considerable value.

Wheat, another component of tribute, also could be a major source of income, but was unreliable in comparison with cloth. According to a lawsuit brought by Indians against a number of encomenderos in 1579, after the devastating floods of 1578, which destroyed not only that year's crop but affected subsequent plantings as well, a fanega of corn or wheat, which normally sold for half a peso, was selling for three to four pesos, if it could be found at all.[63] Wheat was subject to cyclical fluctuations, and in a bad year could and did make fortunes for those lucky enough to hold it, but there was plenty of competition in the north from nonencomienda farms that helped to supply the valleys as well as Lima. Indigenous clothing, on the other hand, was only produced by Indians, and its steady price inflation was a function not so much of scarcity but of manipulations of the markets.

The more centralized tribute system had another important side effect, the improved opportunities it created for merchants and middlemen. Instead of relying upon relationships with encomenderos, merchants could now work with corregidores and other officials to increase their access to Indians and their products. Encomenderos, corregidores, visitadores, and other bureaucrats and officials tended to come from a small, insular group. In the first decades of conquest, the elite supported large contingents of hangers-on who performed various services for small salaries. But as regional economies developed and it became lucrative to haul commodities between the growing centers of the Americas, new opportunities arose for independent merchants, muleteers, and collection agents. The colonial bureaucracy created so many more niches where an enterprising merchant, even with limited capital and access, could insert himself (and more rarely, herself, though many Spanish women provided capital for these ventures).

And merchants were receiving a windfall.[64] As seen above, debt-pressured encomenderos were often selling *en adelantado*, in advance of collecting the tribute, for lower than market prices. Future sales yielded increased prices as the clothing made its way into stores and markets in Trujillo, Lima, and Potosí. A single lot of tribute cloth might be sold two or three times in Trujillo before being shipped to Lima or Potosí; there are significant numbers of contracts in notarial records in Lima for cloth from "the valleys of Trujillo" where neither party had obvious ties to Trujillo, although encomenderos such as Salvador Vásquez and Luis Chacón had homes in Lima as well as Trujillo. Vásquez often handled his own negotiations, generally bartering for luxury goods such as imported wines and construction supplies, though his sugar *ingenio* (mill) in the Saña valley was probably funded through his commercial activities as well as the large loans and mortgages that proved his eventual downfall.[65] However, the majority of the late-sixteenth-century contracts I have located involved merchants and middlemen looking to large urban areas to resell the clothing.

Companies specializing in the sale and resale of ropa de la tierra were not uncommon in the north. The 1570 last will and testament of the Trujillo merchant Francisco de Villalobos suggests the extent of his businesses: he died holding debts for cloth with many local encomenderos, including Salvador Vásquez, who owed him 2,630 sets of garments for which he had paid 5,000 pesos in addition to various merchandise. Villalobos also had 8,000 pesos invested in a company trading in silver and indigenous cloth, with Francisco Ramírez, who had left the city to sell the merchandise; and Villalobos was suing the merchant Luis Martín, who owed him 1,620 sets of cotton cloth from their partnership.[66] Another such company was formed in 1582 between Rodrigo Hurtado and Alonso de Peñaranda, capitalized with more than 2,000 pesos' worth of indigenous cloth and related craft items from the northern valleys and sierra, which were loaded onto two ships sailing for Lima.[67]

The ultimate customers for these vast stocks of inexpensive clothing were most often mitayos in mining areas. Matienzo estimated in 1567 that 300,000 pesos annually changed hands as Indian workers bought clothing and other goods from Spaniards in Potosí alone.[68] Other major purchasers were urban Indians without the time or skills to make their own, and also the employers of Indian servants and laborers, whose labor contracts generally called for two outfits a year in addition to food, shelter, religious education, medical attention, and a small amount of cash. Slaves may have been dressed in it, although León Portocarrero referred in the early seventeenth century to a street in Lima which specialized in "clothing for Blacks," not necessarily indigenous made.[69] It is likely that poorer Spaniards and free blacks purchased and dressed in cheap indigenous textiles, probably reshaping them to conform to European fashions. The large cloth rectangles were also adapted for other uses, from blankets and household furnishings to sailcloth. The only competition for this market, prior to the rise in the seventeenth century of the great *obrajes*, or larger-scale cloth manufactories, were imported textiles from Mexico and the Far East (generally China, the Philippines, and India), which arrived both legally and illegally.[70] But given the relative scarcity of imported textiles and the need for cheap fabric to clothe workers now removed from the community setting where they might have made it for themselves, there was an enormous appetite for inexpensive cloth and, with the encomienda system, a captive labor force to produce it.

For indigenous populations on the north coast, with extensive and early European contact, the first fifty years of colonization brought greater dislocation than Spanish policy would have acknowledged. Despite the lack of mines in the region, the Indian and Spanish economies were integrated in order to increase the concentration of wealth in elite hands. The effects of the plunder economy reverberated within ethnic groups as indigenous elites became desperate to meet these increasing demands with their own fragmented communities. The major administrative reforms—those of the visitador Cuenca in the 1560s and Viceroy Toledo in the 1570s—responded to perceived abuses, but simultaneously created spaces for greater exploitation as a bureaucratic and mercantile structure grew up in conflict with the encomienda system, in competition for the wealth produced by Indians.

"Not . . of great concern": Nontribute Cloth Production and the Business of Colonialism

Toledo envisioned his reforms as affording expanding opportunities for Indians and Spaniards alike in the growing mercantile economy. He supported the increased participation of Indians in the market and wrote in 1573,

if for the said community tribute it will be a good thing that unmarried Indian women and widows of each Repartimiento help out by making clothing of wool or cotton or cumbi or wools [*sic*], the community giving them the wool or cotton and paying them some moderate quantity for their work, so that the community can sell the clothing that they make and the proceeds remain with the said community, then it could not be of great concern.[71]

Certainly some communities saw production for market as a way out of their constant struggle to produce tribute commodities or as a means to support their local churches or even finance legal actions against their encomenderos. Caciques, often under intense pressure to acquire cash for their encomenderos and other officials, as well as to pay their personal creditors, adapted their political roles and organized their communities for production.[72] They certainly organized weaving for the market, as we saw in the visita of Chucuito, and though archival references to this trade are relatively scarce for many regions, there is evidence that it was quite common. Among the most frequent transactions in the notarial archives of Huánuco in the late sixteenth century are caciques selling weaving services to a Spaniard, independent of the encomienda system. Spalding describes this as a "primitive putting-out system," where the Spaniard supplied the raw cotton and received finished anacos and llicllas.[73]

Such sales may well represent surplus cloth willingly contributed by communities to earn the silver necessary for tribute. But there is also evidence that caciques coerced their subjects to produce cloth, often illegally. The provincial government of the north, for example, authorized punishments for caciques who locked up widows and unmarried women to force them to work beyond tributary demands, suggesting that this was a regular problem.[74] The north has fewer notarial records of legal cloth transactions, but there are extant indications of that trade. In 1581, the cacique of Jayanca, don Francisco Puiconsoli, contracted to sell the merchant Mateo Lazcano one hundred *capuces de algodón pintado* [painted or dyed cotton cloaks, a prehispanic craft for which the region was known] at four pesos a piece.[75] And in her last will and testament, doña Ysabel Pacho, wife of the encomendero of Ferriñafe, wrote that don Alonso, the cacique of Ferriñafe, had sent her fifty capuces, which she had sold for 115 pesos.[76] Capuces were not a tributed commodity, so any sales must have involved production outside the legal encomienda system, and they formed part of the burgeoning colonial economy not directly answerable to the law.

But most of the nontribute production of cloth was organized by colonial officials and merchants, and caciques received relatively small shares of the income. From early on, individuals with commodities or services needed or desired by community members could informally bargain for cloth. One of the earliest records of the improper use of power to acquire Indian cloth appears in the report of Cuenca's visita of 1566–67.[77] In his summation of the various charges leveled against clergy in the north coast and recommendations for new ecclesiastical policy, Cuenca noted that "[s]ome priests when they baptize adult Indians ask of them an offering for the baptism and they make them offer *chumbes* [woven belts] and pieces of clothing and the poor Indians that have nothing to offer fail to get baptized." It may be that the priests, unable to get cash payment for their services, took advantage of the prehispanic practice of using fine cloth as part of religious services or sacrifices and then turned to the market to redeem the products.

Cuenca argued strongly that laws prohibiting the involvement of priests in businesses and trading companies should be enforced, since priests were using third parties to set up businesses in indigenous cloth and other products, often with the cooperation of the local cacique. Unfortunately many of the early ecclesiastic records for the north have vanished, so it is difficult to estimate the extent to which the Catholic Church was involved in cloth production and trade, but it is clear that priests saw their charges as a labor force available to supplement their salaries on large and small scales

The Church had less direct but equally powerful effects through its demands on the growing number of converts in Andean communities. As we saw at the beginning of this chapter, in 1567 Garci Díez discovered that the caciques of Chucuito had contracted with upwards of nine merchants for 4,000 sets of clothing over a twenty-month period (in addition to their annual tribute of another 1,000 sets of garments). Díez blamed the corregidor for agreeing to the contracts, but failed to call to account the church: according to the caciques they spent the money on a chasuble, altar cloths (*fronteras*), clothing for the altar boys, and even the construction of one of the churches.[78] One cacique claimed that he spent his pesos in this way because "the doctrinal priest asked for them, and another 170 for a chasuble."[79] Aggressive church demands were pushing the caciques into business. Chucuito, in the sierra halfway between Cuzco and Potosí, was highly monetarized from early on due to its proximity to the mining industry, and the Church was not restrained in its demands for ostentatious if empty proof of Indian conversion and piety. In the poorer and less densely populated north coast, the Church seems to have been somewhat more circumspect in this regard. Other market-oriented needs and tastes, however, would easily arise in its stead.

Colonial administrators, especially corregidores, also found opportunities to augment their income through extralegal indigenous labor.
Although a certain amount of abuse was apparently expected (or at
least endured), political disagreements might well up into indignation
at the flouting of the law. In 1590, Pero González de Ayala, son of the
last encomendero of San Pedro de Lloco and Jequetepeque, brought
charges against Antonio de Urraco and Joaquin de Aldana, the bookkeeper (*contador*) and treasurer (*tesorero*), respectively of Trujillo, which
became the foundation for an investigation of their tenures in office,
called a *juicio de residencia*. After his father's death the encomienda had
reverted to the Crown's possession, but González de Ayala remained
entitled to a share of tribute, to be distributed by the corregidor and
these officials. He claimed that they were withholding his pension and
that the officials were exploiting their access to the community and its
tribute to extract wealth illegally. The *residencia*, which was a standard
review of an official's tenure in office, quickly turned into a full-blown
criminal investigation of Urraco and Aldana. The many charges included lending funds from the community chest to themselves and
others to start small enterprises, gambling and otherwise living
beyond their means, keeping improper accounts, selling grain at lower
than legal prices to friends, and a number of income-generating schemes
involving indigenous cloth.

The encomiendas in question were extremely valuable, mainly, as I
have shown, for their textile production. During an earlier juicio de
residencia, the tasas for the Chicama valley were published, having
been reduced by the last corregidor from Toledo's rates due to depop-
ulation. Jequetepeque had a tributary population in the early 1580s of
700 to 750 adult men, who with their households were responsible for
contributing between 700 and 800 pesos in silver twice a year, as well
as 350 sets of clothing, anacos and llicllas.[80] The encomendero sold his
share of the textiles in 1583 to a local merchant for three pesos four
reales each, yielding significantly more than the other components of
his share of tribute combined.[81]

Apparently Urraco and Aldana were well aware of the wealth-
generating possibilities of the local cloth. According to evidence presented in the trial, they not only arranged to "auction" off tribute from
the royal encomiendas directly to friends for below-market prices, allowing them to undercut other merchants, but they also had their own
(illegal) putting-out system in the Indian communities. Salvador
Vásquez, the encomendero of Reque and a "sworn enemy" of the two

officials (due, he said, to the "mistreatments which he saw them make of Pero González") testified that he heard that "some Indians . . . were making ropa de la tierra called capuces for the bookkeeper Antonio de Urraco and this witness likewise heard it said that said capuces were bought from said bookkeeper by the said Portuguese [merchant] Pereyra." The local merchants and encomenderos were having these capuces made outside of the tribute system, probably with the aid of local caciques.

But the most interesting testimony bore upon the social relations governing cloth production within the community, bringing us back to the question of how the tribute system and the introduction of regional markets affected the day-to-day lives of women and men. Don Juan Chinmis, a cousin of the cacique of San Pedro de Lloco, described the operation in detail:

> A little more than four years ago the bookkeeper Antonio de Urraco came to San Pedro de Lloco, where this witness lives, and one day . . . [Urraco] entered the church and went to the door with a chair and a table and all the Indian women were inside the church and the said bookkeeper called them each up, from a memorandum, and he weighed for them with a scale the cotton that the bookkeeper gave them and to each woman whom he had given cotton for a whole piece of clothing they later gave her for the manufacture eight reales and to the woman who made a half piece they gave four reales.[82]

Juan Batista, a thirty-eight-year-old translator and native of the community, noted that in Jequetepeque,

> the said bookkeeper himself distributed the cotton to the Indian women when he made the orders and he left the money for them with the priest for the weaving, in order that they might pay the Indian women for their work . . . and this witness also said that some Indian women ran out of the cotton the treasurer gave them for the clothing and they supplied it out of their own stores and they have complained that the said bookkeeper has not paid them for the said cotton which they provided.

Since at this time cloth was being sold for between three and five pesos (of eight reales each), Urraco was receiving a profit of 200 to 400 percent, minus the minor cost of the raw cotton (the price of a *costal* or bag of cotton from Los Chachapoyas at this time was 6 reales[83]). Other witnesses asserted that Urraco had never paid the women at all, nor was he willing to issue receipts to the caciques.

Thus, by the end of the sixteenth century, in a small rural community outside Trujillo, a system was in place, with the apparent blessing of provincial officials and the local priest, to organize women's labor to produce cloth for market. And, as we saw in Chucuito a few decades earlier, these women not only participated in this small enterprise, but fully expected to receive payment in cash (rather than within an Andean system of reciprocity) and complained when the terms of their implied contract were not met.

Why would these women demand coin for their labors? Here we find the final piece of the analysis linking the encomienda system to production for market, and the key to understanding how economic stresses in rural areas were creating local crises and the pressure for urban migration. In his testimony Juan Bautista explained that "sometimes . . . the said Antonio de Urraco, when he collected the tasas for His Majesty, sold to the Indian women who did not have clothing to pay their tasa, or to the widowed Indian men, the clothing to the said Indians for the said eight pesos a set." He went on to note that this was the same price—eight pesos—that clothing went for in the town or in the *tambos* (inns). In other words, Urraco was reselling their own handiwork to these women at eight times what he originally paid them for it, so that they could return it to him as their tribute. And the price charged to Indians was two to three times the price paid by merchants.[84]

Urraco and Aldana claimed that none of this was true. Urraco in particular said that if he had any weaving done at all, it was but a small amount and for his personal household, and he paid the just price to a noncoerced labor force in the presence of the Indian officials and the local priest.[85] Nevertheless, both were cleared of all charges *except* for having businesses outside of their official duties, and exploiting the Indians. For these crimes they were fined eight hundred pesos, plus various small restitutions, including a total of thirty pesos to be divided among the hundreds of women who had made the cloth, a sum which would not even purchase a fraction of the next season's tribute.

But even so public a trial had little effect on this lucrative informal economy. During the 1611 residencia of don Gabriel Doria, the outgoing corregidor of Chiclayo, the new corregidor raised charges that Doria had had illegal businesses producing clothing, wine, chicha, soap, and bread; he was also charged with diverting water away from Indian communities to his own vast agricultural properties and with general violence against and mistreatment of his charges. Doria's response to the clothing charges were that he, echoing Urraco above, only ordered the women to make what was necessary for the service of his own house, not more than fifteen sets of garments, and that he compensated them well for it. He added that if they made more, it was at their cacique's orders and not his, "for they have the custom of ordering them to make many pieces of clothing in the name of the corregidor, but being for the said caciques, as is public and notorious, and thus if the said caciques have deposed in this case against (him) it is for fear of the punishment which might come to them for having ordered the making of clothing.[86] Doria was eventually cleared of most of the charges, fined thirty pesos, and allowed to hold public office again.

Elite Spanish women were accused with regularity of similar abuses, on their own or as wives of corrupt bureaucrats and encomenderos. In the above-mentioned 1611 residencia, doña Niculassa, the wife of the corregidor, seems to have been at least partly in charge of running the corregidor's illegal taverns and bakeries, and she personally came to Chiclayo to request that the women make her some cloth.[87] Female encomenderas, who usually inherited their position from a husband, father, or a son, were a small but powerful presence in the early colonial period—as many as a quarter of the total encomenderos of Trujillo and Lima in 1601, for example—and, from the archival record, apparently as likely to exploit their subjects as their male counterparts.[88]

While there is little direct contractual evidence for nonencomienda production of textiles, the record of litigation and bureaucratic self-investigation reveals that it was indeed a considerable business. The expanding economy of Trujillo was closely tied to the production and sale of indigenous clothing. This production was, however, extremely dependent upon the existence of the encomienda system: groups of organized Indian laborers, subject to their own caciques as well as to state and church authorities.

Although colonial officials argued that the encomienda system was simply the reorganization of an Inca tributary system, it is clear that it made new demands on colonial subjects and affected not only standards of living, but also mentalities. As many other historians have demonstrated, colonialism brought new institutions—new laws, new forms of economic life, new religious practices—to indigenous communities, which made of these what they could. In the case of the communities of the north coast, the dependence upon handwoven cloth as a source of wealth meant that despite the male Indian's position as the nominal tributary, women (and presumably elderly and infirm men, and children of both genders) functioned as the main textile producers from the perspective of encomenderos, merchants, bureaucrats, priests, and even their own caciques. The flourishing colonial economy was successfully altering the gender division of labor within the indigenous household by subtle pressures and expectations rather than edict or plan.

Conclusions

Although indigenous women's tribute production is more or less invisible in most of the literature on colonial Peru, a careful reading of both chronicles and archival documents indicates that these women were anything but invisible to participants in the colonial economy: the indigenous communities, caciques, encomenderos, priests, merchants, and administrators, many of whom became wealthier through their involvement in the appropriation and circulation of tribute in clothing. Certainly Viceroy Toledo, one of the architects of the mature tributary system, understood their roles. While explicitly relieving women of the nominal burden of tribute production (which basically meant that the amount of tribute assigned to a "tributary" male was the amount that could be produced by a male and female worker together, a simple arithmetic elision), he authorized not only that they should produce the tribute in cloth, but also surplus production for sale in markets. In so doing, he merely gave official imprimatur to changes that had been underway for at least a decade: merchants and bureaucrats were discovering a way to expand markets further by making women responsible for the production of woven textiles.

Toledo described this as a deeply moral mission, asking visitadores to ascertain

> whether if the said community tribute it will be good if the Indian widows and single women of each repartimiento to make the clothing of wool or cotton, or cumbi, supplying (wool or cotton) out of community stocks so that they can make it, and the product would thus be for said community, which could be for the common good, although one should not order each Indian woman to make more than one piece of clothing each time, so that the said widowed and single women don't go about unoccupied, setting a bad example to married women, and living dishonestly, as has been seen and is seen from experience.[89]

Women needed not only to work, but to be *seen* working all the time. As in the case of Indian men, often vilified as lazy and shiftless, this characterization served to justify a coercive, even violent labor system.

This apparently small change, one among many new or increased demands made by a panoply of officials, Spanish as well as indigenous, caused an important and lasting shift in gender relations in colonial Peru. Not only have we seen a socioeconomic as well as ideological transformation, whereby Andean women became wholly identified with the spindle and backstrap loom, and men, when they wove at all, did so on a European-style standing loom and for a wage, but we have also seen this process put into motion a series of social, economic, and cultural changes. Rural women came to expect cash remuneration for some of their labor and sought recourse in the courts or other branches of the colonial government when they considered themselves cheated, and clothing—both locally made and imported—arose as a prime commodity in the burgeoning consumer markets. By examining the earliest workings of the economy through the prism of gender relations, we have seen on a very personal level how individuals as well as communities experienced colonization.

The supposed distinction between rural and urban life is likewise complicated by the evidence presented in this chapter. Rural women were learning firsthand the new economic discourses of their relatives in the cities, those of wage labor and of commodities bought and sold in markets rather than self-produced or distributed through kin networks. And, more important, the very excesses that wrought disaster for indigenous communities in the highlands became pressures for them to emigrate to urban centers, where they could evade tribute (and their children, if born there, would not be subject to it) and purchase, rather than make, the clothes they would wear on their backs. Indeed, that clothing would come to be their own stock of capital, to be sold or pawned in need or auctioned after death to pay the cash demands of Catholicism and the credit economy.

All this production, far from the silver mines for which Peru was famous, had enormous economic implications. A manuscript from the first years of the seventeenth century speaks of the "abundance of business" that characterized Trujillo during the period of the encomiendas, because merchants from Tierra Firme (Panama), Lima, Cuzco, and Potosí travelled there to buy "cloth and other goods" from the repartimientos, as well as sugar, conserves, leather, soap, and other local products.[90] Encomienda wealth was quickly parlayed into other business ventures: Ramírez estimates that by 1565, at least two thirds of Trujillo's encomenderos had set up cattle ranches in Lambayeque, and many also had small mixed farms, wheat mills, and sugar estates.[91] A significant amount of profit probably went also to luxury consumption: Salvador Vásquez, as noted above, appears in the notarial records buying wine and other imported goods with his tribute in cloth, and encomenderos such as Juan Chacón de Lara, who lived in Lima, were probably not investing their capital in northern industries. But by 1563 there was enough nonencomienda wealth, at least in part generated by all this local trade, to found Saña, convenient to ports and encomienda populations. Given that Saña was settled by those excluded from Trujillo politics, further research might reveal closer ties between the merchants and middlemen of indigenous clothing and this new urban settlement.

The production and distribution of Indian clothing illustrates as well the intricate interconnections of the colonial economy from this early period. Despite law and ideology, there was not one economy of Indians, and another of Spaniards, but a complex and interdependent system of coerced and noncoerced relations, where some markets were created by force but others flourished unexpectedly. Wherever commodities circulated at a profit, society changed at all levels. As we have seen, regional needs were more determining of local growth than transatlantic ones, and it was the performance of this predominantly indigenous, black, and casta or mixed population that dictated the specifics of economic expansion rather than Europe.

The Trujillo region in particular illustrates economic development in the absence of direct access to mines. Certainly, mines created the "growth poles" that structured colonial "economic space," in the felicitous phrasing of Carlos Sempat Assadourian.[92] But regions far from these centers prospered and waned through the production and circulation of commodities that were almost never seen in Europe, except as trophies of the exotic. The ropa de la tierra is thus almost neatly symbolic of the status of indigenous women: it was a source of great wealth for some, but so ubiquitous and necessary as to be invisible. Its study illustrates the heterogeneity of experience in the early years of the colony, where class, ethnic, and gendered relationships were being simultaneously constructed, not in a vacuum but on long-contested terrain.

CHAPTER 2

"With Our Labor and Sweat":
Creating the Urban Economy

Introduction

In February 1635, a Spanish-speaking Indian woman named Catalina
Carua found herself ill and, fearing imminent death, she called upon
the notary of the Cercado, Antonio de Tamayo, to come to her house
and take down her last will and testament. Carua was a vendor in
Lima's plaza, where she sold clothing and jewelry; her second husband
Cristóbal Gonsales was a master tailor and perhaps made some of the
goods she sold. She was a wealthy woman by the standards of most Indians in Lima: she owned, in addition to beautiful clothing and jewelry,
two African slaves she called María Angola and Sebastiana Folupa.[1]

Although she had been born far from Lima, Carua had deep connections to her adopted city, as evidenced by her desire to be buried in
its Mercedarian convent, in a chapel devoted to Nuestra Señora de la
Consolación. She further asked that she be buried in a Franciscan habit,
with a procession of "orphan children" accompanying her casket, as
well as a full complement of masses for the souls of herself, her two
husbands, and her parents. She clearly had strong ties to her urban
community, and mentioned no properties or bequests outside of Lima.

We get another glimpse of Catalina Carua in a census of the Indians
of Lima, recorded two decades earlier. Then she was a young woman of
about twenty, married to her first husband, an Indian who assisted a
Spanish tailor. The census taker did not record much about her, but we
learn that she was originally from Cajatambo, in the highlands north of
Lima, and she had only the slightest recollection of who her cacique and

encomendero had been, suggesting that she was not a member of a noble family, and that she had left at a young age, before the stresses of tribute production and local politics had impressed their names upon her.

Carua asked to record a will for a number of purposes. She arranged for the specifics of her funeral, an important public and social occasion for her community, including the participation of her cofradía or religious sodality. She had a number of charitable and personal bequests to make, including the gift of her slave María Angola to her husband. There were debts to be collected as well as paid off. And all of her worldly goods, after the bills were paid and her own share was separated from her husband's, were to be liquidated in order to pay for years of masses, to assure her soul's route out of purgatory.

We have to ask how a woman of apparently modest beginnings, from a small rural community, came not only to a position of economic comfort in the viceroyalty's capital but also acquired all the trappings of colonial society: a profound Christian religiosity, successful participation in the booming market economy, possessions including human chattel, gold jewelry, and clothing made of imported fabrics in styles that were as much borrowings from Europe as from the Andes. Catalina Carua became, whatever her origins, an urbanized Indian woman, part of what we will term a "creole" world, characterized by new attitudes toward language, religion, dress, and the economy. While her will is episodic and leaves narrative gaps that we cannot fill, Carua's life was not so unusual, and in the following pages we will draw upon this and other life stories to learn how indigenous women and men became "colonial" in the urban centers of the sixteenth and seventeenth centuries.

This chapter and the two to follow draw upon a large sample of wills taken from notarial archives in Lima and Trujillo, spanning the years 1565 to 1698. The majority of these wills were left by Indian women and are concentrated in the period 1565–1650. A smaller sample of wills left by Indian men as well as men and women of other ethnic groups were examined for the purpose of comparison. In some cases, we will see that men's and women's lives diverged, but in many ways their experiences ran parallel, and where possible, this chapter's conclusions will be generalized beyond the lives of Indian women.

Wills were legal documents, generally written in Spanish by a Spanish, or occasionally a Spanish-speaking Indian, scribe.[2] Making a will thus cost money, at least a few pesos for the notary's time and paper, and notes for the document would be drawn up either in his office or in the home of the infirm person. But these were also religious documents. Their formulaic yet flexible openings included a statement declaring the testator's acceptance of the "sacred Roman Catholic faith," an invocation of especially beloved saints as intercessors at judgment, and instructions for burial and masses, all generally appearing prior to any discussion of the testator's wealth or its distribution.[3] A small minority of wills excluded discussion of religion, and some preferred to issue purely legal "declarations" of their possessions, or to alienate property before a notary prior to the end of life, but the vast majority of wills, made by men and women of all ethnic groups, asserted a similar, profound outward expression of integration into the Andean Catholic Church, at least via its community organizations, the cofradías.[4] Fear of a long stay in purgatory, as well as of leaving the earth without the benefit of an elaborate funeral attended by loved ones, were certainly motivating factors for writing a will in early colonial Peru.[5]

But apart from an expression of a particular kind of Christianization, wills also reveal much about the patterns of life and culture of colonial Indians in their creolized contexts. Wills present the accretions of possessions gathered over decades, as well as a lifetime's worth of personal obligations and memories. They rarely present a holistic picture, and I have used other sorts of documentation to fill in gaps where possible, but even so, wills give a much more complete and dynamic view of the life cycle than do censuses or court testimonies. The major revelation of this large group of wills is the sheer complexity that Indian women (like men) faced upon arrival in Lima or Trujillo. Making a living apparently entailed mastering multiple occupations, if not at the same time then over a lifetime. The constant refrain of these documents, that the testator's estate consists of those things earned "with our [or my] labor and sweat," marks how the upwardly mobile segments of the population would scrape to purchase or acquire a valuable piece of capital—a piece of expensive clothing that could readily be pawned for a few pesos, a small house with a garden plot, a piece of prime real estate, even a slave to help with making chicha—that would assure the owner of security at the worst moments.

In this chapter we will begin with the route out of those rural communities, many devastated by disease and economic and social changes, and examine how this group of testators made their way in the colonial city. Although these men and women were surely exceptional, in their deep religiosity and in their relative success in the economy, they were not unique, and they formed part of a creolized community in their urban homes.

A Route to the City: Domestic Service

Many indigenous women, like Catalina Carua, came to cities without their families and at very young ages. The 1613 census of Lima's Indians reports that some 95 percent of its indigenous informants had immigrated there from other regions. Although the census is quite incomplete, nearly 50 percent of male respondents who provided information as to when they had immigrated had come to Lima within the past four years. On the other hand, this was true of only 34 percent of women, who were as likely to have come between five and nine years (28 percent) or ten to nineteen years (23 percent) ago. Relatively few respondents had spent more than twenty years in Lima, though nearly twice as many women (15 percent) as men (9 percent) had done so.[6]

This gender gap is best explained by the different routes indigenous men and women took to urban centers. Males generally migrated as young adults, sometimes fleeing the mita, or taking advantage of their arrival as mitayos in urban areas with high labor demand by staying on as wage workers.[7] A number of adolescent boys appear in urban notarial records in apprenticeship contracts, but they were generally brought forward by their parents, suggesting that they were second generation or at least had migrated with family members. On the other hand, large numbers of very young girls came to Lima and Trujillo as domestic servants to European households. Of 140 Indian *niñas* recorded in that census between the ages of six and twelve years, 44 of them worked as domestic servants.[8] This pattern is supported by existing employment contracts: in 1631, six-year-old Francisca was hired to work for the widow doña Francisca Rengifo in Lima for a six-year period; in 1620, ten-year-old Beatriz of Contumaso was placed in the household of Alonso de Montiel in Trujillo for a two-year stint.[9] Former servants who left wills also demonstrate this tendency, sometimes manifested as an inability to remember their parents' names, as in the case of Catalina Chumbi, who had served Pedro Pomelo in Chérrepe, a good distance from her home in highland Cajamarca, for fourteen years; or more explicitly, as when Ysabel Yauri Saco called herself a *"ladina* [Spanish-speaking] Indian who has been raised by Spaniards since she was tiny."[10]

In many cases, these young girls were contracted in their hometowns and brought to the city by their employer's family. Degrees of coercion may have gone into these relationships; caciques were sometimes required to provide *indias de servicio* for their encomenderos. But in some cases domestic service may have been seen by families as the road to a better life for their children, or at least to regular meals and an escape from the miseries of tribute. The same route would be followed by thousands of adult migrants.

Of course, the life of a domestic servant might not have been perceived as an improvement, particularly by a child or adolescent with no community to protect them from the demands and even predations of their employers. Most domestic servants did not receive written contracts establishing the limits of their services or their rights to remuneration.[11] Even when they did, the contract only offered the most general outline of duties and obligations of both parties, stating that the servant would, for example,

serve [the employer] in everything that she is ordered as long as it is licit . . . and [the employer] is obligated to give and pay her each year twelve pesos of nine reales, an anaco and lliclla made of cotton and a skirt made of *paño* from Quito and two *ruan* shirts and whatever shoes are necessary, a room and food and to cure her when she is ill for up to fifteen days, to collect from her the donation for the Holy Crusade and teach her Christian doctrine.[12]

The studied vagueness of this typical agreement from 1630 probably only hints at the overwork and indignities domestic service could entail, not to mention the extra hazards of rape and pregnancy. Contemporary critics were not silent about these un-Christian relationships. In 1604, Fray Miguel de Monsalve complained that among the abuses Spaniards visited upon indigenous women was

making use of them like slaves: taking daughters away from mothers, putting them to work sewing and embroidering hand towels, pillows, *toques* [headscarves] and women's objects, sending all these commodities to Cuzco and Potosí, [and] Charcas to sell, keeping them as a profitable enterprise, doing great damage to the poor and the mothers of these miserable Indian women by taking away their daughters, who ought to help them sow and reap crops, raise their daughters, spin and weave clothing; such that many of these women seem desperate, seeing the offenses done them by encomenderos.[13]

As many have asserted, domestic service could be an extremely exploitative form of employment.[14] Servants themselves attested to their miserable working conditions. Women complained bitterly that they were not paid even the small compensation promised them, and some tried to use their wills to collect back wages, as did Catalina de Agüero in 1570.[15] Others used more immediate means. An Indian woman appeared in civil court in Trujillo in 1633 demanding the wages due her mestiza daughter Angelina from ten years' service to Martín Ydalgo de Llanpo and his wife. She stated that her young daughter had worked "washing their clothing, caring for their children and cleaning for them, cooking, and sweeping the house, serving the table and doing everything which they would have paid a Black woman fifty *patacones* a year to do . . . and by common estimation Anjelina would deserve thirty patacones for each of the ten years."[16]

Though the life of a domestic servant might not seem enviable, a number of extant wills indicate that some Indian women benefited economically from their roles in Spanish households, often receiving significant bequests and gifts that enabled them to lead comfortable lives. Their introduction into urban life also had effects that could favor them later. They learned Spanish, and some came to use the legal system to their advantage, not least of all by recording wills. They became Christians and joined cofradías, community religious organizations that could provide financial, spiritual, and social support through the rest of their lives and into death. They acquired a taste for new goods, especially real estate, elegant clothing (which they might get as hand-me-downs), and the labor of slaves and servants of their own. The numerous wills that have come down to us are, in a sense, the vestiges of these acquired traits, a manifestation of the creolization of these urban Indian men and women.

Coming to a city at a young age also meant that female Indian migrants would tend to be unmarried. An unusual 1684 census of domestic workers in La Paz tells us that some 741 servants lived in 213 households there, plus their approximately 500 dependent children. More than two-thirds of the servants were female, and the majority of these were single women. In contrast, the majority of the males in service were married.[17]

No such census exists for Lima or Trujillo, but the patterns that emerge from other documentation suggest that the demography was similar: domestic service was predominantly an occupation for single women. One author has described this situation as a "feminization" of poverty, which it surely was.[18] But it also leaves room to suggest that service might have been the occupation of women before marriage and perhaps again after widowhood; that they might have left service to raise families and participate in the economy in other ways.

This was indeed the case for Elvira Carua, who stated that she worked for Alonso Ortíz until her marriage to Francisco Cusmango.[19] After her time in service, she and her husband rented agricultural fields and raised livestock for a living, and earned enough money to have purchased a *solar*, a piece of real estate, in Trujillo. And in the case of Secilia de Avila, servant to a family in Lima in the middle of the sixteenth century, her employers provided her with a dowry of one hundred pesos when she married, which was opportune given that she had been unable to collect the agricultural properties left to her at her father's death.[20]

Not all domestic employees were single, of course. Ysabel de Montenegro, a mestiza woman, served a Dominican friar jointly with her husband for many years. The priest was so concerned for the well-being of their daughter, born in his house, that he created a capital fund of three hundred pesos, employed so as to increase over her childhood, to serve as her dowry or her entrance fee into a convent.[21] Montenegro speaks in her will with great affection for her employer, whom she appointed her coexecutor, along with her husband.

Domestic servants were often expected, in addition to cooking, cleaning, taking care of children, and attending to the various personal needs of household members, to engage in petty industry, like making chicha or prepared food to sell in the market, or weaving or sewing.[22] As it did for enslaved Africans, such an occupation might lead to acquiring some funds of their own, as well as learning skills that would serve in another career or placement.

And sometimes the notoriously sexualized relationships between master and servant might lead to greater remuneration, out of feelings that we cannot judge from this great distance, on behalf of an illegitimate child. In 1579, a Huánuco merchant named Juan García de Xerez took time during a stay in Lima to write out a legal "donation" of a house and agricultural plot in his hometown to his two illegitimate sons, Pedro and Diego, and their mother, Catalina Chimbay, because he had not paid her adequately for three years of service in his home, and in order to provide for their children's support. There is no hint of affection in the legal document, as there may or may not have been in the relationship, but there is recognition of the need for adequate compensation as well as the responsibility for one's children, with or without marriage.[23]

Not all sexual entanglements ended so happily. Ana Velázquez, who ended her life married successively to two established Genoese merchants, began her career as a domestic servant in the Velázquez household, where she bore her master's daughter. He took the child to Spain, where Ana Velázquez heard the rumor that she had become a nun, though she was no longer sure if the girl was alive or dead. After leaving service, she became a successful trader in the market, earning herself a dowry of four hundred pesos for her second marriage, and she regularly sent hundreds of pesos in currency, clothing, and other merchandise to her illegitimate daughter. Her will asked that her husband ascertain if the child was alive and, if so, that he send her two hundred pesos more.[24]

Velázquez's life story, though tinged with tragedy, demonstrates as well how remarkably mobile colonial lives could be, from a pregnant servant to a wealthy vendor with a share in her husband's business. Thus it is probably a mistake to see domestic service as only a dead end for women. In some cases it surely was, but for many other women it was a temporary arrangement until they could create a household of their own or acquire enough capital to start another business. Given that making a will implied a certain amount of economic success, the domestic servants who came to leave a testament were exceptional women, but they were not entirely unusual. Few wills offer a complete life story, so a career in domestic service is usually gleaned from a debt to be collected or a hint dropped about an illegitimate child's parentage; for this reason it is likely that many more of Lima and Trujillo's female testators had spent at least some years in service.

Because they moved into service at young ages and lived among Europeans rather than their own ethnic group, some historians have surmised that indigenous domestic servants were culturally isolated, with limited ties to their birth communities.[25] Such a definition of culture is impoverished and reductionist, as recent studies of the vibrant multiethnic urban spaces have demonstrated.[26] Urban residents clearly created new connections and social identities. Even so, not all migrants lost connections to their natal communities; many testators who identified themselves as having been domestic servants made reference to properties and relationships in their hometowns.[27] For example, Catalina de Agüero was originally from Cajamarca, where she still maintained a large group of livestock in the care of an indigenous nobleman, but when she testated in 1570 she was raising her two mestizo children in Trujillo, where she owned two solares. Some of the sheep she left as a bequest to a kinsman in the sierra, and the rest she ordered sold for the benefit of her son. She was also trying to collect small bequests from one former master, who had himself worked for a Cajamarca encomendera, perhaps the connection behind Agüero's initial move to Trujillo.[28] Long distances and slow travel made it difficult for urban migrants to retain their connections to rural properties, but large numbers of testators either listed holdings in their natal communities or had acquired agricultural lands in closer Indian communities, like Lati or Huarochirí.

A relationship with an elite family could prove beneficial in ways that went deeper that just economics. Servants learned techniques for dealing with colonial life, they acquired new tastes, and sometimes the means to fulfill them. Doña Mencia de Balyde served doña Florencia de Mora, a wealthy Trujillo encomendera and patron of numerous charitable works. Doña Mencia was the illegitimate daughter of a prominent Spaniard and an Indian woman, and service might have been a way for her to enjoy the perquisites of her birth, albeit at some remove. Her will, written in 1584, strongly resembles one written by a woman of her employer's status, with dozens of masses to be said all over the city and numerous charitable bequests including large sums of cash, and she asked that her burial site be chosen by doña Florencia herself. Moreover, doña Mencia owned a fifteen-year-old female slave, which she willed to her mother. For this mestiza woman, domestic service in an elite household was probably a means to live within the ambit of her father's world, when the condition of her birth kept her from inheriting those prerogatives directly.[29]

Those of more humble origins could occasionally enjoy the patronage of elites through service. María Enriquez was one of the few women in either sample who wrote a will while she was still in service. She had been born to a plebeian family in the port town of Huanchaco outside Trujillo and spent much of her life as domestic servant to the family of Juan de Castañeda Bustamante, a wealthy farmer in the Chicama Valley, recently arrived from Spain. Enríquez probably came to the Castañeda family very young, for she took as her last name the surname of Castañeda's wife, Leonor Enríquez. Castañeda left María Enríquez seven hundred pesos in his March 1642 will, "for the good service she has done me, and for having raised my children and taken care of my illnesses." This was an enormous sum for a plebeian woman to come into, given that annual salaries for servants hovered around twelve pesos, and María Enríquez decided to take immediate measures to assure its employ for her benefit. In October of that year, with Castañeda dead and his estate not yet distributed, she testated before a notary, accounting for "seven or eight hundred pesos of eight reales, or whatever sum was left to me by the late Juan de Castañeda under a clause in his will under disposition of which he died, from which I order that my burial and masses be paid."

Enríquez was apparently correct to take legal measures regarding her bequest, since it took more than a year for her to collect the money. But her problems seem to have lain with Castañeda's executor or the state official in charge of estates, for the Castañeda family was also fighting on her behalf. Doña Gerónima, Castañeda's daughter, commented in her own will in 1643 that

Item, I declare that the said Juan de Castañeda, my father, by clause in his will . . . left to María Enríquez india seven hundred pesos of eight reales in payment and remuneration for the personal service which he received from her; that she has not been paid as of now and I order that the said seven hundred pesos be paid with another three hundred pesos of eight that I desire be given from my estate to the said María Enríquez india for the love and will that I have for her, and for having raised me from childhood.

In May 1643 the bequest still had not been carried out, according to yet another will made by María Enriquez. In 1650, Enríquez stated that she was now living with doña Gerónima and her husband, who were holding the seven hundred pesos for her. The relationship between Enriquez and the Castañeda family was clearly close, given that the boilerplate protestations of affection here were accompanied by repeated legal action on her behalf. But we can also see how Enríquez's upbringing in service to an elite Spanish family gave her the tools to contest her situation within the colonial system.[30]

Indians could be employers as well: many indigenous women made small bequests to their own servants. Ana Velázquez left fifty pesos in cash to "a mestiza child in my service named Francisca who is seven or eight years old . . . for the love of God and because she has served me." Catalina, a less wealthy Indian woman also testating in Lima in 1579, left a bequest of "an old black painted shawl" and an old lliclla to her Indian servant, Beatriz. Then as now, service wages were low enough that people of relatively marginal economic status could afford hired help, and many urban Indians even possessed slaves, as we shall see later in this chapter.[31]

Thus many young girls came to cities such as Lima and Trujillo as dependents upon elite families or found themselves placed in service by their own families. For some, this produced a "cultural uprooting," in the words of Luis Miguel Glave, because of their lack of ties to "indigenous cultural matrices."[32] But as we have seen, that is only part of the story. The urban diaspora had its own culture and institutions, no less authentic or positive than those of Indian ayllus. For some, service meant exploitation, poverty, and misery, but for others it was a step toward acquiring the necessary tools for navigating colonial life, for becoming creole: speaking Spanish, finding institutional support in the Church's cofradías or with a confessor, learning of one's legal rights to a salary, acquiring a skilled trade, and even obtaining clothing, funds, and an urban, multiethnic social network that might assist in other economic activities. Domestic service was simply one of a myriad of activities that engaged urban indigenous women over their lifetimes.

Urban Occupations

As many of their chroniclers tell us, colonial cities were at their hearts vast and lively markets, feeding and clothing their own residents and speeding commodities to distant provinces and countries as well. The highest levels of trade—the international merchants and store owners and the upper end of the grocer trade (*pulperos*)—were dominated by Iberian men. But the everyday buying and selling of foodstuffs, alcohol, and inexpensive or used clothing was mainly in the hands of plebeian women, who were themselves dependent upon a multiethnic network of agricultural producers and transporters.[33]

The cities were organized around large and small plazas, with stores lining the streets around them. Clogging the plazas themselves were the vendors: *cajoneros* selling food, cloth, and notions from rented booths, *mercachifles* or ambulatory peddlers selling used clothing as well as food and small items, and the *vendedoras*, predominantly women, who sold all sorts of products laid out on tables or sheets. These latter were described by Fray Buenaventura de Salinas y Córdova in 1630:

Those who sell are women, *mulatas* and blacks, Indians and mestizas beneath their awnings for protection against the sun. The Indians have all that they sell on the ground on mantles, reed mats, and straw mats, and the mulatas and blacks, on wooden tables. Each one has and knows her . . . place [which is] assigned with such agreement, that they form a street and a main square that they distinguish from all the confusion, and they form two rows with all their awnings and tables covered with large leaves fresh from the trees, and on them they put the fruits of Spain and of this land.[34]

One such vendor was Ynes Quispi, who had migrated to Lima from the highlands of Los Yauyos. Her 1623 will described her estate as including large amounts of extremely fine Indian and European clothing (llicllas made of cumbe, awasca, silk, taffeta, and velvet as well as

Castillian wool skirts, and ruán shirts and bedclothes) and "a canopy with which I sell in the plaza of Lima." She apparently sold chickpeas, the root vegetable *ocopa*, garlic, *membrilla* fruit, corn, beans, and melons as well as her large stock of clothing, and she raised chickens and ducks.[35] Quispi was obviously a successful businesswoman, though the precariousness of trade is evident from the long list of petty debts owed to her by an assortment of women vendors, mainly of African descent, and a number of indigenous men from San Pedro de Mama, where she grew much of her foodstuffs.

A number of recent studies have opened the world of urban marketeers, especially indigenous and African women, to modern eyes.[36] We have learned from these histories of Potosí, Lima, Cuzco, and Quito, among others, of the ubiquitousness of plebeian women vendors as well as the instability of their livelihoods. They have also emerged as active agents for their own interests, as individuals as well as in groups, as in the case of Quito's *gateras* (indigenous female traders), who fought for their rights to sell alongside Spanish merchants in the markets.

We can also see, from Ynes Quispi's story above, just how complicated the lives of such women must have been. She had not one but at least two professions: raising fruits, legumes, and vegetables on fields she owned or rented in Lati and Huarochirí and selling these foodstuffs, along with clothing, under her canopy in the plaza. She herself owned the lands in Lati; the fields in Huarochirí were sown with her husband, who might have been from that highland region; at any rate, she did not hold the title to them. She employed at least one subcontractor (another Indian woman) to sell fruit for her, and she had numerous small debts with Indian and free black women, at least some of whom were also vendors. She also acted as an informal banker to Ynes Ampacha, an Indian woman living in the Cercado, for a hundred pesos in coin, and her name shows up often in wills of the period, for small loans she made to friends and neighbors.[37] The coordination of agricultural production and shipping, of bookkeeping and managing employees and contractors, must have been remarkable, especially for an illiterate woman.

Equally impressive are her rather curt dealings with her husband, Francisco Guacra, whose name does not appear until the final folios of this more than ten-page document. In a brief paragraph she says, "I declare that I am married . . to Francisco Guacra yndio, who brought no goods whatsoever to my power, and twenty years ago when I married him, I brought such a quantity of goods that I cannot remember

which came during the marriage, nor do I have any child from him."
She went on to note that she and her husband had planted fields together, though she was careful to state how much of her own money
had been put into that enterprise.

The apparent lack of centrality of her twenty-year marriage to her
last will and testament was not an attack on her husband. In fact, while
she did not name him as her heir (she left her estate to her cofradía),
she did leave him her own share of their house in the Cercado, something other testating wives often failed to do. What this demonstrates
is how independently husbands and wives might function in colonial
cities: her husband was a co-worker, a coinvestor, and a cosupplier, but
he probably was simply one among many in her economic and social
network. Her quickness to delineate what was hers stems from her
clear knowledge of property laws, which made her dowry plus half of
all community property her own to distribute as she liked.

Another business dominated by plebeian women was the production and sale of chicha or corn beer.[38] Chicha was, like cloth, a product
with much currency in the precolonial Andes, where it served as a
marker of status as well as a lubricator of cacique-peasant relations. In
the colonial period it lost much of its symbolic potency and acquired a
somewhat democratic popularity—though it was identified with the
Andean population, it was a common beverage in households of all
ethnicities, including European ones. Its trade and production became
increasingly interethnic as chicha became more central to sociability in
urban centers.[39]

A great number of women testators in both cities owned a chicha-
making apparatus large enough that they must have sold the drink
from their homes or in the streets, since its production was extremely
labor intensive, and the beverage would spoil within a few days of fer-
mentation.[40] Chicha making required relatively limited capital: in addition to the germinated corn that was to be fermented, a *chichera*
needed various clay pots and bowls, grinding stones, and bottles to
store and sell the drink.

Some chicha vendors were relatively modest, like Lucía Holguín,
whose 1601 will only listed fifteen hens, some new chicha pots, and
seven patacones in debts for chicha and a shawl.[41] Some worked in
concert with others, like María Pazña, who asked in her 1633 will that
Pedro Hernandes, the *mayordomo* of her cofradía "pardon her for the
love of God" for a debt of thirty patacones for the corn he had provided
and which she could not repay. Apparently the cofradía's official pro-

vided her with raw materials, while she contributed "the labor, serving him in making chicha every week without missing one day, selling in the public plaza."[42]

Obviously, selling chicha necessitated access to large quantities of corn, so it is not surprising that it was also a popular craft among women in the rural areas around Lima, who could bring bottles into the city to sell. Ysabel Carua Chumbi had a home in the Cercado, but owned agricultural fields in her hometown of Santa Eulalia in Huarochirí, where she also stored her chicha-making equipment. Her 1628 will suggests that she also made her living selling prepared food, a common trade in the plaza as well.[43]

But others had more elaborate businesses, like Juana Gómez, who had nine *ollas* or cooking pots for heating the corn, three large and one small vessel for brewing, six sets of grinding stones, and a stock of ten fanegas (15 bushels) of dried corn and "a mountain of *jora*," or germinated corn. She also had three African slaves, all women, who probably carried out the hard work of grinding the corn and monitoring the boiling liquid. This was clearly a profitable enterprise. Gómez had an enviable wardrobe and extensive home furnishings and seems to have acted as a bank for some of the enslaved women in her community: she held seventy patacones for "Catalina Bañu Black slave of Gerónimo de Soto Alvarado," as well as twelve patacones for Catalina Conga, the slave of a *pulpera* or grocery store owner.[44] Similarly Francisca Yllay, the wife of the Cercado's scribe, made her own comfortable existence selling chicha, honey and other goods, and earned enough to purchase two slaves on her own, and a third in concert with her husband.[45]

The Indian women of Trujillo also made and sold chicha, though on a somewhat smaller scale than Lima's numerous chicheras. The most substantial operation may have belonged to Francisca Ramírez, who in 1633 owned an assembled chichero, eleven new glass containers, twelve glass pots and pans, four other pots, twenty bottles, and "the necessary pitchers for the making of chicha" as well as twenty bushels of corn and six or seven bushels of fermented corn. She sold Andean women's clothing as well, and her husband, carpenter Pedro de Miranda, was licensed to operate a *pulpería* where they might have sold these alongside European merchandise. In 1653, after Miranda's death, she was selling even more chicha, contracting with a royal judge to purchase bushels of dried corn, with bushels more germinating and awaiting grinding. But by 1677 she had abandoned the chicha trade altogether, only selling imported and expensive textiles and clothing:

the work of a chichera was hard labor, and probably marked one's ple-beian roots.[46]

Trujillo's smaller economy sometimes proved more welcoming to the multiethnic poor than did Lima's. The larger group of indigenous women testators in Trujillo who refer to their past as domestic servants likewise suggests that the rural poor found it somewhat easier to move up there than they did in Lima, where the earliest testators can often be linked to an elite Andean family. And a few indigenous women be-came important shopkeepers and marketeers in Trujillo; certainly not on the scale of the important Iberian merchants and financiers, but cen-tral to the local economy (and well known) nonetheless.

In addition to Francisca Ramírez, Trujillo was home to Juana López, a former domestic servant herself, who took over the business of her husband, a mestizo merchant named Francisco de Ayaste, after his death in 1616. Her will is comparable to that of a Spanish merchant, with pages full of debts to be collected from Indians, Spaniards, and blacks, for imported clothing, conserves, jewelry, wine, corn, and vari-ous loans. Part of her business involved fronting merchandise to repre-sentatives selling goods to the Indians of the highlands: she noted that "Francisco Anton yndio" had taken some cotton shirts and trousers to sell, but had not yet given her the proceeds. She included as well a long list of debts left by her late husband, which she had already settled.[47]

A few wills give us a glimpse of other kinds of occupations for women in the period. Catalina Guissado was named in another woman's will for accepting money in exchange for curing a child (the child did not improve, and the mother used her will to demand a re-fund); curing and midwifery were widely practiced, mainly by women, though wills rarely refer to these occupations.[48] A few women in Lima had invested in boats, as part of the local fishing industry: María Magdalena owned a boat with sails and fishing nets (for catch-ing mackerel) in concert with two men, and doña Juana de la Cruz had also invested in a boat with her husband, contributing half of the three hundred pesos it cost.[49] A few were engaged in business deals with Spaniards, including Ana Esteban, a widow from the Cercado, who left a thousand peso dowry to a young woman she had raised named Juana Batista. The pesos were to be sent to a contact in Spain, so that he might bring back Spanish goods to sell in Lima for a profit. The ex-pected return on the investment would allow Juana Batista to marry or to enter religious orders.[50]

There were certain dealings about which the Spanish community believed Indians to have particular and valuable knowledge and which led to financial partnerships. Ysabel Suyo formed a business partnership with ten Spaniards, male and female, in Lima in 1577 to mine silver near her encomienda. She stated in the contract that

since I have information that in the mountain of Cayquiri beyond the town of San Gerónimo which is part of the said encomienda, thirteen or fourteen leagues from this city, there are silver mines from which I have taken metals and I have shown these to Ysabel de Padilla and to other persons from which there are signs and evidence that these mines are very rich; and so that they may be worked and so that she [Ysabel de Padilla] might take advantage of them she has formed a partnership . . . and I am obliged to show them said mine where I have found the said metals in the said mountain and they will work the said mine and provide their labor and industry and tools and take care of all expenses and costs that are necessary and I and all the abovementioned will have and enjoy in equal parts the silver.[51]

And certainly women had numerous other occupations that would not appear in their wills, some illegal, others simply invisible in this sort of documentation. But for the most part, the indigenous women who left wills most likely earned their income farming, selling goods in the plazas, as landlords, and in domestic service.

Nonetheless, these documents do lead to some fascinating conclusions about how indigenous women managed their economic lives: first, that they were truly and consciously independent of their husbands, even when they worked together and had contented marriages; second, that they had to have multiple careers, either serially or simultaneously, in order to make a success of things.

Unlike the wills of many men, women's wills rarely state their occupation, apart from an occasional "vendor in the plaza." Their professional lives have to be gleaned from their possessions, from debts, and from other clues hidden among the directions for carrying out their last wishes. Male testators were usually, at least in the first hundred years of colonization, indigenous elites like caciques, or artisans, especially tailors, silversmiths, scribes, saddlers, and shoemakers, and their occupation or status was stated after their name in the will's first paragraph. Elite status was generally hereditary; artisans usually required a period of apprenticeship followed by working for a master artisan and, with luck and skill, acquiring a shop of one's own. Thus their work trajectories, as well as we can make out from these incomplete documentary sources, were fairly straightforward, though we must assume that many of them also had more complicated lives than their occupations suggest.

On the other hand, women's careers, as we have seen here, required more flexibility. To become successful, a female entrepreneur might begin as a servant, learning skills and building a community network. From there she might become a petty trader, purchasing or inheriting plots of land or domestic animals that would strengthen her supply lines. Men surely needed these things too, but their wills tended to reflect their professions more directly: a guitar maker owned the tools for his work, raw materials, partially made and fully made instruments, and noted debts for personal items (shoes for himself and his wife, in this case) as well as for his trade.[52] This may be an illusion of the documents: men whose careers were more articulated might not have left wills; these female testators might have been married to artisans, and hence part of a group of will writers, while women with more straightforward professional lives might not have left records. But given our conclusion that men and women migrated to colonial cities under different conditions and at different life stages, this may simply mean that becoming "creole" was a gendered experience and that women had to balance multiple pulls, whereas many men were able to network more directly into their professional lives.

Communities of Credit: Constructing Ties in the Colonial Economy

Supply and credit networks were central to the urban economy. Access to distant agricultural products was basic to nearly all vendors, and cash was always tight. Urban residents depended heavily upon multi-ethnic communities within their city as well as ties to families and friends in rural regions. Most of the women whose wills are considered here noted outstanding debts and accounts, demonstrating both the need for networks of trust and the precariousness of such livelihoods in a cash-poor environment. The enormous number of everyday items—clothes, furniture, small silver objects—on pawn at any given moment is demonstration enough of how credit was central to all levels of society, not simply to elites.[53]

Indigenous testators in both Lima and Trujillo left wills filled with lists of creditors and debtors. These ranged from entrance fees for a cofradía to unpaid-for merchandise to cash loans; although Lima's testators tended to have more numerous and larger debts than did testators in Trujillo, there was no great difference in what was loaned or for what purpose. But what these lists of small and large sums, and pawned objects awaiting eventual return, tell us is a story of necessarily close-knit communities in the midst of these cities full of strangers.

Urban workers had many places where they could seek short-term credit. Some credit ties were created by physical proximity, as when a female trader noted loans from other sellers in tiny amounts, perhaps circulating the same coins back and forth as each came up cash-short. Such would likely also be the case for store owners and artisans, who made small loans to colleagues in a shared place of employ or on the same street. This explains the tendency for a gender "bias" to exist in wills: the majority of men's loans were to other men, as women's were to other women, because most loans were made in and around workplaces and occupations, which were often gender segregated. Relatives and friends might ask to have their purchases placed on account, and even strangers could expect lenience on occasion, especially when secured by a colleague or friend. Testators therefore went to certain lengths to identify their debtors, as in the following from the accounts of a pulpera in Lima: some simply by common names and the generic ethnic markers ("Blas Antonio mulatto shoemaker"), others noting where one lived or worked ("Joan yndio tailor who lives next to San Sebastián"), where one was born ("Martín yndio from Yca who lives in Pachacamac"), or noting who could offer more specific information ("Thomas yndio of Chilca who knows my brother-in-law Bartolomé Hernández").[54] These descriptions provide us with a more profound picture of the interconnectedness of multiethnic communities.

Families, co-workers, and friends were an obvious source of credit networks, but wills suggest that other types of communities were being founded as well. Shared places of origin—communities in diaspora— seem to have mattered socially. For example, Catalina Chumbi, living in Trujillo but originally from Chimú, left a list of debts owed her by men with Chimor names: Alonso Mis, Pedro Chipnem, Domingo Por, and Francisco Collique. Because she called all the debts "loans," they probably represented cash outlays and not sales of commodities on credit; she was presumably engaged in some occupation that involved regular cash income such as selling chicha or other goods, and either her clientele was dominated by men from her natal community, or she preferred extending credit to them.[55]

Similarly, Catalina Payco of Chachapoyas in the sierra east of Trujillo had debts with other Chachapoyanos despite living in Lima: she had loaned don Loreto Mangulla two pesos "for his business," as well as small sums to two other men. These diasporic relations could be made even more concrete by living arrangements. The 1613 census of Lima reveals that people from the same community often shared housing, and the Cercado of Lima was originally divided into lots assigned to mitayo groups by region, though that eventually broke down.

Barter and credit were mainstays of the system for people at the margins in these increasingly monetized cities. One of the most common forms of debt was a rudimentary pawn operation: Angelina de Alvarado claimed that Melchora owed her a debt of twenty patacones and had given her as *prenda,* or pledge, a gold "agnus dei." When the executors collected the debt, they were to return the icon. Small loans and goods on credit or guaranteed by pledge allowed poorer people to make payments, such as tribute or rent, or to purchase the raw materials to make chicha or other items they might sell when their incomes were unstable. In the case of Juana, a small loan probably allowed her to make her will: she reported that she owed "an Indian servant of Francisco de Fuentes" ten tomines and that the servant woman was present with her while she testated.[56]

Credit was also important for the better-off in the colony, and they had a number of options to serve them. Wealthier Limeños of all ethnicities could place their funds in a bank, such as the one run by the prominent Spaniard Juan de la Cueva until its cataclysmic bankruptcy in 1635. Diego Guaman, an indigenous gilder in Lima, had four hundred patacones in de la Cueva's bank in 1624, and the Indian principals in the sale of a house on Lima's Calle Malambo placed the extraordinary purchase price of one thousand five hundred pesos in his bank in 1631.[57] Convents and monasteries played key roles in creating significant lines of credit for elites, both Iberian and Andean.[58] On a smaller level, cofradías also acted as credit agents for members—plebeians as well as elites, and of all ethnic backgrounds—who had paid their entrance fee. As we will see in the next chapter, cofradías were often the recipients of generous bequests and were even made primary heirs in numerous wills. These funds provided the capital for future community lending, providing future generations of cofrades with reason to reward them in their own wills.

There were no indigenous bankers as such, but there were indeed men and women known for trustworthiness with one's cash or for making substantial loans. Luis Pérez, an Indian man who testated in the Cercado in 1623, left word that he still owed two hundred pesos on a five-hundred peso loan he had received from "Beatriz yndia whom they call 'the rich one,' who sells in the Plaza of Lima."[59] Many of the largest debtors and their creditors lived within the Cercado and testated before the same notary, suggesting a close-knit community that provided mutual support rather than an open market for credit. And, as noted throughout, many men and women "held" funds for friends and colleagues without a secure place. A friendship with a priest or a Spanish employer might enable an indigenous woman to keep her savings safe from a gambling husband or the other tenants in her overcrowded rooming house.

But most credit arrangements were less formal, even among businesses. Francisca Ramírez's will of 1653 illustrates the way she operated and financed her store in Trujillo: she owed doña Lorenza Roldán Dávila, a prominent Spaniard, five pesos for candles and soap to be sold in the store, for which Ramírez had given a small desk in pledge; she also owed the balance on an account with Juan Rodríguez de Olmedo for imported fabrics and sixteen pesos for wine to the merchant Juan López. Debts to her included twelve patacones from the Licenciado Cristóbal Ordem for his account at the store and small balances from eleven Indians, blacks, and Spaniards, male and female.[60] Although large loans were sometimes necessary in a crisis, it was these small exchanges that lubricated economic relations and made it possible to keep a business afloat and food on the table.

An extensive literature debates whether markets existed in Peru before the arrival of Europeans in 1532.[61] Whether or not long- and short-distance trade took place before colonization (and where), it is eminently clear that the monetization that swept urban centers was unprecedented, and it must have been profoundly experienced by newcomers to the cities. The rapidity with which indigenous marketwomen and artisans adapted to these new circumstances, and creatively borrowed and elaborated on techniques and instruments brought by the conquistadores and settlers, is nothing short of amazing. As much as Europeans would have liked to maintain tight control over economic relations, they would have been at a loss to produce the vibrant markets that quickly crisscrossed the colonies without the labor and ingenuity of Indians, Africans, and castas. The testators of Lima and Trujillo are certainly a self-selected group, who might not have cared much for the changes they saw in their homeland but were able to take advantage of their grasp of the new culture and often made themselves a comfortable life (and death). In the final section of this chapter, we will look at two of the major types of property that Indian men and women learned to acquire and desire as part of their new self-image as creole citizens: real estate and African slaves.

Urban Dwellings: *Solares* and *Solareros*

The Quechua community institution, the ayllu, is a political and social unit based upon a fictive kinship, often characterized as descent from a single ancestor. More than a territorial designation, ayllu membership entails mutual rights and responsibilities, often involving labor and other economic support.[62] In at least some regions of the prehispanic Andes the ayllu, among its many functions, confirmed usufructuary rights to community-held lands to member households based upon size and need. Some regions of the Andes may have had forms of private property, but much agricultural land appears to have been held communally and distributed in this way.[63]

With the Spanish conquest came a pressure to privatize community property. Urban centers became entirely private (or Crown-owned) zones, with fully alienable property rights, by displacing resident indigenous populations. Rural areas adapted in various ways, particularly once the legal institution of writing wills gave individuals authority over property in such a direct way. Studies of colonial Mexico have shown how rural Nahua families used Spanish notions of property to maintain their own customary inheritance patterns on the one hand, or to alienate their properties, to meet their new needs for cash, on the other.[64] While pressure (and incentives) to conceive of agricultural and residential lands as private rather than community property certainly came through rural interactions with the colonial state as well as with local individuals (like encomenderos and caciques), the culture of property ownership also developed through ongoing relationships with community members and kin who had left for the cities. Their wills make it absolutely clear that urban migrants carried over the concept of private, alienable property to their use of and access to rural lands, sometimes acquired through inheritance, other times by purchase or the ruling of colonial courts.

The possession of private property in the hands of indigenous and mestizo testators had multiple valences, not all or always consonant with the meanings of property ownership for Europeans in the colonies. The first European landholders in America were generally recipients of a *merced* or a gift from the Crown signifying their dominance over indigenous inhabitants in the wars of conquest. For Andeans, the purchase of property was more complicated. For some, it was certainly a means to achieve some sort of parity with their conquerors, and in the cases of dispossessed caciques it was even a way to take back what was theirs or their community's. But it was also a way of finding economic security in a world driven by new rules and rulers. This sentiment was even more pronounced among female testators, who asserted that they bought their homes and property with their own earnings and took care to leave this capital to children or to use it to take care of their own souls.[65]

The vast majority of indigenous testators in Lima and Trujillo owned some property, rural lands, or a city house and garden plot. This was certainly a prime factor in deciding to invest in a will and in most cases represented their single most valuable asset. Of fifty-five women's wills in the Trujillo sample, only thirteen (24 percent) mentioned no real estate whatsoever. In Lima, where less well-off women were more likely to leave a will, of one hundred forty-seven women's wills, forty-eight (33 percent) listed no property.

A large number of urban testators—thirty-six of fifty-five (65 percent) will writers in Trujillo and sixty-three of one hundred forty-seven (43 percent) in Lima—owned a solar, a plot of land, either within the center of the city (the *traza*) or nearby. The solares within the traza were originally divided up for the use of the conquistadors and city founders. In Trujillo, for example, Pizarro and his companions formed a central plaza, then partitioned the land around it into parcels of about a quarter of a city block, each with enough space for a house and a garden plot, encircled by a fence. These solares were intended to be restricted to the residences of Spanish vecinos, but the cities grew rapidly, and necessary expansion away from the center was coupled with a lively market in land that quickly integrated even the centers of town.

We have seen that urban living conditions necessitated multiethnic rooming houses, but this integration proved to be the case for property ownership as well. Despite legal prohibitions, by the late sixteenth century Trujillo's Indians were purchasing small plots of land and living alongside Spaniards, mestizos, and blacks. The Trujillo Cabildo in fact granted the right to buy a solar to an elite Indian in May 1554, "as a married man and one who lives like a Spaniard," suggesting that relative affluence, religious acculturation, and the adoption of European clothing and mores made Indians perfectly acceptable neighbors as well as trading partners.[66]

Wills and purchase contracts illustrate this intermingling of the socially mobile. Many testators took care to describe the exact location of
their homes, naming their neighbors to establish territorial markers.
Because property ownership seems to have been an important consideration in writing a will at all, this fact allows us to trace properties
and even sketch out rough neighborhoods through time. In 1594, Magdalena Jiquil dictated a will stating that she had sold her solar to Luisa
Madalena, another Indian woman. Jiquil said, "I sold the said solar as
my own property, purchased by my own labor, for which she gave me
the price of ninety pesos *corrientes*, paid in full, I declare these pesos as
my property, now held by Pedro Bracamoros."[67] On the same day, before the same notary, she had carried out the transaction, describing it
as within the traza, between the solares of Antonio Faria, a Spaniard
who was the city's public prosecutor, and Catalina Román, another
widowed Indian woman. Román had bought her own solar from Baltasar Rodríguez, and it bordered the property of Alonso de Vargas,
both of whom were Spaniards.[68]

These transactions give the clear sense of an economically mobile Indian population, eagerly acquiring prime properties, often with cash in
hand at a time when the Spanish elite was overdrawn on credit. As well,
the establishment of Saña in the 1560s meant that the Spanish population of Trujillo was somewhat dissipated in the late sixteenth and early
seventeenth centuries.[69] In many cases, Indians moved into the neighborhoods once occupied by important Spanish families. In 1607, an Indian carpenter named Alonso de Castro sold his Trujillo solar to Juana
Cache, an indigenous native of Cao in the Chicama Valley. The documentation reveals that Castro had purchased the solar from the Spaniard
don Diego de Aponte, who was married into the elite Chacón family;
Aponte had acquired the property from one of Trujillo's founders, don
Pedro de Lascano.[70] This phenomenon was so well established in Trujillo at the turn of the seventeenth century that many Indians referred to
themselves as *solareros* and *solareras*, perhaps to them equivalent to the
(mostly) Spanish vecinos who achieved political status through their
ownership of property as well as economic prominence. Women were
most often identified in documents with this adjective, though this may
reflect the fact that males tended to have occupational titles, like "tailor,"
appended to their names, while few women did. Spaniards, blacks, and
castas do not appear to have used the adjective at all, nor does it seem to
have been used outside of Trujillo.

In Lima, as well, Indians bought up central properties, though Limeño testators were slightly less likely to own a solar when they testated. Given that the volume of indigenous testators in Lima was much higher than in Trujillo, we can surmise that Lima had a large marginal population, who could not quite afford to purchase land but were affluent enough to have estates to divide. But the absence of property did not always mean that one was poor. Lucia Cusi, a widow originally from Cuzco who probably sold chicha to earn her living, left an extensive will including cash bequests to cofradías and an expensive collection of European fashions and other household items. She owned no real estate and left a rent payment of three reales to her landlord, doña Gerónima de Peralta.[71]

Lima had, by the late sixteenth century, an important, mainly Indian *barrio*, the Cercado, which became the home to a rising middle class of artisans and home owners, producing a more coherent sense of community and identity than existed in more integrated cities and neighborhoods. Two thirds of the testators in the Lima sample who resided in the Cercado owned a solar, either independently or with a family member. Those with residences elsewhere in Lima were less likely to own their homes; about one-third within the sample did so; the rest tended to live with Spanish families or rent a building or room on someone else's property, like most of the urban plebeian population.

The majority of indigenous women purchased their homes and properties with their own funds, or at the very least, firm credit. Women seem to have not encountered too many barriers to land purchase, beyond the obvious economic constraints. The law required that women have a "protector" when making a transaction; either their husband had to assent to the sale in front of a notary, or the Protector of the Indians (a bureaucrat appointed as legal defender) had to appear in a husband's stead. But in fact this rarely was the case, and most nonelite women carried out their own transactions in their own names. And when they did not, they could be at the mercy of whomever they had trusted: María Magdalena de Urraco asked her lover to purchase a house for her with her own money, and he subsequently refused to turn over the bill of sale to her, claiming that he had to investigate whether it had access to water or not.[72]

While such laws interposed authorities to protect women from being cheated, authorities might well be the ones doing the cheating. Many Indians complained that the inspectors had reassigned or confiscated their properties. And the church was also subject to charges of fraud and abuse. In mid-seventeenth-century Lima, Francisca Chani complained of being tricked by the Jesuits over lands she had inherited from her ancestors in Surco. The Jesuits had "offered" to exchange her lands, which she described as extremely fertile and with access to a spring, for some others that turned out to be of much lesser quality. The Jesuits seem to have gone to the Real Audiencia to take possession of her lands while she tried to get the decision reversed by the local visitador and her ownership reconfirmed, but the officials refused to side with her and confiscated her records of ownership. In her will she asked not only that the lands be returned and the exchange nullified, but that the cacique of Surco, who had been using the Jesuit lands for three years to produce crops for his community's tribute, pay her appropriate back rent.[73]

Beyond providing shelter and community, property ownership could also be a source of income. Colonial cities teemed with rooming houses and crowded multiple-family dwellings, and small garden plots or large agricultural properties were likewise easily rented out. María Cutucunca, a married woman living in Lima in 1572, had inherited her house and garden from her father, don Hernando Monacuyo, and was renting it out to Sebastián de Rivas, *gentilhombre de la companya de las lanzas*. The solar was surely in a very desirable location, and quite possibly she descended from one of the cacical lines of the Lima Valley that had been displaced by the city's founding.[74] More common were rentals among working people of moderate means, as in the case of Luisa de Osorno, a Trujillo native, who rented a solar, with its chicha-making apparatus and vessels, beginning in 1633 for sixteen pesos a year to Juan de Castro, a tailor.[75]

Although a minority of testators (fifty-two of one hundred forty-seven in Lima, eight of fifty in Trujillo) listed rural properties in their wills, the fact that so many did at all is surprising, given that they tended to immigrate so young and to have relatively few other external signs of regular contact with rural areas, like debts or bequests. And many more mentioned livestock they owned in far-off regions. This suggests continued relations with kin groups, although often under difficult conditions, as we shall see below. The smaller percentage of property-owning testators in Trujillo probably speaks to slower penetration of private property and Spanish inheritance practices into the Trujillo Valley, or—less likely, given the short distances—infrequent contact between migrants and the communities of their kin.

Rural lands generally came to urban residents in one of two ways, through inheritance or purchase. In both cities but especially Trujillo, inheritance of properties outside the city predominated; when the properties were closer by—and thus probably not in a region with a kin connection—they would have been purchased for occupational reasons. Though lands were usually inherited from parents, they might also come through marriage. Barbola, a native of Trujillo who left a will in 1608, had inherited her *chácaras* or agricultural fields from her late husband, who had stated that he made this bequest because he had "spent one hundred and twenty patacones of hers that she had inherited from her father," as well as because of the love he had for her.[76]

In contrast, in Lima we see a greater variety of properties and forms of acquisition than in Trujillo, and while the evidence is too thin to make strong generalizations, important and suggestive patterns do emerge. About one-third (fourteen testators) had inherited properties outside Lima from a close relative. The rest either purchased the land (sometimes in a nearby region) or did not clarify how they had acquired it. These women often purchased lands that would provide them with further income or access to agricultural produce that they could sell in the city. Like many solareras, they saw land as capital and saved their funds until they could invest.

As in Trujillo, lands tended to be inherited from parents. Ynes Tamayo declared four pieces of land growing fruit trees in Huarochirí that she inherited from her parents, and Catalina Gualcum, who had lived ten years in the Cercado, was concerned for the disposition of a number of chácaras in the Lurin Valley "that she inherited from her mother and her father more than forty years ago."[77] Some women stated that they had inherited land from their mothers, perhaps a vestige of gender dualism, though there is not enough evidence to support a strong claim. Anna Alli, for example, had inherited a piece of land from her mother, María Malla, and left it to her own daughter, Ysabel Alli, in 1616. Ysabel also received a plot of land that her mother had previously inherited from a male relative, and Juan Solano, Alli's son, received a piece of land whose provenance was unstated.[78] Barbola Guacha, a chichera who left her will in the same year, had also inherited, along with her sister, a good-size piece of land in Lati from their mother. She left her share in equal parts to her sons.[79]

Rural properties could clearly be a source of significant income, if rents could be collected promptly. Women were extremely aware that they could be at a particular disadvantage in dealing with their rural properties, whether they lived in the cities or remained in rural communities. María Cayn managed her late husband's lands in Carabayllo, where he had rented them to a Spaniard named Juan de Guerrero more than forty years earlier. The original notarized contract only specified four years, at a rent of forty-eight pesos. Guerrero had apparently refused to leave the property or pay more rent; Cayn asked that her cofradía intervene to get the lands back and rent them out at a better rate, something she had apparently been unable to accomplish by herself or with her husband.[80]

But not all rental relations were contentious. Magdalena Picona, who testated in the Cercado of Lima in 1630, owned a large parcel of land in the valley of Lati, which she had bought from don Lorenzo de Ulloa, a prominent Spanish vecino. She stated that

> because I cannot work them, and I am alone and a widow, I have rented them out for a long time to Jorge Márquez, a Spanish farmer in the said valley, and I am paid up for all rentals through the first of May of next year, 1631, and since I cannot sustain and dress myself with the rent from these, being very little, and the said Jorge Márquez, in friendship and charity, has paid me in advance for the rents, to supply my necessities for the illnesses I have had, and to sustain myself and dress myself . . . he has given me . . . four hundred and fifty pesos in reales beyond the rents, for which reason I leave him from now on three fanegas of the said lands.[81]

Purchasing land, either for a home or for agriculture, was a major step for urban Indians in the century after colonization. It entailed acquiring a significant sum in cash or negotiating a loan, and navigating the legal system through notaries and sometimes the Protector of the Indians. A few men and women received land as gifts, from parents, grateful employers, or others who would be their patrons. But however they acquired this important commodity, Indian men and women quickly joined the Spanish conquistadors in the cities that the Spaniards founded and the Indians built. In Trujillo, where the population was evenly divided among blacks, Europeans, and Indians, all three became close neighbors even in the most prestigious neighborhood, the traza; Indians celebrated this new status by coining the sobriquet solarero. In Lima, some wealthy Indians likewise moved near to the central plaza; others populated barrios that were less heterogeneous, like the mainly Indian Cercado or predominantly black San Lázaro. But no neighborhoods in either city were exclusive, within a generation or so of the conquest, and the sample of wills gathered here demonstrates how radical social mobility was in these two coastal centers.

Indians and African Slavery

Another clear, if less pleasant indicator of the status achieved by many Indian women, as well as men, was their possession of black slaves.[82] Slaves had come to Peru with the first conquistadors and, though not yet plentiful, were an important labor source, especially with the decline of the indigenous population, as well as a symbol of prestige. Slave ownership was generally concentrated on the coast, and particularly in and around urban centers: in 1614 Lima's population included 10,386 blacks, nearly one for every Spaniard, and three times the contemporary total population of a city like Cuzco or Potosí.[83] A household replete with liveried slaves was the marker of status for wealthy Spaniards, and they also employed slaves (as well as free blacks and Indians) on the growing estates that emerged to feed urban populations toward the end of the sixteenth century. In particular, as the Spanish Crown began to legislate against the coerced use of Indians in agricultural mitas as well as in sugar mills and olive fields and on vineyards, cities like Lima and Trujillo became more and more dependent upon African slaves for food production.[84] However, gangs of slaves, even on the coastal sugar estates, tended to be small. Frederick Bowser's survey of forty-one estates between 1580 and 1630 reveals that only three had more than forty slaves, and only one had as many as one hundred; the majority had fewer than twenty.[85]

Within urban centers, slaves were symbols of ostentation and luxury, as when elite women notoriously had themselves carried in sedan chairs by slaves through Lima's streets. Households employed them for cooking, cleaning, and gardening; as wet nurses; and in all sorts of petty trades, including producing items for sale in the markets. But slaves were also important capital for people of lesser means, including Indians and free blacks, though to a far lesser degree than property ownership or ostentatious dress. Despite the fact that Spanish laws were repeatedly promulgated prohibiting free or enslaved blacks from serving Indian men or women, these seem not to have been widely enforced in Peru. Only one indigenous woman in the Trujillo sample mentioned a slave among her possessions, but twenty-six of one hundred forty-seven (18 percent) Indian women in Lima reported owning slaves. The middle sectors of Lima and Trujillo, including established Indian vendors and artisans, did use black slaves to further their own economic projects.

African-born (bozal) and American-born (creole) slaves were both extremely expensive commodities. In his study of the period 1560–1650, Bowser reports average prices for African men and women in Lima ranging between four and six hundred pesos, depending upon scarcity in the markets.[86] This was an enormous outlay, far more than a solar and certainly more than the minimal cash savings reported in most Indian wills in the sample. Given the extensive markets for credit that we have seen developing, it stands to reason that Indians might have received loans to purchase slaves, but slave traders extended little credit to purchasers before the economic downturns of the 1620s.[87] Few Indian men and women could afford the hundreds of pesos in cash that an adult slave cost and lacked informal options for loans of this size other than employers or patrons and a few wealthy Indians like Ynes Quispi, who loaned Francisca Yllay thirty patacones to help her purchase a creole black child in the 1620s.[88] This structural problem—the lack of credit available to make such a large purchase at once—certainly explains the relatively few Indians who owned slaves in Lima and Trujillo, alongside the de jure illegality of ownership or the high prices in and of themselves. Many of the women studied here bought young children or cheaper creole slaves to serve them; this was far less expensive than purchasing an adult bozal laborer.

The most likely to own slaves, of course, were the hereditary elites. Caciques were accustomed to having servants, and owning African slaves was a way of signifying prestige in the new property system. Don Juan Panas Payco, the cacique of Huarmey (in the Santa Valley, between Lima and Trujillo), left an estate containing five black slaves in 1635, two of whom he had purchased for 907 patacones at the estate auction of another Indian. His executors reported that one of the five men had died, they had given an elderly male slave to his widow, and that the other three had been sold for a total of one thousand pesos.[89] The 1622 will of don Luis, the cacique of Colán (north of Trujillo, near Piura), enumerates seven male and female slaves, of various ages and mainly bozales, as part of his massive estate.[90] But most of the cacical wills within my sample listed no slaves whatsoever, suggesting that many elites continued to rely upon customary indigenous labor and used other, more achievable means of signifying their authority and prestige to colonial society.

Indians of plebeian origins acquired slaves as their own fortunes rose. Juana Gómez, born and raised in Lima, made a comfortable living selling chicha and renting out rooms in her house. Her fine wardrobe (including a skirt of "black Castillian paño . . . with a border of braided gold") was purchased in part with the labor of three African women, two named María Bañu and the third, the newborn daughter of one of these two Marías, called Lucía.[91] Ana Velázquez, an Indian from Los Cañares, and her husband, the Genoese merchant Juan Batista, employed a number of slaves in their businesses, whom she had brought from her first marriage to another Genoese trader. According to her 1579 will, Velázquez had married with a letter of dowry that listed a house and garden plot and "three slaves, one named Sebastián, and the other Andrés, and Catalina his wife." Velázquez seems to have made her living selling assorted items in one of Lima's plazas.[92] For the rising classes, African slaves were sources of labor and income (if rented out) as well as domestic servants and markers of a newly opulent life style.

Chicha vendors in particular seem to have found slaves an important capital investment, as chicha production was so labor intensive. Catalina Payco, a chicha vendor originally from Cuzco, did not own her own house, but she did own a twelve-year-old creole boy called Juan who presumably helped her with the onerous parts of chicha production, like monitoring the boiling liquid for hours at a time. Other than this valuable child, the bulk of her estate was ninety pesos and a collection of Andean anacos and llicllas. Agricultural labor might likewise be a reason for purchasing a slave rather than hiring seasonal workers. María de Jesús, who testated in 1598 in Lima, owned a chácara or agricultural lot in San Lázaro where her slave, Cristóbal, likely labored.[93]

In addition to providing additional labor for jobs like farming and brewing chicha, slaves were a common source of income through rental arrangements. Doña Catalina Llacla, a prosperous landowner in the Ica Valley who was residing in Lima in 1606, owned two slaves, an adult named Pedro Angola and a six-year-old boy named Juan Angola. Pedro Angola, at the time of her testating, was "pawned" to don Geronymo Barreto for the sum of 450 pesos; he was likewise renting some of her land in Ica. Similarly, a free black woman named Mencia López had five slaves when she testated in 1578, one pawned for an unnamed sum.[94] The Cercado, and likely other neighborhoods as well, had labor systems whereby Indians hired out other Indians' slaves for a daily wage. Religious organizations such as cofradías and hospitals might also have such arrangements.[95]

Indians in Trujillo did not invest in slaves to the degree they did in Lima. Only one of the forty-nine women's wills in the sample (and none of the men's) named a slave, and this was Juana López, the widow of a prominent mestizo merchant in the city. In 1616 López no longer owned the slave herself, but rented him back from Captain Francisco Guillén de Herrera, a Spaniard who had purchased the un-named man from her to settle her late husband's debts. Captain Guillen charged her ten patacones a month for his wages.[96] Even the illustrious Francisca Ramírez, who worked her way from chichera to wealthy shopkeeper, did not mention a slave in any of her many wills.

One reason for less access to the ownership of slaves among Indians in Trujillo than in Lima may be that the laws against their holding slaves were more strongly enforced there.[97] In 1639, the cacique of Je-quetepeque, Don Carlos Chamo Chumbi, had to petition the Real Au-diencia for control over the black male slave his mother-in-law, Luisa Magdalena, had left in her will to his daughter and her granddaugh-ter, Juana Centeno, who was still a minor. The petition granted him possession of the slave but not the ability to sell him in his daughter's name, despite his guardianship of her. The fact that he had to go through legal channels for this access indicates that there was indeed closer scrutiny of Indian slaveholders in Trujillo than in Lima. Luisa Madalena did not herself mention a slave in either of her two wills dated 1617 and 1626; there was probably a subsequent will not yet lo-cated. While clearly already well-off by the 1620s, when she owned a solar and other large possessions, she must have acquired the slave during the final decade of her life, possibly due to the enhancement of her position after her daughter Leonor Centeno married into the indigenous elite.[98]

The majority of interactions between blacks and Indians, however, were *not* that of slave and master. Although free blacks and Indians had a sense of a separate ethnic identity that derived from more than just economic relations, the cities were places where they recognized their interdependence and often a sense of connection. In contraven-tion of the stereotype—promulgated by colonial governments—that blacks and Indians were natural enemies, in many cases they demon-strated a sense of affinity, as members of a "lower sphere" in the colo-nial hierarchy but also because of their experiences of negotiating heterogeneous communities in their travels to the coastal cities.[99] These feelings of affinity were expressed in their wills, through debts, be-quests, and other social ties.

The clearest ties were certainly economic ones, predominantly tiny loans or pawns for cash. As we have seen, blacks, both free and enslaved, showed up regularly as small debtors in Indian women's wills in both cities. Chicha sellers and plaza vendors, the most ready sources of petty, informal credit, were generally the most likely to generate debts with Africans. The plaza was, in fact, the place of employment for numbers of black and Indian female vendors: Ynes Quispi, an Indian vendor, listed debts with seven free black women who shared her selling location in Lima's central plaza. These were all moderate debts, ranging from seven reales to nine patacones, and were probably for the fruit and vegetables that Quispi sold under her canopy.[100]

Even more interesting are the numerous small loans that vendors were willing to make to enslaved men and women, with or without pawned objects, demonstrating that they were perceived as autonomous economic agents by at least some strata of urban society. The chichera María Pazña was owed three patacones by Anton Terra Nova, an African man enslaved by a religious order in the Cercado, as well as twelve reales for a bedspread bought on credit by another slave named Joan Bran.[101] These small debts speak to the relative freedom of domestic slaves in the cities, where they acted much as we have seen indigenous servants did, earning some wages for themselves under these adverse conditions and spending them on small luxuries and necessities. The vast majority of Indian women's debts were with other Indians, suggesting that ethnic identification played a role in both the formation of trading links and the communities of trust necessary for credit. However, the regular appearance of free and enslaved blacks in notarial registers establishes that commercial links did not only follow ethnic lines.

Economic and social relationships went both ways. In 1604 in Lima, Pedro Biafara, the freed slave of Cajamarca's encomendera doña Jordana Mejía, declared a debt for men's clothing and jewelry he had sold to the Indian Andrés.[102] Mencia López, a wealthy free black woman and a slave owner herself, indicated through her 1578 will a rather explicit level of ethnic transculturation: she wished her burial in the Cathedral of Lima to be accompanied by "four Indians with their torches," each to be provided with a suit of clothing, and she made small bequests to both the hospitals of Indians and of Spaniards, so that each might say masses for her soul. López also owned, in addition to a large and expensive European wardrobe, "a shawl and a lliquilla of cumbe . . . and a cotton and cumbe shawl."[103] These may have been gifts from Indian friends or were simply luxury items to be possessed by any elite woman.

One final statement of ethnic interdependence comes from the 1578 will of Catalina de Ysásaga, a free black woman who lived in Lima. She stated,

Item, I declare that I have as a possession a black woman named Juana from Zape [Sierra Leone], and because I, as long as I have lived in this city, have dealt with Indians and in order to ease my conscience, I bequeath the said slave to the Indian hospital of this city, to be its possession, and to serve the Indians for as long as she shall live, and the hospital shall make use of her as their own property, and I beg and charge the mayordomo of the said hospital to treat said black woman well.[104]

In summary, the varied relationships between Indian and black women remind us that ethnic designation, in sixteenth-century Peru, was not a stable nor a segregative signifier, although ethnicity clearly had meaning for people. Some Indians were able to achieve a relatively privileged position and even come to possess slaves, the ultimate marker of status among their colonizers. But blacks too were sometimes slave owners, and it is likely that free blacks had Indian apprentices or servants from time to time. The majority of Indians, however, related to blacks as to another subaltern group, with all the tensions as well as commonalities which that might imply.

Conclusion

The extensive body of testamentary and other material from Lima and Trujillo analyzed here reveals that there was a great heterogeneity of experience between regions as well as within them. Studies of Indian towns, like Huarochirí, or predominantly Indian cities like Potosí and Cuzco, have given us great insight into how indigenous communities, migrants as well as long-time residents, managed their encounter with colonial domination. But Lima and Trujillo presented different opportunities and obstacles, because their permanent Indian populations were never a majority, and were primarily composed of immigrants. As a result, those Indian populations shared many qualities with their non-Indian neighbors, but also came to forge their own specific identities.

Lima and Trujillo were also notable, though not unique, for having such a large body of wills produced by their non-Spanish populations. It is obvious that wills were not usually made by the poorest strata, though a number of the women testators had very insignificant material possessions. More heavily represented are minor landowners, vendors, and artisans, but many of these evidenced great transformations of fortunes, such as must have occurred to many others who conversely died at a lower socioeconomic level than they had once attained. Urban colonial society was one of great mobility, in opposition to the static picture offered by numerical censuses.

This heterogeneity, while frustrating from the point of view of categorical analysis, should be seen in a positive light. It reveals an obvious truism, that little of use can be known from an ethnic designation; colonial Indian women were not all of a type, and their life stories were intertwined with those of non-Indian society as well. These wills certainly represent the most acculturated segments of Indian society, as demonstrated by these women's acceptance of Spanish social values (the possession of properties, cash-based worth, the use of legal instruments to document wealth); but also the most transculturated, for they created new identities involving the forging of diaspora or neighborhood communities through new economic networks, reinterpreting Spanish laws and society for their own benefit, and serving as models themselves to black and casta residents as well.

We have seen that many Indian women migrated to urban centers as domestic servants, an occupation which, in its worst forms, was sometimes akin to slavery in terms of the boundlessness of its workload and the misery and humiliation that might be visited upon the worker. At the same time, domestic service was not slavery for the most obvious reasons: servants were regularly remunerated and their contracts were defined within a chronological period. Many women in service appear to have used their occupation as a temporary means to an end, eventually leaving in order to take on other jobs, marriages, or other responsibilities. Although service could thus lead to a certain level of financial independence (especially through paternalistic relations with employers), it also, through acculturation, led to an acceptance of the material value system of the colonizers. The service contract that dictates that the employer take from the servant's salary a sum to pay for the Crown's Holy Crusades at other ends of the empire is but a trenchant example of the way commodification was reinforced as an adjunct of other ideologies. Similarly, the ownership of black slaves by an Indian elite reflected the interrelation between the upper levels of both Spanish and Indian society and also legitimated a colonial hierarchy based in part upon ethnic categories.

Our reading of colonial wills has illustrated the ways in which the ownership of certain kinds of property quickly created economic distinctions among Indians as well as Spaniards, turning some Indians into more prestigious solareros just as some Spaniards (and others) became vecinos. Even the poorest women, as we shall see below, would purchase an item of clothing with extra cash or credit, partly to demonstrate a social position, and partly as an investment because clothing was easily pawned. The wealthier would invest in land—houses, solares with gardens, or larger agricultural plots. These too could be easily sold or, better, rented out to generate income over a lifetime. Slavery presented a whole new way of acquiring access to labor, and though few Indians could afford to lay out hundreds of pesos in cash before credit became more readily available with slave traders, the possibility of renting a slave meant that large sums of money did not have to be amassed to take advantage of this dismal form of labor.

In this rapidly changing society, women seem not to have been held back by legal barriers to the acquisition of properties. What legal disadvantages they might have faced were shared by Indian men, and it appears that the law's gender bias was enforced unevenly. But women did find themselves confronted by different social problems than did men, and they sought different means of resolving them. The next chapter examines some of the strategies women learned to use to strengthen their positions.

CHAPTER 3

"Because I am a woman and very old . . .":
Indigenous Women's Testaments
as Legal Strategies

Introduction

Catalina Gualcum approached Lima's city magistrate and a public notary in August 1582.[1] She was a native of the Lurín Valley, but she had resided in Lima for the past ten years, where she owned a house and now "intended to bury herself in the Church of the . . . Cercado . . . where she had received charity." She described to the officials a series of parcels of land she owned in the Lurín Valley, inherited from her parents forty years earlier. Her continued involvement with that community is obvious from the incredible detail she provided about each parcel: its name, geographical and social landmarks describing its precise location, the amount of wheat or corn each yielded, and who was presently tending it. Gualcum had come before the officials, she said, "because I am a woman and very old, I cannot take advantage of these [lands] nor do I have an heir, and if I should die, they will enter the lands and take them." The assumed "they" of her speech was most likely the ruling elite of her rural community, who might seize vacated lands as private or community property.[2]

Rather than see her family's lands revert to control of her community or her caciques, Gualcum asked that her confessor, the Jesuit Father Diego Anton, take control of her estate and use its value to pay for her funeral and for alms for the poor, because "she did not have the means to bury herself." Gualcum approached the institutions that had supported her and had the means to carry out her will, despite her own weak social position as a cash-poor if land-rich single, elderly, Indian woman. Not only was she responding to the charity of religious-based community institutions, but she was (like many of her urban peers) participating in constructing a powerful and uniquely Andean Catholic Church.[3]

It is possible to take Gualcum at her word, as someone who was prone to be victimized due to her lack of political or economic power. Yet her decision to approach the colonial authorities in order to carry out her wishes reveals that some women did believe that they had socially given rights and the means to redress through law and institutions, hardly the posture of victims. Early colonial wills, as we have seen, demonstrate a savviness about the legal system and a real tension between the practices of changing rural communities and new urban centers.

Studies of indigenous towns in Mesoamerica have investigated the degree to which testators used colonial law (via indigenous-language as well as Spanish-language wills) either to uphold or to undermine local preconquest practices, particularly with respect to the inheritance of property.[4] In the Andes, Irene Silverblatt analyzed the will of a noblewoman from Cuzco named Juana Chimbo to assert that Chimbo rejected a patriarchal Spanish legal system that produced a loss of traditional rights for women. Chimbo had explicitly disinherited her husband and instead had chosen female friends and servants as her heirs in the document.[5] This study differs in its conclusions from these others because, unlike Culhuacán or Cuzco, neither Trujillo nor Lima had a majority indigenous population, and the Indians who did live there came from culturally and geographically diverse regions of the viceroyalty. Because of the radical diversity of the population and the lack of significant corporate support, urban Indians were less likely to use colonial law to provide continuity with a recent past, especially one that no longer spoke to their needs. Instead, they used law in much the same way that Spaniards and Africans did, as a particular response to their circumstances, and their perceived rights, as creolized subjects.[6]

This chapter investigates the ways that women sought advantages by recourse to law and institutions, especially cofradías or Catholic sodalities. Women and men seem to have adopted different strategies to deal with their economic and social powerlessness; women clearly saw their wills and their involvement in the Andean Catholic Church as means for exercising some amount of discretion over their lives and property. The arenas in which women sought to influence or determine outcomes included the inheritance and disinheritance of property, debt collection and score settling, protection of illegitimate children, and control over property to which they believed they were entitled. Wills introduced the colonial legal and religious systems—and their agents, generally but not always Spanish males—into indigenous life. But wills also reveal the extent to which indigenous society was already part of the colonial system.

For women such as Catalina Gualcum, their status as poor, female, and elderly compelled them to provide written instructions for the colonial authorities regarding their death. In the absence of such directions, lands might be absorbed by their birth communities, personal property might be appropriated by unwelcome kin, and they might receive a pauper's burial rather than the comforting social and religious occasion desired by so many. The circumstances of their existence—often with tenuous connections to originary communities, but social and institutional ties to an adopted city and the Catholic Church—led elderly and infirm women to adapt a colonial legal framework and instrument to articulate their final wishes, even when they had local family who might do so for them.

Spanish Property Law in the New World

According to the seventeenth-century *Recopilación de leyes de los Reynos de las Indias*, a compendium and critique of existing colonial law, there was much disarray among the heirs of those who died intestate.[7] A bureaucratic structure, the *Juzgado de bienes de difuntos* or "Tribunal of the Estates of the Deceased," was devised to deal with legal questions and complications due either to the lack of a will or conflicts over the carrying out of last wishes. There were apparently numerous conflicts even when wishes were clearly specified; executors were allowed one year to give final accounts of the property of the dead, and the ecclesiastic and civil courts were full of suits over noncompliance, corruption, and dereliction of duties. In any case, when inheritance was not clearly mandated by law, a will provided some modicum of support for the wishes of the dying; and when the testator's plans were likely to raise conflicts, it was a necessity.

Thus, don Diego Cossanosan, who worked as accountant in a storefront in the plaza of Trujillo, declared that he made a will in 1627 because "I have stated in this testament that I have two legitimate children, one male and one female, so that between the two abovementioned children there should be no lawsuit, but that they should enjoy my possessions in a brotherly fashion, as they are brother and sister, and share the estate by halves without any difference at all."[8]

The will was not the only or even most common means of distributing property before death. Some wills were accompanied by notarized sales of property, which both raised money to pay expenses brought on by illness and ensured that the proper individual or group received the property expeditiously. Much small property surely passed through less formal means, but wills were important when informal means could be contested or were unclear. The five contracts made by Catalina Román in 1611 are illustrative: although she had left her solar to the cofradía of San Antonio de Padua in her 1607 will, in 1611 she sold the solar, wrote a new will leaving half of the proceeds to the cofradía, and then in a series of codicils changed back and forth the distribution of those proceeds between her own funeral arrangements and two cofradías.[9] In her case, formal contracts followed on informal agreements and discussions (as described in the various wills), and the wills and codicils served as clarifications of her changing transactions and desires. The fact that these formal organs also contradicted one another led to the possibility of legal actions, although in this case it seems that the principals understood and respected her (final) instructions.

Medieval Spanish legal codes, including the *Siete Partidas* (of the mid-thirteenth century) and the *Leyes de Toro* (1369), both recodified for Spain and her colonies as the *Nueva recopilación de las leyes de Castilla* in 1567, established that, upon dissolution of a marriage for any reason other than adultery, dowry (*dote*)—the cash, real estate, clothing, and other assets that a woman brought to her marriage—was the property of the woman, and the groom's estate, minus a 10 percent contribution to his wife called the *arras*, reverted to him.[10] In elite society, these transactions were witnessed and set in writing, in a "letter of dowry" (*carta de dote*), so that they might be enforced in the future. In plebeian society, explicit dowries and dowry contracts were unusual. Instead, nonelite women seem to have taken dowry as a conceptual model for maintaining personal property within the marriage; the will was then used as a means for legally establishing and redistributing that property upon death or dissolution of the marriage. Indian men and women in colonial Lima and Trujillo spoke in their wills not so much of dote and arras but of the "goods brought to the marriage" by each individual.

Upon dissolution of the marriage, the wife's share was not seen as belonging to the parents of the bride but to the woman herself. Any property earned within the marriage (*bienes gananciales* or joint property) was treated similarly to the traditional "fruits of the dowry," the multiplication of property due to the proper management of capital in animals, money, or land, and thus was divided equally between the partners.[11]

Despite this impartial attitude toward marital property, Spanish law did treat men and women differently. Adult women were not considered minors, nor imbeciles before the law, as some have argued, but they did have certain restrictions placed upon them, such as the inability to hold a public office, for example lawyer or judge. Like their male counterparts, single women under the age of twenty-five had to have the express consent of their father before entering into legal contracts. Married women were supposed to have their husband's express consent but, as we have seen, this was rarely enforced. In most other ways, married women were as free as widows or single women who had reached majority to engage in economic and legal transactions.[12]

And this was the case in practice as well as in theory. Women of all civil statuses appeared before notaries with great regularity, only occasionally with the formal dispensation of husbands or fathers and sometimes in direct opposition to them. At times they found it necessary to defend their own interests through the colonial judicial system, rather than rely upon male relatives to do so. In Trujillo in 1563, doña Luisa de Cabrera, a Spaniard, requested the court's protection of her dowry from her husband Diego de Alarcón; she had received from him a receipt for her dowry of two thousand pesos, and she had placed another two thousand pesos in the hands of the prominent citizen Juan Daça Carabajal. Before she would transfer the second sum to her husband, she demanded an additional letter of receipt to protect her interest, such that "should the marriage be dissolved, (the money) would return to my power and to my heirs." The court granted her request and the transfers took place.[13] Other women stood before notaries in order to make declarations that their husbands misused their properties or otherwise abused them. It is apparent from the voluminous archival record that men and women of all classes and ethnicities found the legal system to hold out at least the possibility of justice.

But given the law's predisposition to see married and single women as dependents, it is not surprising that widows were overrepresented among early colonial testators. In Trujillo, more than one-third of all female testators in the sample were widows, and an equal number were married. In Lima the numbers are similar: nearly 30 percent were widowed, though half the sample was married (see Table 2). These numbers are surprising when placed against the male samples for the two

TABLE 2

Marital status of indigenous testators

	Single	Married	Widowed	Unknown	Total
Trujillo:					
Women	15 (27.3)	20 (36.6)	20 (36.3)	0 (0)	55 (100%)
Men	2 (8.3)	21 (87.5)	1 (5.1)	0 (0)	24 (100%)
Lima:					
Women	14 (9.5)	75 (51)	44 (29.9)	12 (8.1)	147 (100%)
Men	9 (14.7)	44 (72.1)	8 (13.1)	0 (0)	61 (100%)

SOURCE: Documents from AGN, AAL, ARLL, and BNP.

cities: in Trujillo, nearly 90 percent of male testators were married, and in Lima it was 72 percent. Because both cities had more Indian men than women, and the wills themselves demonstrate that marriages tended to be endogamic, we can draw the conclusion that married women were less likely to testate than their spouses (and possibly that men were less likely to remain widowed than women).

This situation might well reflect socioeconomic factors rather than legal ones. Widowhood occasionally brought the inheritance of substantial enough property to make a will necessary. But the fact remains that more than one-half of the female testators in Trujillo and nearly as many in Lima were unmarried at the time of making their wills. It may be the case that unmarried women found needed protection in colonial legal instruments and institutions.[14]

Urban Indians, perhaps assisted by priests and the notary, demonstrated a cogent knowledge of colonial property laws. Indigenous women as well as men generally mentioned the division of their possessions into "goods brought to the marriage" and "joint property" in their wills, and many compulsively listed the smallest items according to their provenance as well as their desired destination. Periodically, women protected their share of the property by asking a respected member of the community, often a Spaniard, to hold it for them. Catalina, a Spanish-speaking Indian from Quito, stated that "I declare that I brought in dowry and marriage to the said Juan yndio one hundred and seventy pesos in silver which I have had and currently have in the power of Simon Beltran, of which I have received from the abovementioned thirty four or thirty five pesos, and the rest is owed me by the said Simon Beltran."[15]

Men also generally referred to the separate estates they and their wives brought to the marriage. In 1590 Miguel de Paz, a Spanish-speaking Indian resident in Lima left a will clarifying the situation regarding his wife, Madalena, who was still living. In this case, he stated that he had "received nothing" (that is, no dowry) from her, and likewise "when I married the said Madalena my wife, I had no possessions and those which now might appear except the house which I inherited, the rest of the estate are *bienes multiplicados* during the marriage; I order that they be distributed in the usual fashion, [half] to my wife."[16]

The joint property was literally thought of as an entity to be divided in half. An evocative example was offered by María Sacha Chumbi, married to Mateo Guaman, with whom she owned a farm in Pachacamac. She asked her executors to "make a mountain" of all the vegetables and beans from their upcoming harvest "and distribute it proportionally; and with what belongs to me, do good for my soul with the half that is rightly mine, and the other half [of my half] give to my daughter Ana Gregoria, because this is my will."[17]

Similarly, Catalina Carguay Chumbi, who testated in Lima in 1608, made arrangements such that her half of the estate would benefit her soul, as her husband's would benefit his. Her estate included

First, two hundred and fifty pesos of eight reales, one hundred and twenty five of which are mine and the other hundred and twenty five belong to Francisco Poma, my husband, because we have earned them with our labor and sweat; of which said pesos must be distributed on the above-declared masses and in the rest of the bequests made in [this will], those being the pesos belonging to my part.

Poma was likewise sick in the hospital. If both died, she ordered, the executors should spend the entire amount on masses for both souls; if Poma recovered, he was to keep his half.

Urban Indians, many of whom had grown up under different (albeit changing) property rights structures in their natal communities, quickly internalized this framework and saw their wills as a means of creating and enforcing these rights. Inés Guamguam, who testated in Lima in 1614, stated vehemently that her late husband's executors were violating her property rights by selling off their joint property to pay his personal debts: "and I also declare mules and other things [as debts] to be collected that [my husband's executors] have sold on credit; I state that these objects were acquired during the time when I was with him, as matrimonial property, and this half pertains to me; settle accounts with the executors of my said husband and give me what belongs to me."[18]

In the not-uncommon case where she was more successful than her husband, a woman could be quite definitive about the sources of her income as well as what she intended done with it. Francisca Ramírez had married a Spanish carpenter named Pedro de Miranda around 1630. In a will written three years later, she was explicit in separating her own substantial property from her husband's, noting even the fact that "from my possessions there was purchased a quantity of tools so that the said Pedro de Miranda might work, and wood for his work," leaving these few items as a bequest to him. Miranda, she added, "brought no goods whatsoever to my power and thus what I declare are my own which I had prior to marrying him." Her ultimate heir was her own soul, although she did leave her husband an additional bequest of a mare and a saddle "so that he might go about on her." Miranda was not even to remain in her house: he was entitled to one year free of rent, then the house should be rented out to "whoever offers to pay the most and would treat it well."[19]

Her financial concerns were perhaps borne out by her second marriage, to another Spaniard named Francisco Sánchez Cortés, whom she sued for ecclesiastical divorce "because of his bad treatment of me and the diminution of my estate . . . moreover he spent and dissipated part of my goods in his vices and distractions and in the paying of his debts, pawning my jewelry, which was the cause that moved me to make the demand for divorce, such that today I believe before God and my conscience that he is my debtor for many pesos."[20] Ramírez was certainly among the more conscious tacticians in her use of the legal system, and her acute business sense served her well in terms of property, if not in her choice of spouses.

Delineating preconjugal and joint property in such apparently petty ways could be a means of punishing or disinheriting an unworthy spouse, but it also might be a way to protect other survivors. Juliana de Mendoza, the owner of a successful pulpería or grocery store, asserted that her husband, a shoemaker who had been absent from Lima for over a year, had brought nothing to the marriage and she even "established and filled a shoemaker's store for him." Her declaration meant that her entire estate, including agricultural lands inherited from her ancestors, slaves, houses, clothing, furnishings, and numerous cash loans from her pulpería and rental properties, would be divided equally between their two children, leaving nothing at all to her absent husband.[21]

Leaving a testament by no means guaranteed the absence of legal claims, and the civil and ecclesiastical courts brimmed with challenges to wills. But litigation was expensive and risky, so many preferred to work out arrangements privately. An agreement notarized in Trujillo in February 1624 speaks of the contentious claims of Francisca Chunbe and Luisa de Mendoza, the widow and daughter (by another woman), respectively, of Diego de Mendoza, who came together to avoid a lengthy lawsuit in the aftermath of his death. Chunbe demanded two hundred pesos of premarital property, as well as a fifty peso bequest, as stated in her husband's will. Mendoza challenged Chunbe's claim, but "in consideration that lawsuits are risky and the costs are high and that neither side has the law with them so securely that the other could not challenge, and so to resolve all the abovesaid and maintain friendship and the family relations that exist between them," they came before a notary to record their compromise. In the settlement, Francisca Chunbe received one hundred and fifty pesos rather than two hundred and fifty: half of her dowry plus the fifty peso bequest.[22]

The ubiquity of indigenous and plebeian wills in colonial archives make it clear that colonial law and legal instruments were perceived as providing relief to those fearing the chaos that might ensue with their death. Relief took the form of control over property, as well as provisions for proper burial and celebration of masses. As was the case in Mesoamerica, Andean testators showed an adept use of legal instruments both to establish private property and to arrange for its transference. But as we will continue to see, testators in Lima and Trujillo disposed of their property in ways specific to their cultural location.

"Forcible" and "Universal" Heirs in Colonial Wills

Spanish law was simultaneously specific and flexible regarding mandatory inheritance patterns. Direct inheritance went through lines of first, descendance (testator's legitimate children) and second, ascendance (testator's parents). Ascendant and descendant heirs (called collectively *herederos forzosos*) could not be deprived of their share of the estate, except in cases where heinous actions, such as attempted murder in order to acquire the estate, would preclude inheritance. When there were no mandatory heirs, testators could specify anyone at all to inherit. In the absence of a will, legitimate children and grandchildren inherited all possessions equally, regardless of gender or other factors. If there were no living children, grandchildren, or parents, the closest family member would inherit; and if there were no blood relatives at all to be found, a husband or wife would be the heir. In the absence of any heirs or will, the state took possession of the estate.[23]

In a written will, the testator had a number of options. First, she or he could assign property to specific individuals as a bequest. But whether properties were assigned or not, an *heredero universal* or universal heir had to be appointed, in a final clause, to inherit all nondistributed property (equally, if more than one universal heir was named). Susan Kellogg found this practice uncommon in colonial Mexican wills written in Nahuatl, occurring only when an Indian was consciously imitating the style of Spanish wills; in urban Peru, however, appointing a universal heir was the norm across ethnic groups.[24]

An adult's universal heir was generally his or her legitimate child or children, if any. If childless and with no surviving parents, a testator could name whomever she liked. Once all bequests and debts were met and the funeral paid for, the remaining property would be sold at a public auction and the proceeds distributed to heirs equally, except in the case of a *mejora* or small increase in one share over the others.[25] Illegitimate or "natural" children (those born to two unmarried parents) were dealt with differentially. If named in a will, they became mandatory heirs of their mothers. Fathers, on the other hand, had to recognize children officially in order to make them mandatory heirs. Thus we can imagine that for those who wanted to provide for their illegitimate children, a will was a necessary tool. But those who wanted to pass over their out-of-wedlock offspring could simply fail to name them.[26]

Consistent with the law, nearly all the testators in the sample who named living children made them their universal heirs (see Table 3). Of nineteen mothers in Trujillo, only two failed to name their children as universal heirs: Catalina de Agüero left her two illegitimate mestizo children substantial bequests but made her own soul her heir in 1570; and Elvira Alacaxa disinherited her daughter because of abusive treatment.[27] Indigenous men also followed the letter of the law by naming their legitimate children as their universal heirs, though they were less likely to do so with illegitimate offspring. Although nearly a quarter of the male testators in the Trujillo sample acknowledged a child outside of wedlock, only two made them their heirs. Only two men in the Lima

TABLE 3

"Universal Heirs": Lima and Trujillo

	Soul/ Church	Spouse	Child/ Grandchild	Parent	Unstated/ Other
Lima:					
Women	44	15	63	6	21
Men	10	13	31	3	3
Trujillo:					
Women	26	2	22	0	6
Men	1	4	17	1	3

SOURCE: Wills from AGN, ARLL, AAL, and BNP.

NOTE: Some testators split estates between multiple heirs, thus entries do not add up to total number of wills.

sample acknowledged natural children, and in one of these cases made them his heirs.

Children, Legitimacy, and *Mestizaje*

As we have seen, legitimate children were mandatory heirs of their parents' estates, in roughly equal parts. But when parents had illegitimate children, they faced important decisions. The way that a child was described in a will, while not beyond contestation, could affect their social status or *calidad*. Clearly, some indigenous testators wielded these legal documents in order to advance their children's prospects.

Illegitimate children suffered discrimination in colonial Latin America, but, as Ann Twinam notes, illegitimacy was a continuum, where the public circumstances of one's birth were both a decisive and a malleable factor in producing social status. There was a vast range of ruses as well as legal means that could obfuscate or change birth status, from marrying after the fact (if both parents were single) to purchasing legitimation from the Crown with an ample fee and evidence of one's honorable life. Of course, wealth would be a major factor in discounting the stain of birth, but even the poorer classes found other ways to contest calidad. Wills, as notarized statements of personal history, could thus be part of an attempt to affect the perception of a child's natal status or at least provide material relief to offset the loss of honor.[28]

Providing a dowry to better the life chances of an illegitimate daughter was clearly an incentive to write a will. María de la O had two sons, one legitimate and one not, and an illegitimate daughter when she testated in 1660. She asked that they inherit equally, but with a mejora or improvement for her natural daughter, María de las Nieves, composed of furniture and clothing. Her legitimate son was plaintiff in a lawsuit to gain possession of the estate of his father, the late governor of the town of Virú, and would presumably be quite well off should he succeed. Juan Ramón, her natural son, would receive his legal share of María de la O's estate, which mainly consisted of a house and solar in Trujillo. María de las Nieves received her mejora either because of a special relationship with her mother, or because, as an illegitimate child, she would require a larger dowry in order to marry well.[29] This pattern held true in many other cases as well: illegitimate daughters were likely to receive larger portions of their mother's estate than did sons.[30]

Illegitimacy might be even more complicated in the case of mestizo children, with a Spanish and an Indian parent. Early Crown policy promoted crossethnic marriages, especially between elite Andean women and Spanish conquistadors, the better to get access to community lands as well as political legitimacy. But *arriviste* colonists demonstrated a strong preference to wait for marriage with elite Iberian women, and while they continued to have sexual relations (consensual and not) with Indian women, they by and large failed to formalize these unions. As Nancy van Deusen and Kathryn Burns, who have both provided important studies of this complicated period, note, the Crown shifted policy around 1549, when it declared that mestizo children of encomenderos could not inherit their father's estates. This ruling was accompanied by other restrictive policies against mestizos, who were not tributaries like Indians, but were increasingly marginalized by Spanish society. However, the slow immigration of Iberian women to the Americas meant that the first generations born after the conquest included a large number of children born of informal relations between Spaniards and Indians. Some of these, as Elizabeth Kuznesof has argued, were certainly absorbed into "Spanish" society, particularly those with elite fathers. But many were marginalized, bearing the stigma not only of illegitimacy but also of not belonging to one community or the other. By the middle of the sixteenth century, when the samples of wills begin, the two terms, *mestizo* and illegitimate, were nearly interchangeable.[31]

According to the 1613 census, about eight percent of Lima's female Indian residents were married outside their ethnic designation.[32] An even smaller percentage of testators in the samples—just two or three in each city—spoke of such marriages, although ethnic designation (of the testator or the spouse) is often not given, and there is reason to believe that such designations were fluid, especially in the sixteenth century.[33] Unformalized sexual relations between ethnic groups were more common, though less so in Lima (where four Indian women in the sample claimed relationships with Spaniards, and none with blacks or mestizos) than in more integrated Trujillo (where ten Indian women acknowledged relationships across ethnic lines). These numbers probably underestimate actual practice, which may have been even greater among those without the means or need to make a will, although we have seen that having an illegitimate child might well provide additional reason to testate.

There are no accurate measures of illegitimacy in Lima or Trujillo for this period, but María Emma Mannarelli has compiled some compelling evidence from baptismal records. According to her study, of approximately 10,000 registered births in two parishes of Lima in the seventeenth century, only 39.2 percent in one parish and 50.7 percent in the second, were "legitimate." A very small number, 11.5 and 4.6 percent, respectively, were registered as illegitimate. But the rest—nearly half—appeared without information as to the marital status of the parents. And, even more interesting, the incidence of these births with no recorded information was highest for couples of mixed ethnicity, that is, 76 percent of those births. A reasonable interpretation of this data is that a large percentage of crossethnic births were indeed illegitimate.[34]

We have seen that Indian men and women used their wills to recognize their illegitimate children, often establishing them as heirs to substantial estates. In the cases of assymetrical, usually crossethnic relationships, outcomes were mixed. Some offspring of wealthy Spaniards and Indian women were raised as Spaniards and even sent to Spain to marry or join religious orders. Francisco Pizarro possibly began this tradition by handing off his illegitimate children by Inés Yupanqui (the daughter of the Inca Huayna Cápac) to his half-brother Francisco de Alcántara, when Inés married and set up her own household.[35] A number of Spaniards explicitly "purchased" their mestizo children, through the courts or more informal agreements, in order to bring them up in Spanish society. In 1577, Antonio de Medina, a Spaniard living in Lima, signed a letter of debt to Ysabel Yanaguar, an Indian woman from Cuzco, for fifty pesos. The debt was incurred for the

upbringing and costs you have incurred for María mestiza, aged eight years, your daughter and my own, who has been given to me by the courts so that I keep her in my care as her father, and although the said birth and care you

have taken of the said María deserves more reward, we have come to an agreement between you and I that I only give and pay you the said fifty pesos.[36]

A slightly better deal was offered in Trujillo in 1616 by Pedro de Tarasco,
a Spanish merchant from Nasca, who had traveled north on behalf of
his brother Miguel, the father of a child with a then-unmarried Indian
woman named Luisa Díaz. Pedro de Tarasco was entrusted to offer
Luisa Díaz, now married to an Indian man, "in order to do her good
and a charitable work," one hundred pesos plus a substantial quantity
of imported textiles in exchange for the daughter. The payment was to
be considered compensation for her past upbringing, and the mother
and stepfather agreed to have no future claims on the child.[37] It is difficult to evaluate the circumstances that might lead a woman to agree
to give up her child, though the courts favored fathers over mothers
in questions of custody, and in many cases, the perceived benefit of
raising a child in more privileged circumstances must have been considerable. In most cases, these illegitimate mestizo children would
have been kept in Spanish families as secondary members, or even as
domestic servants, but would have received lodging, sustenance, and
education.[38]

But even when material support was limited, wills could also help
establish status. As we have seen, illegitimacy was considered a stain
on honor, but one that could be rectified. In the absence of wealth,
women utilized more subtle means to provide for their children. One
common strategy appears in naming patterns. There are no identifi-
able patterns for transmission of names within plebeian Indian families in Trujillo; a child might take a mother's or father's name or one
with no relation whatsoever to either parent. But when the father of a
mestizo child was Spanish, the child was likely to carry his surname.[39]
Hence Jerónima Martines was the mestiza daughter of Jusepe Martines
and Ysabel, and Doña Melchora Marañón was the illegitimate daughter of Doña Lucía Chumbi of Lambayeque and Don Esteban Marañón,
a Spanish official from Chiclayo. Doña María de la Oliva y de los Santos, the daughter of an elite family from the Saña region, left her
worldly goods to her three illegitimate children, whose paternity was
not disclosed but who bore the surname "de Castro"; it is perhaps not
coincidental that she had received the gift of a large solar in Trujillo
from one Licenciado Antonio de Castro, the sexton of the Cathedral
Church in that city. Naming her children "de Castro" might have been
acknowledgment of his patronage or of his paternity.[40]

The interethnic naming pattern could be seen as a case of indigenous women adopting a cultural practice from Spaniards, who already tended to give children the patronym of the more powerful or elite side of the family. As Lockhart has noted, the intense elitism of Spanish families led them to adopt any "higher-sounding surnames to which they might have some claim," however tenuous.[41]

But more likely, in the case of illegitimate mestizos, this was an attempt to establish patrimony when economic resources might be at stake. Further evidence comes from the fact that this pattern did not hold when the child was the result of a union between an Indian woman and a black man. The son of Catalina Guisado, an Indian, and Antonio Bigo, a free black, was called Sebastian Rodríguez; the daughter of the Indian Barbola Guay and a black man named Cristóbal was named Joana de Rivera. While the Spaniards who were named in Indian women's wills could offer their children social if not economic status, fathers of African descent were less likely to provide either.[42]

From all this evidence, it seems that some indigenous women believed that they could use colonial legal instruments to pressure Spaniards into supporting their illegitimate children. It is unlikely that this strategy worked on a regular basis, as wills were so often contested and an obvious ruse would be recognized by the community where reputation was constructed. But the fact that the patterns of naming and recognizing herein described were consistent over the century and a half investigated suggests that it was successful enough to produce ongoing hope.

"I name my soul my universal heir"

But whom did testators favor when the law gave them no guidance? Perhaps surprisingly, indigenous women rarely named their husband as a universal heir, even when they were childless. Fifteen of seventy-five (20 percent) married women in Lima and only two of twenty (10 percent) in Trujillo named their spouse as their universal heir, and not many more left substantial bequests to their husbands. Men in both cities were slightly more likely to make a surviving spouse their heir.[43] The decision not to leave a significant bequest to a spouse is understandable in cases where there were children who would inherit, but overwhelmingly, when women were childless, they made their own soul their heir, using their estate to fund charitable acts and masses for themselves and their kin. This act did not impoverish or disinherit their husbands in general, since, as we have seen, each spouse kept half of the marital property as well as whatever estate they had brought to the marriage, but it does strongly indicate that indigenous women who testated were interested in establishing and maintaining their own property after death, and thus carving out a legal and economic identity separate from a husband's.

Benefiting one's soul with an estate could take many forms in colonial Latin America, most simply by spending all the remaining money on numerous sung or spoken masses, which could cost up to five pesos each, at the time of the funeral and at subsequent anniversaries.[44] More formal arrangements included endowing one's cofradía, which would provide for masses and also create a pool of credit to be used by community members; and placing a *censo* or lien on personal property, in this context usually a transfer of the property to a religious institution, which would then lease the property to a third party and use the income to pay for masses. The most expensive arrangement, seen only in the wills of the truly wealthy, was a *capellanía* or chaplaincy, the establishment of an ongoing income for a cleric, who would be in charge of ensuring that anniversary masses would be said in perpetuity.[45]

Fewer indigenous men named their soul as their heir, perhaps an indication of a gender difference in relationships with religious institutions. Only one childless, married man in Trujillo made his soul his heir, while the others named their wife or another close relative. In Lima, where more single men appear in the sample, souls and cofradías were more often their beneficiaries, but few married men failed to provide at least in part for their widows, at times dividing their own estates between their wives and their souls. This certainly reflects the paternalistic discourses of Spanish and ecclesiastic law, which explicitly sought to protect women from impoverishment during widowhood, but it may also reflect women having closer or different kinds of relationships with priests, cofradía officials and members, or even with the notaries who guided their will writing.[46]

Naming one's soul as heir ensured that masses would be said in perpetuity, shortening the soul's stay in purgatory, consistent with the religiosity we have already seen common in these wills. In addition to speeding one's way toward salvation, it aided the persistence of memory, so that the community continued to remember and celebrate the dead for years after burial. Although the Catholic Indians of Lima and Trujillo were no match for the excesses of their European contemporaries, who demanded increasingly opulent ceremonies and processions upon their death, even plebeian wills demonstrated a desire for ostentation and the performance of remembrance.[47]

The most elite enjoyed funerals with vast processions of candle-holding cofrades, orphans, and the poor, followed by sung masses in many of the city's churches and the cathedral. Less grandiose arrangements were more customary but still occasions for ostentation: Ana Esteban, an indigenous resident of the Cercado, planned that her unusually large estate—more than 1,700 pesos and seven slaves—be used to pay for over two hundred masses, the accompaniment of seven cofradías and representative orphans in her funeral procession, and a capellanía.[48]

Although we should not underestimate the profound religiosity of urban residents, including Indians, funeral arrangements were also public signifiers of status. Francisca Ramírez in Trujillo did not make any remarkable requests concerning her funeral in her 1653 will, beyond asking to be buried in the habit of San Francisco in a burial site she had already purchased in the Franciscan convent; but she did set up an extensive capellanía to benefit "my soul, parents, husband, brothers, kinsmen, relatives, niece, those who have done me good, and persons to whom I may owe something." This permanent and expensive institution would be funded by the sale of all her houses and possessions and would endow the chaplaincy of one of the sons of the prominent Spanish couple who would maintain the capellanía on her behalf.[49] The highly secular language used by Ramírez throughout her wills and her lack of cofradía memberships suggest that her desires were less religious and more mundane: solidifying her ties with elite families, making public demonstration of her gratitude for good works done for her, and implicit criticism of those who had done her wrong.

A last will and testament was an exercise in counterpoint to the law and thus presents us with clues as to the desires and concerns of the testator, here clearly inflected by gender and social status. Though the state established that no child (or surviving parent) could be deprived of their share of an estate, it also left substantial flexibility in terms of bequests and, in the absence of descendents, universal heirs. The patterns of inheritance discerned from the wills in the sample demonstrate that Indian men and women used the law to provide for their families, including, in some cases, for illegitimate children. Those married women who wrote wills were often spurred on by concerns for illegitimate children as well as for their own life after death; married men seem to have been driven more by a concern to provide for their widows. Well-to-do widows expressed fears that their estates might be commandeered after their death, and thus they turned to writing wills to protect their interests. Childless single and widowed women often chose to expend their fortunes on masses and charitable works in their name.

Wills as Alternatives: Intervention and Coercion

Because of the flexibility of colonial law when there were no mandatory heirs, the naming of a universal heir reveals much about testators' state of mind and *mentalité*. We have seen that Indian women sought final solace in the Catholic Church in a different form than men did. Our samples reveal that they also occasionally used their wills as instruments of coercion or punishment. Wills and inheritance were probably part of the discourse of everyday life in many families, and it is clear that some women used their property, however small, to try to affect social relations. At the same time, there is evidence that some women were manipulated by others, including family members and the religious community.

Many women were explicit about their own use of a will to manipulate family members or punish them. As mentioned above, Elvira Alacaxa, in a codicil to her 1573 will, revoked her gift of half a solar to her daughter Leonor, because "[Leonor] had been disobedient and had mistreated her and laid her hands upon her."[50] In a society that condoned a certain amount of mistreatment of wives, wills were part of an armory of threats available to women to use against their husbands or other family members.[51] Few women mentioned in their wills that they had been physically abused, although Mencia Mayuay in Lima in 1631 stated that she was testating when ill "due to a wound given to me by my husband during a disagreement between the both of us, therefore I forgive him."[52]

A number of women made outright declarations that they were *not* mistreated, suggesting that spousal abuse was indeed a concern. María Carua Sacsa was seriously ill when she made the following vehement protestation in her 1615 will: "I declare and state that I have been well with my husband without any occasion whatsoever and that I have received no mistreatment from him and even if I had received such, I pardon him, and I declare that not now, nor at any future time will I or my heirs ask anything of him; I declare this to unburden my conscience." Although she apparently bore her husband no ill will, she did not make him heir to her property, instead dividing it among her brother, nephew, and father. It is hard to say what discussions among the testator, family, priest, and notary might have led to such a statement, though it is easy to guess at coercion or prodding from some party or another.[53]

Wills and the threat of their enforcement seem to have been significant weapons. Ynes Bravo, a widow, lived unhappily with don Pedro Jimeno de León for more than ten years, providing company and care for him at the request of his family. During this time she (and her two female slaves) took care of don Pedro and his house, all the while earning their own living by selling firewood, raising chickens, and sewing. In a codicil to her will, Bravo was able to take her revenge: she demanded that her executors collect a two hundred peso debt that don Pedro owed her. But a few days later she returned, accompanied by don Pedro, and issued a second codicil, forgiving the debt "because he is poor," under the condition that don Pedro ask nothing more from her; but should he attempt to collect something from her estate, she would reimpose the demand for repayment of the two hundred pesos. Thus Ynes Bravo's will served as a blunt instrument to forge peace in their household.[54]

As we have seen, funerals, capellanías, and perpetual masses provided important income for the church and other religious institutions, which partially recirculated to communities through the church's loans and charitable works.[55] A fee schedule for burials and masses in Santa, on the central coast, in 1569 sets the cost of a funeral for a prominent Spaniard at twelve pesos, including the presence of the high cross and one mass; the same for an Indian cost six pesos. Vigils cost six pesos for a Spaniard, two for blacks and Indians; a sung mass cost between three and five pesos.[56] With hundreds of masses being said on some occasions, the church stood to gain substantially from the death of its faithful.

The income-generating aspect of institutional bequests raises many questions, including the degree to which will writing might have been a function of pressures on the sick and dying. We know, for example, that hospitals encouraged or coerced the seriously ill to make their wills. Santa Ana was the facility founded by Archbishop Loaysa to serve the indigenous community of Lima (another hospital, San Andrés, was for *españoles*, though in both cases class probably became a more important factor than ethnicity) and was known as a "dumping ground" for impoverished people, especially domestic servants whose employers did not wish to pay the costs of their care. Even the poorest could be buried in its pauper's field, called *Monte Calvario,* and masses for their souls said in its chapel, which became central to an important evangelizing parish in Lima. But all these services came at a price, and many of Santa Ana's patients died without paying their bills.[57]

The hospital ordinances of 1597 were an attempt to establish fiscal responsibility for sick Indians through various measures: domestic labor contracts were now to include the promise of medical care; patients were to register with the hospital officials to make it easier to track down persons who might pay medical bills; and the hospital mayordomo was charged with seeing that those in danger of dying made wills, in order to dispose of their goods and settle accounts, including medical bills, after death. Priests and notaries were a common, if not always welcome, sight in Santa Ana's corridors, and certain notaries were either assigned to the locale or chose to do regular business there, as their registers include sequences of wills made in the hospital.

It is likely that San Sebastián, Trujillo's hospital in the Indian parish, was also a losing financial proposition, and thus "encouraged" patients to write wills that would pay for their stay and burial. Beyond acknowledging in the will that the testator's hospital and burial costs should be met by their estate, this could also take the form of naming one's soul as universal heir and establishing a capellanía in the hospital's chapel or benefitting its cofradía, Santísimo Sacramento. Elena de Faria did just this in her "Memorial" of 1600: it was not a will because her wishes were "presented" in her name to the notary by the priest of the Indian parish and by the mayordomos of two cofradías, Santísimo Sacramento and San Antonio de Padua. The Memorial left her solar to the two cofradías.[58] Of course the financial and religious concerns of these hospitals were not mutually exclusive, as religious institutions they were also charged with making certain that last rites were administered and wills were written to provide for the soul's rapid passage out of purgatory.

Other likely sources of pressure were family members and the Catholic Church. Many women spoke explicitly of the presence or absence of "persuasion" when testating, and some went to great lengths to ensure that their wishes would be met despite the ability of others to affect their actions. Doña Juana Julia had her will written by the Cercado's notary in 1630, while suffering a long illness. She made extensive bequests, to religious and charitable institutions as well as to friends and relations who had taken care of her during her illness, and set up a capellanía. She left the remainder of her estate to her husband Francisco Sánchez. But this was not her first will, nor, she feared, her last. She had been coerced to write wills previously (by unnamed individuals) and was, she stated, "afraid that the same will occur again." To safeguard against future coercion, doña Juana Julia established a code for determining her "true" testament: if a later will should begin with the words of the "Our Father," it should be considered legitimate; otherwise it should be assumed that it was made under persuasion.[59]

A last will and testament was a mediated dialogue between a dying person and her God, as well as a legal document concerned with the mundane. Early modern Spanish law, adapted for the colonies, granted men and women significant flexibility in disposing of their possessions, within certain constraints, and how they chose to utilize that flexibility gives us insight into the pressures on daily life as well as the cultural ambit within which people lived. Women, who often outlived multiple spouses, were particularly likely to take advantage of the flexibility of the universal heir, often in explicit response to social pressures. Though coercion did enter into will writing on occasion, more likely the choice of an heir reflected a desire to improve the life chances of a friend or relative or expressed a deep religiosity that grew out of the vibrant community-based religious organizations, the cofradías.

Cofradías and Community Power Structures

Cofradías were religious sodalities, with origins in European Catholicism, founded in particular churches or convents for devotion to a saint. They required a membership fee (which was often paid upon death, by the evidence of wills), and depended upon donations to support their charitable work within the community. Cofradías also played an important part in creating an urban identity in Lima and Trujillo, one that was Catholic and looked to urban neighbors rather than rural birthplaces for support and community. It is likely that membership in a cofradía was strongly correlated with leaving a will—membership connoted deep piety, which would necessitate a final confession and testament, and cofrades tended to leave explicit instructions for their funerals as well as bequests and payments of debts to their sodality—and the samples of wills studied here show a strong propensity to be a member, if not an officer. Thus urban cofradías represented not only a strengthening of bonds within urban areas, between and within ethnic groups, but also a draining of resources away from rural communities and toward an Andean Christianity.

Table 4 shows a sharp peak in membership in Lima in the period 1621–60. This bump reflects a peculiarity of the sample: for these years,

TABLE 4

Cofradía *Membership Mentioned in Women's Wills*

Period	Trujillo: Cofrades	Percentage of Testators	Lima: Cofrades	Percentage of Testators
1565–80	6	67%	2	9%
1581–1600	2	50%	5	38%
1601–20	6	37.5%	11	46%
1621–40	6	46%	24	65%
1641–60	5	83%	19	63%
1661–1700	0	0%	11	55%
Total	25	47%	72	49%

SOURCE: Wills from AGN, BNP, AAL, and ARLL.

the majority of wills collected were written by women living in the Cercado. The Cercado, which alone had four cofradías by the end of the sixteenth century (almost as many as the entire city of Trujillo), was supervised by the Jesuits, who ran the hospital and eventually two schools as well; it was a center for evangelization in Lima. It also may have had stronger community institutions, including its cofradías, though this still remains to be demonstrated.

Cofradías were more than centers for evangelization; they were foundations of civic life. They provided economic support, including charity and loans to members; they sponsored the burial of their members as well as religious festivals; and they allowed for the exercise of power relations within the community, although always under the authority of the religious orders. Like men, indigenous women were active members, often belonging to three or four different sodalities, and they used their memberships to advocate for themselves.

Cofradías grew rapidly toward the end of the sixteenth century: so rapidly, in fact, that the Crown placed limits on their growth. Trujillo in particular was increasingly in the hands of the Catholic Church, especially as encomendero power waned and their former properties found their way to direct and indirect Church ownership. Juan Castañeda remarks that so many properties carried liens to the Church that "it was necessary to think twice before purchasing a hacienda."[60] The increasing power of the Church was also felt in rural communities, where Indians also made bequests to cofradías as safeguards for their souls.

Cofradías clearly played an important role in Indian men and women's lives, sometimes representing their only access to official power and its privileges. Juana Chumbi, in her 1625 will left her Lima house to the cofradia of Nuestra Señora de Copacabana, but in a subsequent will left it to the Jesuit cofradía, Niño Jesús, of which she was also a member. After her death, her confessor, the Jesuit priest Padre Alvaro Pinto, produced a memorandum supposedly dictated to him by the dying woman after he had thrown out the official notary and all Indian witnesses during an argument. The memorandum called for the eviction of her husband, Pedro de los Reyes, from her house two years after her death so that the cofradía could begin renting it for income, and it threatened to fully disinherit him if he objected. It also stated that the secrecy was necessary because she feared mistreatment at her husband's hands if he knew of her plans.

The two cofradías went to court over possession of the house. At the trial a Spanish woman friend of Chumbi's hinted that her original illness had been caused by a beating she had received from her husband. Witnesses rapidly took sides regarding the accusation of domestic violence: Indian members of Copacabana testified that they had never seen Chumbi and Reyes fight, while the Jesuits maintained that there was abuse. The indigenous testimony must have been ultimately more convincing, as the high court overturned a lower court decision and awarded the house to Copacabana but left a memorial with Niño Jesús, providing a living for Padre Alvaro Pinto.[61]

Although it is difficult to gauge what Juana Chumbi's real wishes were in this matter, it is clear that there were many pressures upon her, and she responded to these within the communities provided her by the various cofradías to which she belonged. If indeed she feared her husband, she turned to Spanish friends and a priest to protect her property and body. Another possibility is that she fell under the influence of an aggressive local priest who manipulated her (and possibly forged her final will).[62] In any case, Chumbi saw the cofradías as sources of support as well as means to exercise her will.

Leaving a house or part of one's estate to an institution such as a cofradía offered many direct benefits to the testator beyond the spiritual. The cofradía could assume the costs of one's funeral service, burial, and masses against the future returns from renting or selling the property.[63] This was particularly attractive to women who had little cash, but was not always the preference of the cofradía, which had to make extensive outlays up front. In 1643, Isabel de Ayala, the widow of a silversmith in Trujillo, arranged that her brother Agustín Ramírez should inhabit her solar and house for the rest of his life, and he should pay the censo on her house to the convent of San Agustín. After his death the Franciscan cofradía of Madre de Dios de la Concepción would inherit it, but they would pay for her funeral and masses in the meantime. That this was not necessarily the most desirable setup for the cofradía is evident in that Ayala made provision that a second cofradía should inherit if Madre de Dios refused the arrangement. Nevertheless, this became a more common strategy during the seventeenth century, possibly because individual executors were perceived to be less trustworthy or competent than institutional ones.[64]

In such ways, cofradías "offered a collective power to their members vis-a-vis the colonial elite."[65] Indians who had trouble collecting debts, salaries, inheritances, and the like could name the mayordomo of a cofradía as their executor, who would then have to collect on their behalf and pay off all their debts and expenses. Another related strategy was to make a Spaniard or other member of the elite an executor, especially if there was already an outstanding debt that would make them take the task more seriously. Executors were notorious for taking longer than the year mandated to carry out their duties, thus economic and moral incentives could speed completion of the testator's wishes.

There are many examples of this sort of last-ditch strategy, which generally yielded more of a moral than substantive victory for the testator. An Indian named Isabel, for example, had had an illegitimate mestiza daughter named Ynes with Esteban Rodríguez, a servant of a local encomendero. Rodríguez left a will naming their daughter as his heir before his death, but she also died before collecting the inheritance. Ysabel declared that she had also been unable to collect the inheritance, which should have fallen to her as her daughter's obligatory heir, probably due to recalcitrance on the part of his executors. In response, Ysabel named the mayordomo of the Indian hospital as her own executor and made the hospital heir of two-thirds of her estate, the final third to be spent on good works for her soul at the discretion of the mayordomo. Thus the hospital official—a prominent Spaniard—not only had the power to collect, but a great incentive to do so as well.[66]

Widowhood also brought economic crises to some women's lives, especially when a husband's estate was mishandled or debt-ridden. These women learned from this experience to invoke more powerful patrons to salvage their properties. María Chuqui, who testated in 1649, had gone from poverty "with no estate or goods at all" to owning two slaves with her third husband. But since her husband's death eight years prior, her brother-in-law, his executor, was renting the slaves out and not paying her anything for them. She expected her own executors, a Spanish man and woman who had acted as her patrons before, to collect on the debt and sell the slaves for her.[67] In these and other cases, Indian women of various classes demonstrated their ability and willingness to use the colonial system, including their own relationships with Spaniards, for their own purposes.

Indigenous women made use of their wills to force society to accommodate their needs when other measures failed them. While legal codes usually express themselves in absolute categories and dichotomies, experience is rarely so clear cut. It may well be the case that those women who wrote wills were the ones whose lives were the most complex and who felt the greatest need for security and clarity. In this sense, as well as the fact that they took legal action, they may be said to be "exceptional." But while their final actions were exceptional, the circumstances under which they lived were not. Although the law could not protect them all, it apparently offered some hope of justice or power in the end.

Conclusion

This chapter has demonstrated some of the ways in which indigenous women negotiated the complex circumstances of their lives in two colonial cities. We have seen that patterns in naming illegitimate children, or appointing powerful executors, or reserving one's estate for perpetual masses might be seen as moments of resistance in colonial society. At the same time, some of these might well be signs of coercion or of the persistence of earlier customs into the colonial period; because they take place within a hegemonic legal discourse, they are rife with ambiguities that cannot be sorted out easily.

Most of the women discussed here felt it necessary to invoke legal instruments because they were keenly aware that they were doubly disadvantaged, as women and as Indians. Most were also ill or elderly at the time of testating and were even less likely to be able to exercise their will personally. "Because I am female and very old" was not only a statement of victimization, however. Although women recognized the limitations and constraints placed upon them as subalterns, they also identified and utilized the institutions that could act on their behalf.

We have seen some of the more unfortunate circumstances that Indian women faced in this period: abuse from spouses and others, theft and incursion into property, problems arising from the illegitimacy of their children's birth, as well as the lack of legal standing for many of their relationships. Overall, though, the substance of their wills indicates that these women felt strongly that they had labored long and hard to accumulate small amounts of property or cash, and they wanted to control its distribution in a society that ostensibly did not favor either Indians or women. The women who approached notaries or priests in the hopes of exercising some of this control were generally neither victims nor exceptions, but individuals who had learned to operate within the new, hybrid institutions of colonialism.

CHAPTER 4

Dressing Like an Indian:
Producing Ethnicity in Urban Peru

Introduction

In . . . the house of the accountant Sebastián de Mosquera, there was found in his service a young Indian boy called Martín, he knows no other name, and he said that he is a native of La Chimba in Arequipa and he was born in the home of the said accountant, and he does not know who his parents are, other than that he is said to be a mestizo. And the accountant certified that said boy is a mestizo although he was wearing the clothing of an Indian, and that he is twelve years old.[1]

So reported the royal scribe Miguel de Contreras in his census of the Indians of Lima, carried out via a house-by-house survey in 1613. Contreras was charged with counting the Indians of Lima in order to assess tributary responsibility among the growing urban population: identifying ayllu-born Indians who were evading payment by living in the city. The apparent contradictions around identity given voice here—what constitutes an "Indian" or a "mestizo" at this moment in colonial history, and for whom?—were seemingly easily resolved for government officials like Contreras; his marginal notations indicate that, in his estimation and in contradiction to the testimony of the boy's Spanish employer, this "mestizo dressed like an Indian" was, in fact, an Indian tributary.[2]

The "Indian dressed as a mestizo" or the "mestizo dressed as an Indian" is a familiar character in colonial documents.[3] Sometimes, as in the case above, he or she is pointed out in order to assert a hidden "true" identity, for the purposes of assessing tribute or otherwise placing the individual in the social order. But it would be a mistake to ascribe a single explanation to all these "misdressed" individuals in the colonial world. It is tempting to argue that some Indians dressed in European garb in an attempt to "pass" into Spanish society (thus avoiding the obligations of tribute and mita), or conversely that mestizos donned Indian fashions to make claims on indigenous communities, to avoid the harsher sentences of Spanish justice, or, as in the words of the King of Spain in 1568, "[mestizos] are many. . . and badly intentioned . . . and they hide among their [Indian] relatives and can't be found" in order to foment trouble.[4] But such reductionist explanations ignore significant internal aspects of identity under colonial rule, and they gain their powerful credence from our retrospective understanding of the ills of colonial society. We may rather question what identity might have meant for indigenous, Spanish and casta actors at the end of the first century of colonization.[5]

But it is just this internal aspect that is lost to us in the colonial archives. In this chapter I do not claim to recover voices for these individuals, but I hope that through a close, textual analysis of a small but diverse set of wills, we can complicate more instrumentalist readings. What identities were most important to these early testators? Surely we can extract clues as to how they presented themselves in the worlds that wills described.

We have seen that colonial wills offer inventories of the possessions most valued or perceived as most valuable by testators, since the main object of the will was to distribute and liquidate the estate to pay expenses, debts, and the passage out of purgatory prior to passing on property to heirs and loved ones. While a number of testators in cities like Lima and Trujillo had significant property and even cash, another large group did not. Their limited estates were anchored around wardrobes, ranging from fashionable to threadbare, which, in addition to covering the body and signaling status, also served as vehicles for the accumulation of wealth. An expensive garment might serve as a pledge for a small loan, as would a silver vessel or a religious icon. And when contemplating the means to the afterlife, even a cash-poor woman in urban Peru would quickly turn to her small wardrobe as a source of funds.

Costume and fashion are also important to understanding the structure of particular societies and individuals' self-presentation, experience, and perception within those structures.[6] Studying changes in fashion under colonization provides important social insights, but it also requires discretion. In early colonial Peru, where hierarchies based upon class, ethnicity, calidad, and other factors were contested, being able to speak of wardrobe as it related to status is particularly important. This is a delicate process, running the risk of viewing some costume as "authentic," and thus the move to another form of dress as "deculturation" or even cooptation.[7] Instead, I propose that knowing the range of what people of various positions wore, and thinking about how they were perceived by others or even saw themselves, is indeed key to thinking through concepts such as ethnicity. Clothing (like hairstyle, which was also of great importance but cannot be deduced from testamentary materials) provided visual cues, but ones that were ambiguous and malleable. By studying the way that colonial testators discussed clothing as well as accumulated it, we can consider the ways that members of the nonelite classes participated in creating social difference, rather than simply suffered under it.

As we have already seen, costume had great importance in parts of prehispanic Peru. The Incas in particular were said to have encouraged a visual stratification for the purposes of imperial control, and local weaving techniques as well as other stylistic differences were of clear cultural importance, at least judging from the archaeological record.

Under colonial rule, as native populations were reduced to juridical "Indians," and communities were broken up by migrations (forced and voluntary) and high mortality rates, many individuals found themselves in the position of being able to consume products previously unavailable to them. The markets and shops of Lima, Potosí, Cuzco, Quito, and the like were novel in at least their scope in the Andes, and they were filled not only with imported goods but regional specialties, like the unique tributed clothing of Cajamarca, Lunaguaná, and the valleys of Trujillo. As well, specialty cloths like cumbe became more widely available, some still being produced by artisans, but the majority surely recycled from the wardrobes of elites.[8] As we will see, as indigenous individuals became "Indians," they could and did reach into this broad and politically charged visual discourse that referred simultaneously to a prehispanic pan-Andean moment and to the specificities of region and status now being eroded.

Spain too had its own discourses of signification through wearables.[9] Iberia was itself a crossroads for cultural signification at the time of the conquest of the New World: fashion from the Muslim world as well as other parts of Christian Europe played roles in the production of a Christian-Spanish identity. At the time of the conquest,

Spaniards wore fabrics and fashions produced in Spain, but also imported from all over the world—silks from Valencia, Madrid, and Barcelona, but also from the Far East; French ruan; Milanese serge (*raso*); Dutch and Flemish linens. Baroque Spanish costume valued heavy, dark fabrics, covering and even hiding the body under expensive layers; the somber style of Philip II dominated the dress of the upper classes.[10]

These tastes followed to the colonies: in 1577 two Spanish merchants in Trujillo filed charges against an African slave who had stolen 650 pesos from their store. As part of their complaint, they included an inventory of their wares, including hundreds of yards of black and colored satins, silks, velvets, taffetas, and woolens. In fact, the greater part of the 6,500 pesos of original capitalization was for uncut yardage of textiles imported from Europe and the Far East.[11]

So elite Spaniards, like their Andean counterparts, were used to demonstrating their social position through expensive fabrics and up-to-the-moment clothing styles in a society where the poor might have only the set of clothes on their backs. They were also accustomed to sumptuary laws that sought to restrict access to finery to certain classes and used clothing to mark religious communities. The medieval *Siete Partidas*, for example, had required all Jews to wear a distinguishing mark on their heads, since "many crimes and outrageous things occur between Christians and Jews because they live together in cities, and dress alike."[12] Given the impossibility of living apart, classes and ethnicities would have to find other ways to know one another's place.

But the Spanish American colonies were largely founded and settled by social climbers, men and women of undistinguished families who acquired wealth and titles through their actions rather than heredity. The conquest did not produce a free-for-all, but instead a newly stratified society with a great deal of anxiety about social position. To a Spaniard of the sixteenth century, sumptuous dress represented high status, and thus public dressing was part of a contestation over political power.

But public dress also carried the danger of misrepresentation. Colonial rulers and administrators demonstrated deep concern about how fashion and inappropriate excess would destabilize imperial relations, ostensibly by depleting wealth and resources, but also by signaling incorrectly. In 1509, King Ferdinand issued a royal order prohibiting settlers from bringing with them clothing made of costly and ostentatious silk, especially taffetas and brocades, or decorated sheaths, saddles, or even expensive furniture, in the hopes of convincing them to spend their new wealth on less "disorderly" and more appropriate things. Certainly, part of Ferdinand's concern was that the rapid ascent to wealth offered by conquest would lead to the appearance of high rank or status before it was officially bestowed by the Crown.[13]

But laws regarding dress tend to be difficult to enforce, especially when distinctions between groups are already ambiguous. Although the Crown and its agents attempted to modulate the dress styles of their subjects, including prohibitions on the wearing of silk by black and mulata women, and the famous seventeenth century attacks on Lima's *tapadas*, women who veiled themselves nearly from head to toe to engender a liberating anonymity, the dominant culture was rarely successful at restricting the appearance of its others.[14] And it was hardly in the economic interests of the merchant class to restrict their already scant consumer base. On the other hand, we will see how plebeians themselves participated in the construction of ethnic categories through fashion, unwittingly, perhaps, aiding the construction of a colonial hegemony.

Conquering Fashions: Clothing in the Sixteenth Century

Fashion is always highly time- and place-specific and sometimes deeply personal. We cannot reduce the diverse wardrobes of regions like Iberia or the viceroyalty of Peru to a simple uniform, and certainly not over long epochs of rapid social change. We can identify certain garments as having iconographical cachet within a society, as demonstrated by their appearance in portraits and sculptures, their manifestations in burials, and their descriptions in period narratives as well as in wills. It is from this range of information that I have extracted what follows, a description of what were the key elements of Iberian and Andean wardrobes at the time of contact and colonization.[15]

In prehispanic Peru, indigenous men and women tended to dress in garments made of rectangular woven cotton or wool, women wearing a wrapped dress called in Quechua an anaco, sashed with the woven *chumpi* belt, and with a shawl called a lliclla pinned around the shoulders, sometimes with a cloth headdress (see Figure 3).[16] Men dressed in the long tunic called unku, with a draped mantle across the shoulders (see Figure 4). These gendered sets of pieces—anaco and lliclla, manto and unko—became the template for tributary goods across the viceroyalty, though different regions used different fibers, dyes, and

Figure 3. Indian noblewoman, circa 1600. From don Felipe Guaman Poma de Ayala, *El primer nueva corónica y buen gobierno.* (Courtesy of Siglo Veintiuno Editorial.)

design patterns. Thus the sets of two garments, though not necessarily equivalent across all regions, came to be considered the general costume of Andeans under colonization.

Figure 4. Indian nobleman, circa 1600. From don Felipe Guaman Poma de Ayala, *El primer nueva corónica y buen gobierno*. (Courtesy of Siglo Veintiuno Editorial.)

European fashions of the time were somewhat different, though not as radically dissimilar as some chroniclers argued. European men and women wore far more layers than their Andean counterparts; their garments were cut and sewn rather than made of one length of cloth; and they preferred dark, somber colors to the bright stripes and patterns that many Andean regions favored. Sixteenth-century Spanish men wore a white shirt, *camisa*, with a waistcoat, *jubón*, over it and often another overgarment, the *ropilla*, which might have an extra set of hanging sleeves or *mangas*. Their legs were covered by *calzas* or stockings, and they wore a short skirt, the *sayo*, around the waist. Over the latter part of the century, stockings were replaced with *calzones*, calf-length breeches, and colored socks. Over all of this went a long, dark cape, the *capa* or *capote*, which covered the body and presented the strong, severe aspect known from colonial artwork.

Early modern Spanish women also wore a jubón, with its detached sleeves, over a white blouse, camisa, with their necks modestly covered by a collar, the *gorguera*. They famously wore the French-style *saya*, a wide skirt, usually black, sometimes with elegant embroidery or gold and silver thread trims, and often with an underlayer called a *fustán* to give it body. Like indigenous women, Spaniards wore a long shawl across their shoulders, which they called a *manto* or *mantellina*, and they covered their heads with layers of cloths called *tocas* or *paños de cabeza* and the hairnet called a *cofia* (see Figure 5).

Spanish men and women both wore shoes made of leather or fabric, and they might wear leather gloves and felt hats, the women's usually adorned with feathers or ribbons. Indigenous men and women might wear leather sandals, and on occasion had headdresses that indicated ethnic affiliation and/or rank, most remarkably in the case of the Inca *mascapaicha*, the red fringe only to be worn by the *Sapa* (unique) Inca.[17]

Thus we see obvious points of comparison between the dress styles—the shawls across the shoulders and over the hair, the layers of fabrics, the interest in pattern and fine textures, and the belief that status was revealed through appearance. Some Europeans recognized these similarities, even calling Andean garments by European names, as when the chronicler Zárate noted that Indian men wore a short camisa over bare legs (exposing their "shameful parts") and women wore mantas (for anaco, likewise a single length of cloth). Other Europeans brought attention to disturbing dissimilarities, for example, expressing concern that Indian women exposed their legs with the wrapped dress.[18]

The resonances between styles of dress present us with an interesting problem: how to tell when a garment has changed versus when a different term is simply employed? As we will see, Andean and European

Figure 5. Elite Spaniards' dress, circa 1600. From don Felipe Guaman Poma de Ayala, *El primer nueva corónica y buen gobierno*. (Courtesy of Siglo Veintiuno Editorial.)

styles did shift across the first century of contact, but given that our records are literary rather than visual, it is possible that we are occasionally seeing shifts in vocabulary rather than in garments themselves, and vice-versa.[19] But it is these very ambiguities that underline the process of change that we are analyzing. Rather than hunt for absolute authenticities and continuities, we will imagine all these as elements of a developing creolized language, literally fashioned by colonial subjects.

Finding the Comforts of Colonial Life

As Ferdinand had complained, European travelers to the New World brought with them all the luxury goods they could carry, with the knowledge that whatever fortunes they might acquire, imported consumer products would only be available at irregular intervals. J. H. Parry estimates that by 1608 forty-five thousand tons of goods—Spanish oils and wines, but also furniture, textiles, paper, weapons, glass, and other goods produced outside Spain—were shipped annually from Seville to New World ports.[20] But because of the hazards of weather and privateering, the convoy of ships known as the *flota* system only made its round-trip once a year, although local resales, pirates, and other aspects of the "informal economy" provided some periodic relief. By the end of the sixteenth century, local production supplemented necessities quite well but could not replace the charm of the import.

Thus the first generations of successful colonial settlers craved European consumer goods and were willing to pay for them. Wills demonstrate this avidity, both through their loving descriptions of these prized possessions and also because they are inventories of commodities easily liquidated in the estate auction. Dressing in imported fabrics was particularly expensive, though there was a range of quality that signaled the niceties of status, and testators were careful to declare the constituents of each piece of clothing. According to documentation from the 1570s in Trujillo, black satin, *veinticuatreño paño* from Segovia, Milanese serge, and red velvet all sold for six pesos the yard—a significant amount indeed when you consider that a domestic servant in this time and place earned only twice that each year. A piece of silk or silk and wool crepe (of unspecified length, often used for mourning) cost fifteen to twenty pesos. A pound of Florentine gold thread, a luxurious decorative element, cost twenty-four pesos. At the lower end of the scale, and more accessible to those of moderate income, were French ruán, less than a peso the yard, or taffeta, a stiffer silk fabric of Persian origin produced in Spain and Pisa, a yard of which could cost up to a peso depending upon color and style.[21] Despite inflated prices and limited stocks, the wealthy of the sixteenth century accumulated at least respectable trousseaus, and the less-well-off purchased or inherited the odd elegant piece as complement to their well-worn, everyday clothes. For example, María Daça, a Lima shopkeeper originally born in Madrid, testated in 1573 as a moderately well-off widow: she owned a female slave named Geronyma and claimed fifty pesos in cash as well as a few pieces of silver. Her relatively small charitable and religious bequests similarly suggest that she was of modest means. Her will asserted her Madrileño origins, as well as the status of her parents as vecinos of that city, and her more precious belongings included four bottles of Castillian wine, three sayas (one of damask, one of fine paño, and a third of ordinary black paño), a light silk cape and another heavier one of wool and silk, a white linen jubón and another of taffeta. The only article that was probably of local manufacture was an anonymous garment (*ropa*) made of bayeta, probably from a South American obraje.[22]

More elite women owned equally few garments of local provenance. The 1577 will and inventory of Ynes Díez, born in Ávila, Spain, demonstrates her great wealth and high status among the elites of Lima, though it gives no clues to her occupation or other personal information. But she had an enormous wardrobe for her time, including seventeen women's blouses, four jubones, a number of long capes, and a complement of headscarfs and shawls to offer the appropriate modesty of her class and gender in Lima's streets.[23] A few cotton items—a cape, a toca—might have (unstated) New World provenance, but the majority of garments appear to have been imported or fashioned of imported fabrics, and the fact that so many of her garments were "used," as the inventory puts it, certainly reflects the difficulty of acquiring new clothing and the preference for wearing older, higher status pieces rather than purchasing more common locally-made fabrics at this time.

Similarly, Ysabel López, thrice widowed and, by her assertion, the wealthier partner in her fourth marriage, testated in 1597. She also boasted an extensive wardrobe of European fashions, both new and well-worn. But she did own a bedspread made of cumbe, an indigenous high-status item that reflected her privileged and transculturated position within Lima's elite.[24]

Elite Iberian men followed similar patterns: the goods they inventoried included imported and ostentatious European garments like "a long cape and a purple waistcoat from London with purple and green trim, and some stockings with a velvet lining," but men's bedclothes and furnishings might include a locally produced "bed covering made of guanaco wool."[25] Residing in a city without a transatlantic port, like Trujillo, apparently did not affect Spaniards' ability to purchase the best new clothes and fabrics. Juan de Ayala, originally of Seville but living in Trujillo, perhaps as a merchant, owned a spectacular wardrobe, including dark red breeches with a gold trim, dark red false sleeves with ten crystal buttons, black velvet breeches, and a waistcoat of coarse Mexican wool with thirty gilded buttons.[26] During the first half century of settlement, elite Spaniards brought their sense of fashion from Europe, but irregular access to imported goods meant that they would wear their once fashionable clothing until it wore out (perhaps covered by a long, dark cape), and they would buy their home furnishings— carpets, tapestries, tablecloths, bedspreads—of high quality local textiles, now often incorporating European, Asian, and Middle-Eastern iconography and techniques.[27]

But despite the exorbitant prices, plebeian fashions would also shift to partake of the various symbolic menus now available, and this is what will concern the rest of our analysis. A successful Indian market-woman could also purchase some old cumbe or a new European or Asian fabric and have a tailor make her a lliclla or a *saya*, or she could buy the ready-made goods of another region's tribute. With decreasing attention to spinning and weaving at home or less access to the handiwork of their rural kin, urban Indians began to purchase their everyday garments and to invest them with their own meanings. Rather than simply invoke an old hierarchy, these new symbols pointed toward hybrid identities in the expanding marketplaces and an ongoing conversation over status between classes and ethnic groups.

Thus urban centers in the New World provide us with a glimpse of the emerging codes of colonial identity in their process of formation. Although many studies of fashion have examined elites and the middle classes—mainly because these are the people most likely to leave their appearances on record—colonial Peru offers greater breadth, because individuals across the social strata did leave extensive wills. By examining early colonial wills, we can draw conclusions about the interrelations of the "Spanish" and "Indian" worlds, as well as see across class lines.

But this analysis comes with a strong, self-conscious caveat. As we have seen, supposedly straightforward markers like "Indian," "mestizo," "Spaniard," and the like are deeply problematic in the early colonial period, given the initial ambiguities of categories and the possibilities for slippage between them.[28] These were simultaneously juridical entities, imposed by royal officials, as well as learned behaviors with complex meanings. Reading colonial wills for ethnic identification and self-presentation provides us with a glimpse of that learning process. Leaving a will involved a dialogue between the testator and the notary, as well as powerful witnesses who could include priests or family members. Part of that dialogue was certainly cued visually—it is by no means clear that the ethnic labels attached to testating individuals were their own declarations, and might well have been suggested or imposed by notaries, following their own formal procedures. Thus we cannot take the term "yndia" that might follow a woman's name, or its absence, as evidence of her own self-identification. But the interesting correlations that we will see occurring between ethnic labels and wardrobes and other possessions tell a story about how self-presentation changed and developed in multiethnic early colonial urban centers.

Transculturating Wardrobes

By the late sixteenth century, important forms of transculturation had already taken place in colonial Peru. We have already seen how legal processes and religious institutions were adapted and reconstructed in response to the specific conditions of life in the colonial Andes. Likewise, an everyday culture developed out of the intermingling of Europeans, Africans, and Indians, from food to language to furniture, whereby old products acquired new valences in the colonial crucible.

This was particularly notable in the realm of luxury goods. Europeans had, of course, engaged in early exploration precisely to locate valuable and scarce resources. Potosí's silver, Venezuelan pearls, and other New World mineral wealth meant that the comfortable classes could boast jewelry collections that measured favorably against those of Europe's elites. Residents of all ethnicities banked part of their income in *cocos* or *keros*, silver cups akin (or identical) to those produced in the prehispanic era, that could be cut into chunks and used as cash.[29]

And the most prominent transculturated commodities were textiles. We have seen men and women of Iberian and African descent choose fine woven cumbe for their bedclothes, if not their outerwear. It is likely that with the constant shortages of imported fabrics, European settlers depended upon the innumerable and multiethnic tailors of Lima and Trujillo to cut and sew locally manufactured bayetas and paños, even handwoven awascas, into acceptable daily wear, even if these garments did not always find their way into their wills. Similarly, indigenous men and women increasingly adopted fabrics and clothing styles imported from Europe as components of their wardrobes, as well as buying from other regions of Peru.[30] In many regards, clothing styles transcended class and ethnicity, in part because of the strong culture of passing on even worn clothes of any value to relatives and servants, and in part because there was such a large number of tailors in colonial cities that expensive fabrics and trim, rather than style per se, indicated status.

But this did not mean that all came to dress alike. As ethnic categories were acquiring more social and economic resonances, visual cues also became more pointed, although these signs never lost their ambiguity. A few examples will make these emerging social lines clear. In the new convent of Santa Clara in Cuzco, in 1560, the small minority of nuns of Spanish descent forced the mestizas, mainly illegitimate daughters of the conquistadors of Peru, to wear permanently the white veil of the novice, rather than take the black veil of the professed nun.[31] In 1632, a dispute between Franciscan monks and local priests over the right to minister to a mixed community of Indians and Spaniards in the Audiencia of Quito was resolved with a decree that the monastic orders should give sacraments to those dressed like Indians, while the lay clergy had spiritual authority over those persons who dressed like Spaniards; the defining garment that made mestizas into Indians rather than Spaniards would be the lliclla, the shawl worn by nearly all women of either ethnicity in that region.[32] As elites realized the dangerous ambiguities produced by miscegenation, migration, and generally unclear ethnic boundaries in a world predicated on status divisions, they repeatedly, usually via the state, attempted to clarify juridical identities, but rarely with any degree of finesse.

In this context, it is not surprising that fashion did not remain static. We saw at the beginning of this chapter that the notary responsible for counting the Indian tributaries of Lima in 1613 found numerous "misdressed" men on his roles. Some of these, he apparently surmised, were trying to evade tribute by claiming the legal status of mestizo despite their appearance. But in twenty-four cases, Contreras noted that men called themselves "Indians" yet were "wrongly" dressed as Spaniards. The vast majority of these were domestic servants or artisans who could not even name their natal cacique, suggesting that they no longer had ties with those communities. While they were not attempting to claim a non-Indian identity, they had clearly acculturated to (or were born into) urban colonial life, whose visual culture they deployed as a matter of identity rather than deceit. In twenty-seven more cases, Contreras disagreed with the self-ascription of his respondents, men who claimed to be mestizos and argued that they had no relationship with caciques, but wore the clothing of the poor—handwoven "Indian" cloth. Contreras registered all these men as Indians in the margins, even those who brought forward impeccable (Spanish) witnesses to support their parentage. It was crucial for the Crown to maximize the number of Indian tributaries, and the cynicism of its agent suggests that changing dress style was seen as a common way to evade economic and social obligations.[33]

It is, of course, unlikely that evading tribute was the sole motivating force in adopting new dress. Abandoning the anaco, lliclla, and the unku, or taking on the blouse and skirt, even temporarily, had multiple meanings for migrants out of rural communities and urban dwellers escaping poverty. An artisan or shopkeeper desiring a more upscale clientele might choose to dress like his social "betters." Those with new wealth might choose to show off their purchasing power with a variety of goods. Illegitimate children of mixed ethnicities might present themselves in a way that suggested higher status and obscured their birth. And even the poor might acquire different dress styles in a way that demonstrated their subservient status: contracts for domestic service routinely included one or two sets of clothing to be provided by masters; as well, servants were often the beneficiaries of their masters' cast-off clothing. In a fluid society such as Lima or Trujillo, individuals were, through their own agency or not, clearly acquiring these physical symbols of their new colonial status.

"Living like a Spaniard"

Indigenous elites were most likely the first to respond to European dress styles in the colonial world. Gifts of clothing were exchanged between the conquistadors and the Inca, since both societies shared a concern with textiles as symbols not only of status but of political domination.[34] Once colonial rule was established, the gains to the conquered to be made from acculturation were evident. Diego, the Indian who petitioned the Cabildo of Trujillo in 1554 for a solar within the traza was granted the property specifically "because he is married and lives like a Spaniard."[35] "Living like a Spaniard" presumably encompassed a variety of characteristics: being Christian and properly married, speaking Spanish, perhaps participating in the urban economy. But certainly fashion and hairstyle played a substantial part as well.

Spanish and indigenous elites after the conquest recognized one another's social positions and entered into all sorts of dialogues about legitimacy in their new circumstances. Forging these new ties proved expensive for caciques, who found themselves caught between legitimacy in two systems. Spanish merchants quickly saw a new consumer market and issued substantial credit to caciques who wanted to purchase the novelties appropriate for their rank. The 1579 will of Domingo Fino, the son of the cacique of Lunaguaná, acknowledges an outstanding debt of forty-two pesos to Fernando Maldonado, merchant, for clothing: a suit of paño, a cape, a frockcoat (sayo), and a doublet (jubón). In addition and apparently free of debt, he had ruán shirts, a red damask jubón, and two pair of shoes, one imported from Mexico.[36]

Such debts could amount to serious legal difficulties, especially as caciques faced financial pressures stemming from their communities' hardships. In 1604, don Pedro de Mora, the cacique of Chicama, found himself thrown in jail for an outstanding debt of one hundred twelve pesos to a prominent mestizo merchant. All of the debt was for imported fabrics—damasks, silks, and cloth from Florence and Segovia. Don Pedro acknowledged his debt but argued—successfully—that the law required his release, "Because I am a minor, as a native, I cannot be held prisoner for debts; additionally the Viceroy don Francisco de Toledo has ruled that no cacique nor Indian can be imprisoned for debts to a merchant." Toledo's ordinance (of 1572) demanded that merchants and shopkeepers not extend credit to Indians at all, beyond a few bushels of corn or potatoes, and that those who broke this ordinance could not seek help from the justice system to recoup their losses. Notarial registers make it clear that vendors paid little attention to these ordinances.[37]

But the mixture of Spanish visual symbols with Andean ones was not simply a case of conspicuous consumption or an apolitical hybridity. The colonial world proved to be a visual contest between symbolic realms, and indigenous as well as Iberian critics made pointed complaints about transculturating practices. Indigenous elites (and would-be elites) deftly manipulated the symbols of Inca power as well as those of Iberian *hidalguía* or nobility. The chronicler Garcilaso de la Vega, son of a Spanish conquistador and a member of the Inca ruling family, complained in the early years of the seventeenth century that the Inca insignia made of *corequenque* feathers was being donned by plebeians, "all of them now say they are Incas and *Pallas*."[38] Wearing the visual symbols of the vanquished rulers had great power for indigenous men and women struggling to assert their status in the colonial hierarchy, as well as for their Spanish audiences. Men dressed as "Incas" were a common sight in Catholic feast day processions, and descriptions of their participation were entered into the legal record as evidence for noble status and exemption from tribute. Such "Inca" costumes came to include the symbols of Iberian hidalguía—a status that could only be conferred by the Crown—as the parallels between the ruling classes were emphasized by the conquered nobility.[39]

Elite indigenous women enacted their own versions of the Inca-hidalgo performance with their personal wardrobes. A particularly impressive case comes from Cajamarca, where a Cuzco-born woman calling herself "Angelina Palla" testated in 1571. "Palla" is a Quechua word used to refer to females of the Inca line, a status, as Garcilaso noted above, many women were claiming, since authenticated descent from the Inca offered substantial material privileges. Angelina Palla made no such genealogical claims in her will, but her bequests and the inventory of her goods portray a high-status woman who used her positions in indigenous as well as Spanish societies in deft symbiosis.[40]

Angelina Palla's wealth manifested itself mainly through numerous wooden chests full of fine clothing, as well as assorted silver jewelry and other objects, a few domestic animals, and some home furnishings. But the clothing was splendid: she wore anacos and llicllas made of a variety of colored cottons, velvet, sturdy linens, twill, and cumbe. She had relatively few garments cut in a European style, but these were not run-of-the-mill: mangas, the false sleeves that Spanish women wore hanging alongside their arms, woolen stockings, gloves, embroidered shoes, a black cape, a toca or headscarf, and a velvet cap. What is interesting about Angelina Palla's wardrobe is how she contrapuntally used these few items of elite European clothing (few Indians owned embroidered shoes, gloves, or velvet caps at this time) to accentuate her expensive but unmistakably indigenous costume of anaco and lliclla. Her more urban and less elite compatriots would make very different costume decisions.

Thus it is clear that clothing was readily perceived by colonial subjects as having political and identitarian implications. Elites recognized that their position in Spanish society was in part contingent upon limiting others' access to the tokens of that status. They equally understood that the pull of European finery could dilute their distinctiveness and undermine their social position. Guaman Poma, who had himself failed to achieve the prestige he sought in either the Spanish or the Andean world, took up this note when he bitterly called upon his compatriots to maintain their "own dress . . . so that each is known and respected and honored." In particular, he called upon caciques to differentiate themselves from plebeian Indians, mestizos, and Spaniards, eschewing European beards and haircuts, and dressing in native finery as their office required.[41]

Like the nobility, the popular classes found themselves both enticed by new fashions, as well as coerced to some degree. Early Christian chroniclers, beginning with Columbus, were often disturbed by the inadequacy of native clothing to the European eye, particularly in the warmer climates. To deal with this problem, usually described as "nakedness" (though this was certainly not meant literally), the church and the state intervened. The Laws of Burgos (1512–13) required that encomenderos provide their subjects with a gold peso's worth of clothing each year "in order that henceforth the Indians may have wherewith the better to clothe and adorn themselves."[42]

This ordinance soon became the expectation that any labor contract (for domestic service or apprenticeship, for example) would include acceptable clothing as well as Christian doctrine, care when the laborer was ill, and room and board. Thus Martín Taco, a domestic servant in the household of don Diego de Carabajal in Lima, reminded the executors of his will in 1577 that don Diego owed him twelve pesos for a year of service plus a set of clothing.[43] This clothing was often inexpensive ropa de la tierra, the product of some region's tribute purchased from a local merchant, but could also be the master's or mistress' cast-offs. And the family servant might find him- or herself the recipient of clothing as a final bequest from an appreciative employer: Beatriz de Escobar, daughter of one of Trujillo's founding citizens, left cash and clothing to "Francisca yndia who raised me . . . Catalina yndia who cared for my daughter María . . . María my Black [slave] who has raised the child . . . [and] to each of the rest of my slaves."[44]

Purchases of clothing could also be coerced in some circumstances. *Repartimientos de mercancías* or the forced sale of surplus goods to indigenous communities was illegal for most of the colonial period, but was too great a temptation for royal officials, priests, and even indigenous elites to pass up. While imported cloth and clothing were certainly not high on the list of commodities needing a captive clientele, there is evidence that less costly items like ruán and certainly obraje-made textiles like *paños de Quito* were "distributed" to communities at exorbitant prices.[45]

But much of the incorporation of European items into everyday dress took place more or less voluntarily, especially in the urban areas where individuals were less likely to make their own clothing and thus more apt to purchase it. In a cash-strapped economy, this meant that plebeians, like the nobility, were drawn easily into debt. According to a 1577 lawsuit, the debtors to a pair of Spanish merchants who had formed a company to sell European clothing and fabrics in Lima included not only a number of caciques and *principales*, but Indian hosiery makers, masons, and many individuals simply identified as "yndio" or "yndia," as well as African slaves and freepersons.[46]

Nor were those who sold imported goods to Indians always Spaniards. In early seventeenth-century Lima, the most common occupation for indigenous men was tailor, followed distantly by domestic servant.[47] Certainly, some of these tailors sold locally woven goods, but many of them worked with imported fabrics and designs as well.

Tailors and clothing vendors are also well represented as testators in the cities, so we do not have to guess as to the range of their clientele and stock. In Lima, we see from relatively early on indigenous tailors and vendors selling imported stock to a multiethnic clientele. In May 1570 the indigenous tailor Domingo Hernandez included among his possessions a new black taffeta hat (trimmed with gold), a new black sayo of paño, a slightly used black cape, a red taffeta frockcoat, velvet-trimmed socks, Castillian shoes, and a number of Spanish-style shirts, as well as a blue paño saya that he was making for a mulata servant, and a debt for some leather he bought for an "Indian mestizo." These goods, which seem to have represented his own possessions as well as those for sale, included no clothes described with Quechua terminology or any handwoven cloth at all.[48]

On the other hand, in 1606, Diego Lastara, apparently a vendor or shopkeeper in Lima's Cercado, had a clientele that demanded more ethnic diversity of goods: a handmade purple cloak and painted tunic from Guayaquil; a camiseta of a green thin silk (*jerguilla*) with its trim and breeches of blue paño from Mexico; and a lliclla of Chinese damask with a gold and silk trim; a length of black taffeta from Mexico; a white cloak; a tunic of ruán to be used as his shroud; two hand cloths of cotton and wool; and squeezed into the bottom margin a list of colored threads, silks, and linens.[49] The unusual array of bright colors in this list raises the question of whether the lower classes and the nouveau riche took a more ostentatious approach to dress than their more somber "betters." Certainly, as we will see, Indian men and women were likely to have colorful items among their wardrobes.

And Francisca Ramírez, the Trujillo vendor whom we have met previously, demonstrates this trend toward transculturation within her own lifetime, albeit on a slower trajectory (perhaps due to Trujillo's slightly less commercial environment). She began her career as a petty marketwoman, probably selling from a cajón in the plaza.[50] From her possessions in 1633, it appears that she then sold "painted" or dyed shawls—a local indigenous craft—and an assortment of indigenous-style women's clothing like anacos and llicllas, although some of these were cut from fabrics imported from Europe and Asia. She also owned some domestic animals, equipment for making chicha, a few pieces of jewelry, and some furniture. From this first inventory it appears that she was already relatively well-off, but firmly established within the network of Trujillo's indigenous community.

But by 1653, Ramírez had her own store (perhaps jointly with her husband), where in addition to large quantities of chicha, she sold imported fabrics and clothing (silk, damask, taffeta, and velvet), soap, candles, furniture, jewelry (especially pearls and gold), and religious icons. Her debts indicate that her clientele and credit network included a royal official and a local cacique, among an assortment of Spaniards and Indians. And by 1677 her inventory no longer included indigenous clothes of any type, nor chicha.

When we recall that cities like Lima and Trujillo were, more or less, "new" spaces made up entirely of immigrants, the relatively rapid transculturation of wardrobe for certain sectors of the population makes a great deal of sense. Changes in self-presentation certainly facilitated the shifts individuals wanted to make in their economic positions, occupations, and community ties. In the colonial environment, dress was part of a process of cultural mediation, whereby individuals took items out of one context and deployed them in another, layering old and new meanings in complicated ways.

Dressing Like an Indian, 1570–1599

As we have seen, the sixteenth century marked an early move toward transculturation, the influence of indigenous, African, and European cultures on one another, to differing degrees. Now we turn to the material culture of the popular classes, the range of indigenous, casta, and

African-descent individuals who were making their livelihoods in urban Lima and Trujillo.

We can begin by examining the material aspects of two wills, left in similar circumstances during the same year, 1570. Both women, called Juana and Ysabel in the documents, were identified as "yndia" and with no surname.[51] Both testated in the Hospital of Santa Ana before its ubiquitous notary Esquivel. Neither was remarkably well-off, though Juana had left seventy pesos in safe-keeping with a third party, while Ysabel listed about twenty pesos' worth of debts to be collected on her behalf, some from members of a Spanish household where she may have been employed. But each woman had left a wooden chest full of clothing with a friend, and the contents of these show us how, by 1570, material culture among the lower classes was already changing.

Juana tells us nothing of where she was born and raised, but she dressed in what might be thought of as a colonial indigenous style: she wore the anaco and lliclla typical of the highland, closed with a silver *topo* pin and sashed with a woven belt, a chumbe. But her llicllas were now made of paño from an obraje and of cotton rather than handwoven camelid or sheep's wool, and the anaco was homespun from Lunaguaná, a coastal city south of Lima. She also had an "old shirt," in the European style, and she slept on bedsheets made of imported but inexpensive ruán. Ysabel, born in Huarma, did not list many items of clothing contained in her chest, only a lliclla made of linen, but she had a great number of what she called "mantas" that were actually anacos, handwoven wrapped dresses, in this case the tributary goods of Cajamarca and Chachapoyas.

That Ysabel (or, less likely, the notary) termed these items "mantas" rather than anacos is of particular interest: the Quechua anaco was a dress made of a single length of cloth wrapped around the body; the Spanish manta was a large shawl probably of the same general size and shape. As well, she claimed as part of her estate a little under nine meters of French linen and "in two pieces" another five meters of ruán, conceivably the raw materials for another couple of wrapped dresses or shawls. It seems quite likely that these items were physically equivalent, as cloth rectangles, though the language used to describe them and the means of acquiring the items were in the process of changing: the length of cloth translated from anaco to manta, the source of the cloth from woven tribute goods from Cajamarca to obraje-made paños and imported if relatively inexpensive French linens. The indigenous lliclla, usually draped around the shoulders, also came to have a counterpart in the Spanish toca or headscarf, as in a 1573 will that inventoried "five cumbe lliclllas of the type you wear on the head."[52]

Ysabel might well have been selling these wares; her inventory lists far more garments than did those of other testators of similar characteristics, and she had numerous small debts for her executors to collect. If so, we may then also interpret her debts as credit extended to clothing purchasers—who in this case turn out to be mainly women of African descent: Ynes, the enslaved cook in the household of Ysabel's own probable employ; Juana, a free black woman from Biafara; and Beatriz, the slave of another elite Spaniard. A little imagination offers the tantalizing scenario that Ysabel was selling or making clothing that was consistent with older indigenous styles, but called by a new name and sold to a clientele that included African women.

Even more well-off Indian women were at this time dressing in ways that both reflected change and continuity, but still set them off from their colonizers. According to the will of a woman named Elvira, in 1572 she was the wife of an Indian silversmith and herself sold merchandise, possibly clothing, in the market.[53] She and her husband had joint savings of eighty pesos, and as befit the wife of a silversmith, she had a number of silver, gold, and gold-plated topos and two pairs of silver cocos. The garments she inventoried were two sets of cumbe clothing and a linen lliclla. Similarly, Beatriz Utca who testated that same year, had joint property and collectable debts with her husband valued at three hundred ninety pesos and stated that she had brought a dowry to that marriage of "seventy pesos in cash, moreover two horses worth forty pesos, and in my clothing and a chest, [the value of] fifty pesos."[54] She boasted six outfits (each anaco and lliclla), one of cumbe, one of paño, and the rest presumably of more common handwoven material, as well as a ruán lliclla and a large bolster of that material. These wills underscore the fact that testators usually only listed items that they felt would have resale or sentimental value; everyday items do not always show up in inventories. Thus we cannot know whether, in everyday life, these women wore the same dress as their more rural relatives, but we do know that they were slowly beginning to purchase (and sell) the new fabrics and that their own notions of fashion were beginning to shift. They were, in a small degree, becoming conspicuous consumers in colonial society.

As they became wealthier, Indian women acquired not only European fabrics but the form of elite costumes as well. The first will in my survey attributed to an "yndia" to mention the Spanish saya belonged to Ana, originally from the northern highlands of Guamachuco, who testated in Lima's Santa Ana hospital in 1576.[55] She may also have been one of Lima's well-off chicheras, for she had all the apparatus for making and bottling it, as well as thirty chickens. She left part of her estate to one don Diego Carua Curi of Huamachuco, who might have been a relative (though not a father or a son, since she had no mandatory heirs), and the rest went for alms for the poor, for the benefit of her soul. Her business must have been successful, since she mentioned a significant amount of money, in most of the many forms available at this time: thirty-two pesos in coins, eighteen pesos and one *ducado* in marked and weighed silver, nine pesos in *plata corriente,* and a debt of eight pesos she wished collected on her behalf.

Her clothing represents the fashionable hybrid and mixed style we have come to see as the emblem of the well-off working Indian woman: a lliclla made of paño; an anaco, lliclla, and two shawls made of cumbe; another lliclla of red damask. But she also had acquired a "sturdy red" saya and a skirt of blue paño. These were the style of Spanish elites, though made of inexpensive and rough fabrics, probably by one of Lima's indigenous tailors.

But Ana's acquisition of the saya was unusual for this time; women identified as Indian in Lima before the turn of the seventeenth century still tended to dress in the anaco and lliclla, even when they were wealthy. A final example comes from the 1589 will of Madalena Carua Sisue, born in Quiquis, who stated that while she and her (second) husband had brought no estate to their marriage, since then he had given her an incredible assortment of anacos and llicllas made of velvet, silk, damask, and taffeta, trimmed with silver and gold thread, as well as more everyday cotton pieces from Lunaguaná.[56]

In this early period, the indigenous female testators of Trujillo bore a strong resemblance to their kin in Lima, though they were far fewer in number and less wealthy. These women—predominantly domestic servants and ex-servants, wives or widows of artisans, and often owners of solares themselves—demonstrated their relative affluence largely through the purchase of real estate and clothing. Ysabel, the Spanish-speaking widow of a shoemaker, counted as part of her estate in 1570 some cotton anacos and lliclla, some old faldellines and camisas, and assorted pieces made of cumbe and silk.[57] Juana, the widow of a tailor, had embroidered camisas, an anaco and lliclla from Cajamarca, and clothes of taffeta and cumbe.[58] Though these women had some access to the new fabrics and styles, they tended to list fewer pieces of clothing in their wills. Given the somewhat smaller scale of trade in Trujillo as opposed to Lima, we are probably seeing a similar tendency but at a slower pace.

On the other hand, urban wills also indicate the pockets of indigenous women whose ties to their natal communities were stronger than those to the urban centers in which they now resided. Consider the situation of Beatriz Guanca, the illegitimate daughter of don Diego Panpa Guanca and Ysabel Yupay. She was described in her will as a native of León de Guánuco but was "presently in Lima." She might have been traveling for a lawsuit and taken ill in Lima, or she was recently relocated, because her will makes clear that her real home was Huánuco, where she had a house and a garden plot, as well as many of her belongings. Her clothes are markedly different from those we have been seeing: although she had with her llicllas of taffeta and *telila* (a very fine wool), possibly bought there, these were not the majority of her clothes by any means. She also had with her a number of anacos, probably of wool, and a couple of these were painted with a prehispanic dye technique not much seen in Limeño wills. She also inventoried her clothing still in Huánuco: a painted anaco, anacos and licllas made of cumbe, and one of Castillian wool. Compared with the Limeñas we have seen so far, she was less of a thorough-going consumer, having acquired a small number of impressive items to mark more important occasions rather than for everyday life.[59]

Another set of wills from Surco, an indigenous community on the outskirts of Lima, tells a similar story. These women were not integrated as fully into the nearby urban economy, their income seems to have come from agriculture and petty vending (mainly chicha), and they still made their own clothing rather than purchase it. Costança Ticlla listed no clothing whatsoever in her 1596 will, only "four skeins of colored cotton thread and ten smaller ones; I leave these to Pedro Payante, my husband, so that he may make his clothing."[60] Elvira Coyti listed as her only possessions "three pots of brown and white cotton with its seeds; a container for spindles containing twenty-one spindles with thread to be spun; the ornamentation for a shirt of striped blue and white cotton thread; two large skeins of cotton thread dyed blue; five skeins of cotton thread still to be spun, one brown and four white."[61] Since homemade clothing had little resale value in a rural community, these women didn't even bother to waste their money on the paper needed to describe it, although raw materials like uncombed and unspun cotton and wool would likely raise money to pay for masses and burial fees.

Thus we can conclude from these cases that the sixteenth century brought some subtle but important changes for indigenous women in Peru's cities. Since so many testators began their urban lives in domestic service for European families, we can posit that this provided both the first models for high-status dress and a source for the beginnings of their new wardrobes, through hand-me-downs, small cash salaries and access to markets. Urban plazas and stores made it possible for them to purchase the less expensive new fabrics, while the many tailors fashioned their clothes—some of which could be interchangeably anacos, lliclas, and mantas, while others were clearly cut and sewn to be European skirts and blouses. The small population discussed here is surely representative only of an emerging urban middle sector, but it was an important and highly visible group, since they also represented those most involved in cofradías and civic life.

Indigenous men in this early period demonstrate the same range of possessions, with a few interesting differences. As we have already seen, many indigenous men in Lima were tailors, and their estates include the expected range of men's and women's clothing and fabrics. Martín Cungo, who testated in 1572, might have been a successful tailor from the large and diverse inventory of clothing in his will: three sets of women's cumbe clothing, a camiseta made of hand-woven awasca, a linen lliclla, a man's scarlet shirt with a border of colored silk.[62] But the indigenous men in this sample were less likely to inventory clothing than indigenous women did in this time and place, and even those whom we would most expect—tailors like Diego Tanta Quileche (testated 1589) and caciques like Don Cristóbal Xuto Chumbe (testated 1580)—wrote wills that mentioned no clothing at all. The non-noble indigenous men of Trujillo showed similarly muted interest in clothing, apart from a successful shoemaker like Alonso Julca, who dressed in splendid tunics of red damask and taffeta, covered by mantles of ruán; or Juan Quispe, probably a tailor, who listed a large stock of clothing, many described as "camiseta y manta" but now made of ruán as well as cumbe, wool and cotton, and coming from all over the Trujillo Valley and Cajamarca. Quispe also boasted a jubón and a *nagua*, a pleated skirt worn by Spanish men under their outer clothing, both rare in the wardrobes of indigenous men in this city.[63] But these were among the exceptions; many—even well-to-do—testators failed to mention any clothing at all, including don Melchior Carorayco, the cacique of Cajamarca, who made his long will in 1565.[64] This disparity between men's and women's wills may reflect a gendered pattern for wealth accumulation (men purchasing other forms of capital), or it might mean that indigenous women were simply more active consumers of expensive clothing by choice or by access.

Thus, by the final decades of the sixteenth century, imported fabrics and European fashion sensibilities had permeated the multiethnic markets of Lima and Trujillo. More rural communities appear to have been less affected, probably because they continued to spin fibers and weave their own clothes as well as those for tribute, and they had substantially less income to spend on luxury items, though intermittent traders did bring the odd collection of goods to smaller towns.[65] But this urban influx was not abrupt, nor was it a case of simple mimicry. We have seen evidence that the language deployed around clothing changed: the indigenous man's tunic and mantle immediately acquired the names of related European items, *camiseta* and *manta*, and rarely were called anything else in this environment. However, the lack of men's breeches (*calzones*), socks (*medias*), and stockings (calzas) in indigenous men's wills suggests that their "camisetas" were indeed the long prehispanic tunic and not the shorter European garment. Women's garments tended to retain a small range of Quechua names, though the similarity in shape between the Spanish *manta* and the Quechua *anaco* meant that those names could be used interchangeably.

But looking beyond the linguistic influences, we see a serious attempt to integrate new and old vocabularies. The increased access to cumbe meant that a Catalina de Agüero, who moved from an indigenous community in Cajamarca to become a domestic servant in Trujillo, could dress in clothes of that formerly limited material by 1570.[66] Nearly all female testators could purchase the set of anaco and llicIla in one of the cheaper imported fabrics, ruán or paño, if they preferred these to the still-cheaper flood of tribute goods from all regions of the viceroyalty. When cash or credit came more easily, luxurious textiles such as Chinese or Philippine silks, taffetas, damasks, and velvets could also be had. Such clothes allowed women to demonstrate their affluence, to show that they were consumers of taste and worldly knowledge, since they carefully noted in their wills the provenance of each item and the minutiae of its trims and borders. And, little by little, items in European cuts also made their way into wardrobes, a skirt and blouse (of imported fabric, but also of awasca or paño) alongside the anacos and llicllas for when a particular impression had to be made. Bedclothes, towels, pillows, and the like also began to appear in the households of all classes, most often in imported ruán but also in cumbe.

Plebeian women seem to have made this particular transition more quickly than men, perhaps because of their integration into Spanish households through domestic service, or perhaps this is simply an illusion of the document or the sample. But if true, this could stand as additional evidence of the differing forms colonial adaptation took for indigenous men and women in sixteenth-century cities. However, when compared with the rural men and women who made wills while passing through cities, or those who lived in the agricultural villages just outside the urban centers, we can see the beginnings of a basis for an urban, pan-Andean ethnic style that would take form over the seventeenth century.

"Creolization" in the Seventeenth Century

As might be expected, the seventeenth century brought even more goods, including new fabrics and dress styles, from Europe into the New World's urban marketplaces. While tribute in goods slowed, lessening the availability of ropa de la tierra, colonial obrajes geared up to meet internal demand for wool textiles such as bayetas, paños, and jerseys, though these were never perceived as having the high status of imported fabrics.[67] As wealth expanded and, especially, a multiethnic middle sector emerged that owed its position to the increased trade in major cities, imported goods showed up in more and more households. But there was no convergence toward a single "colonial" style; instead, overlapping "ethnic" styles emerged, though there was not a one-to-one correlation between a person's ethnic origins and the figure he or she cut in public. Instead, the cultural encounter produced an array of visual elements, akin to a creolized language, that could be deployed by individuals. Rather than perceive these as instrumentalist actions by isolated individuals, we can see the beginnings of identity formation as individuals imagined themselves as part of larger social groups in the colonial order.

First, we see an important change in the constitution of the population of urban centers. Although the vast majority of residents of Lima and Trujillo over the sixteenth century were immigrants, there was now a growing constituency of Indians born in cities who evidenced a new consciousness. At around the turn of the seventeenth century, they began to call themselves *indios criollos*, creole Indians, a term that appears to mark cultural adaptation as well as place of birth.

In Latin American usage, "criollo" originally marked slaves of African descent either born in the colonies or having acquired the cultural characteristics of colonial society—language, religion, dress. It also was used to distinguish those of Spanish descent born in the Americas, sometimes as a pejorative in the mouths of "peninsular" Spaniards, and eventually by these Americans themselves to highlight their "native" knowledge. And in the case of the indigenous population, which could hardly differentiate itself on the basis of being born in the New World, "criollo" at least briefly had a vogue marking the acquisition of urban characteristics—being born in a city (and thus exempt from tribute) as well as growing up speaking Spanish, as a Christian, living apart from a rural community, and probably looking a certain way.[68] For example, a 1637 trial over a debt for sixty pesos between two Trujillo Indians included as witnesses indigenous men variously designated by the scribe as *ladino*, or Spanish speaking, *muy ladino, natural* or native of small towns in the region, and *criollo desta ciudad* or *criollo* of this city. As we have seen in the case of Africans, birthplace and acquired characteristics could be mutually determining, and so *criollo* here probably referred to a person's ease with urban mores as much as an actual place of birth.

Both of these labels—*criollo* and *ladino*—represent levels of acculturation from the perspective of the colonizers. But they were also invoked by subalterns, as in early seventeenth-century wills that refer to Diego, an Indian silkmaker "criollo born in the City of Los Reyes [Lima]," and Alonso de Paz, who noted that while he himself was born elsewhere his two daughters were "Bernarda criolla, aged four years, and another daughter called María criolla, aged one year."[69] While we have limited sources to untangle all the implications of the social terminology of the colonial period, the existence of such a complicated yet well-understood vocabulary of acculturation suggests a fluid and rapidly changing world not assimilable to static categories, but engaged in an active process of identity construction.

How were urban criollos of the seventeenth century culturally distinct from their forebears? As we have seen, beginning around the turn of the seventeenth century there was a new affluence among many of Lima and Trujillo's Indians, manifested in the ownership of real estate; slaves; and luxury goods including jewelry, furniture, and clothing. There was also increased participation in cofradías, places where social networking took place in the context of Christian fellowship. Lima's Cercado in particular seems to have been a neighborhood where a successful Indian community could take comfortable root while maintaining a connection to rural life (often by buying or renting agricultural properties in the valleys just outside Lima). Concomitant with this, we have seen an increase in debt of all kinds, from petty pawns to relatively large cash loans, as marketeers and shopkeepers became small-scale bankers for the popular classes. And, as might be obvious, the acquisition of fashionable clothing continued apace, reaching deeper into the pool of testators that was itself growing.

Lima's indigenous testators still wore lliclla and anacos, but the bulk of the wardrobes listed in wills and inventories were now European both in fabric and style. In 1600, Catalina Sacsa Nurma, who owned two lliclla of green and purple damask, had a large chest from Mexico filled with skirts and bodices of paño and taffeta and a "blue Spanish *sayuelo*," as well as the layers of headcloths and veils worn by elite Spanish women. She included among her possessions a small sewing case, so she may have been a tailor or seamstress herself.[70] Catalina Carguay Chumbi, originally of Huarochirí but now a landowner in Lima, included a spectacular "lavender silk llicla with a purple and red silk border, and a sash of violet taffeta" among a substantial wardrobe with only a few anacos and lliclla, these mostly "worn out."[71] Though not every female testator boasted wardrobes such as these, they were no longer isolated cases.

The cost of such garments was not insignificant, especially keeping in mind the difficulties of acquiring cash at this time. A tailor named Melchor Payta in 1631 claimed a debt of forty pesos from a female vendor in the plaza for "an olive skirt of Castillian paño with a gold trim."[72] An even more outrageous price of one hundred pesos was attached to a "suit of black *raso*, trimmed with velvet," the security for which was "six shirts, four embroidered and two plain . . . with their hand-embroidered handkerchiefs, all worth ninety pesos."[73] Toward the more moderate end of the economic scale, estate auctions of the period brought eight pesos for a new ruán shirt embroidered with silk; six pesos for a striped silk llicla; six patacones (from a Spaniard) for a black silk llicla bordered with red Chinese taffeta; ten patacones for an anaco and llicla from Lunaguaná.[74]

On the one hand, the increasing economic comfort of a small group of indigenous men and women meant that they could purchase, in addition to slaves and real estate, more and more ostentatious outfits, like the "twelve embroidered and plain gorgueras" and "twelve pair of colored silk socks" that the pulpera Juliana de Mendoza remembered in her wills, alongside agricultural lands in Pachacamac and one female slave.[75] But even at the more moderate end of the economic scale, high fashion was becoming more accessible: the very same year Catalina Ynes, "who said she was an Indian, native of the city of Guayaquil, dressed in the style of a Spaniard," came before a notary with her employer, doña Ana María de Rivera, the widow of a Spanish general, to state for the record that she had received the following as pay for her service: fifty pesos in cash, two silk sayas, two ruán shirts, a shawl made of silk from Toledo, and a mattress.[76]

But rather than see a generalizable movement toward adoption of European fashion markers by urban Indians, instead we can detect a set of styles emerging, analogous to changes in class, geographic, and group behavior. The wealthiest Indian women wore clothes nearly always cut from lengths of store-bought fabrics, from the cheaper paños of Quito, Peru, and Mexico, to the most expensive rasos, silks, and velvets. They no longer wore many anacos, rather they dressed in skirts and blouses, but they still called the shawl they wrapped around their shoulders a lliclla, no matter what fabric it was made of: Lucia Cusi owned a "blue Chinese velvet" lliclla with a gold thread edging, alongside a ruán blouse, a jubón and gorguera, *perpetuán* false sleeves, and a silk embroidered headscarf.[77] Or like Mencia Mayuay, they had now only a remnant or two of handwoven goods, like one woven chumpi belt.[78] These wardrobes (and the jewelry that inevitably accompanied them) appear little different from those of middle-class Spanish women, though we must underline that this was indeed a small and exclusive group.

Wealthy Indian men also appear by now to have shifted to a European style of dress, though they were still much less likely to list all their clothes in their wills, often singling out a few exceptionally valuable pieces. But Luís Pérez, whose second wife joined her dowry of four hundred pesos in cash to his agricultural fields (yielding them another three hundred pesos at harvest), owned a black velvet suit (shirt and breeches) with a wool cape, silk socks and two new shirts, and an Italian cape of lavender fabric. The couple also owned a large house and five male slaves and had significant outstanding debts based on their good credit and extensive capital, certainly placing them among Lima's most established Indian households.[79]

On the other hand, the successful petty traders and chicha vendors had a more hybrid dress style, as we have seen. They continued to wear anacos, llicllas and topos, though increasingly of a variety of fabrics and supplemented by skirts and blouses for different occasions.

The marketeer Catalina Carua, who sold from a *cajón de mercachifle* or peddler's chest in Lima's plaza, was married to a master tailor, presumably the source of her elegant velvet and silk llicllas, skirts and jubones, but she also owned plain woolen llicllas and a *ñañaca*, a small rectangular lliclla originally specific to Cuzco and the southern highlands, worn as a headcovering.[80] In Lima, these men and women tended to live in the Cercado, now expanded from a Jesuit-run residence for mitayos to a multiethnic but predominantly indigenous neighborhood. The Cercado was also home to various institutions that gave Lima's Indians a certain level of power and prestige *qua* Indians: access to land, an Indian cabildo, important cofradías. Although all of these were under the control of Spanish and Jesuit officials, Lowry has argued that "these institutions increasingly became the ground on which Indians began to formulate and express their own interests."[81] Whether because of class issues or relative isolation from kin and ethnic groups, the indigenous women of the Cercado in the early seventeenth century dressed differently from either their European neighbors or their rural relatives, inventing a sophisticated visual language that wove together evidence of their newfound worldliness.

The less well-off Indians and those less connected to the urban community, as in the years prior, were least likely to change their dress style radically. Juan Magdalena, who lived in a relative's house in the Cercado, left his daughter in 1631 a few debts to clear, some lands in La Magdalena, and "an old red shawl, a new painted cotton tunic and an old green hat," an outfit that had not changed much since the previous century.[82] It appears that the shift in clothing style had much to do with a sense of arrival in a new and comfortable space, the convergence of extra cash, and a will to demonstrate some affluence.

In Trujillo, where indios criollos (as they also called themselves, upon occasion) were also achieving a level of accommodation and comfort, we see patterns reminiscent of the two extremes of Lima, without the Cercado's large creative and modulated center. The wealthiest indigenous men and women of Trujillo dressed increasingly like Europeans, while the growing class of people well-off enough to leave a will yet without substantial estates picked up a few new dress habits and purchased new fabrics, but they overwhelmingly continued to dress in the anaco and lliclla. An example is María Magdalena de Urraco, an immigrant from Chiclayo, now the owner of a solar with a stand of fruit trees. She owned a black Chinese satin lliclla, as well as one made of green taffeta, but also two sets of ropa de la tierra from

Cajamarca and "a cumbe belt that cost me eight patacones."[83] A few petty traders, such as Angelina de Albarado, a chichera with a multiethnic clientele, who did not even own the solar she lived in, dressed in the style we have seen in the Cercado (skirts of perpetuán, serge, and paño; llicllas; and mantas, either another form of shawl or the neologism for anaco), but these were exceptions rather than the rule.[84] The rapid transformation of the urbanized Indians of the Trujillo valley into property-owning citizens of a multiethnic city (without an Indian barrio at its heart) may well have meant that a differential ethnicity played a less strong role in the early seventeenth century, though this is a thesis that still demands much investigation.

Dressing Like a Mestizo?

To make the comparisons above more stark, we should examine women and men who were not identified as "indios." As we have seen, women who identified themselves in their wills as being solely of Iberian descent owned no anacos or llicllas, nor did they list any garments made of "ropa de la tierra" or cumbe, though they might own furnishings made of cumbe, or garments made in colonial obrajes. Although we know, from Contreras's census as well as from other places, that the poorest residents of cities dressed in cheap "Indian" clothes, in their wills free Africans, castas, and even mestizos all followed this pattern, calling their garments by European names and favoring imported materials or obraje paños. Luisa Gregoria, the legitimate daughter of a black master saddle maker and an Indian woman, listed only two old Spanish skirts (made of bayeta and jersey) and a pawn of two lengths of blue Quito paño in her will, but no llicllas.[85] Ysabel Gutiérrez, the illegitimate daughter of Francisco de Herrero and María, had been brought to Lima from Huánuco by the Espinosa family as a domestic servant.[86] She complained in her will that she had not received payment for her services— she stated "they only gave me a saya and a manto de la tierra" and these were cast-offs of her employer's wife. The rest of her wardrobe included seven Mexican cotton shawls, called not llicllas but mantas, and a complement of European-style skirts and waistcoats. She was not a wealthy women, and these items were not made of the most luxurious fabrics, most were colored paños, perhaps decorated with velvet borders or silver buttons, and she described many as worn out. But Ysabel Gutiérrez, though born to an Indian mother and of the plebeian class, cut a different figure from the women designated as "indias"—from her saya and jubón to her lace gloves and two pairs of new black shoes. It is remarkable that casta testators, whatever their economic condition, and despite acknowledged descent from an indigenous parent, described wardrobes with no "Indian" content.

Testating casta men were equally unlikely to dress in the style of the tributary. A four-year apprenticeship contract made in 1573 between a carpenter and the Spanish father of a mestizo teenager to be apprenticed called for all the tools of his trade, and it specified "a new outfit of black paño, cloak and waistcoat (sayo) and breeches and doublet (jubón) and two shirts and a cap and a pair of shoes."[87] In contrast, when in 1589 Agustín, an Indian man from Jauja, concerted to serve a Lima tailor, his two-year contract simply called for "twelve pesos corrientes each year and a set of clothing," shorthand for the camiseta and manto of tribute.[88] Given the negative consequences, as we have seen, of being "mistaken" for an Indian by an administrator, it is likely that poorer men and men of mixed descent might go out of their way to avoid the dress of a tributary when they had the ability to negotiate the terms of labor agreements.

We must ask, of course, whether an individual's self-presentation was what ultimately convinced a notary to use the label "indio" or not. Maria Caravajal was the illegitimate daughter of Ysavel Chilca and Nycolas de Alfonchel, none of whom were ethnically identified by the notary, though Chilca was an indigenous surname. Her father too might have been an Indian, but her community and her wardrobe prove a contrast to the other cases we have seen.[89] She certainly represented the multiethnic Lima that we have seen developing in this period—her *comadre* was an African slave named Juana Laama, and she had debts that spanned the ethnic horizon, from domestic servants identified as "indias" to a free woman of African descent who owned a corral, and one Muñiz, a servant in the Gallego household. Despite her illegitimate birth, and her close ties with domestic workers and slaves, she dressed in finery with no apparent nod to indigenous culture, wearing sayas of silk, paño, and *grana* (scarlet cloth), trimmed with velvet, gold, and silk; crystal buttons; a black *mantilla* or veil with a black velvet trim; and a fustán, a cotton underskirt. Seeing her presented in this way—with no explicit ties to a rural community, dressed in a manner resembling elite society, and with some well-placed ambiguity about her parentage—we, like the notary, may assume that she was not an "india," and in fact, for all intents and purposes described here, she was not.

Many other wills describe lives like that of María Caravajal, with an ambiguity around ethnic identity from a categorizing perspective that supports our argument that these identity categories were not altogether useful for colonial subjects. While we have seen that "Indian" was being constructed in different ways by various classes of subjects, "mestizo" and "mulato" seem not yet to have the same resonances. For example, in 1602, María Madalena, natural daughter of Rodrigo de Tapia "and an Indian woman whose name I don't recall," a domestic servant like her daughter, left a will that spoke of the ambivalences of ethnic divisions, at least in terms of occupation, credit networks, and material culture.[90] María Madalena had begun her service in the household of a preeminent merchant, Vasco de Arzane, and was presently selling chicha with the aid of a female slave purchased with three years' back wages as well as her own substantial savings. She was hoping to collect on a two hundred peso loan she had made to the Spanish shoemaker who had fathered her illegitimate child. And her wardrobe befit a woman of her calidad: sayas of taffeta and two kinds of silk, a number of fashionable headcoverings, and veils. Although her life could not be described as affluent in the context of colonial excesses, she had through her own accomplishments acquired comforts and status, despite origins that put her at a disadvantage. Though María Madalena did nothing to hide her origins from the notary, she seems not to have presented herself in any specific visual way as a "mestiza," as opposed to as a hard-working and fairly comfortable Limeña.

Certainly, lists of favored clothing and the odd ambiguities of descriptive labels are not overwhelming evidence of the lack of a mestizo identity, and that is not the argument set forth here. But some sectors of the urban indigenous population did seem to be constructing a positive identity, which made them visually and culturally distinct both from their rural kin and other ethnic groups in the cities. For this reason, not only juridical identities like "Indian," "mestizo," and "Spaniard" came to have meaning beyond the vagaries of colonial law, but concepts like "dressing like an Indian" also came to be meaningful. "Dressing like an Indian" did not mean dressing like an Inca, nor even like the peasants of any particular region of the Inca realm. Instead it came to describe the wearing of inexpensive homespun, and later obraje-produced, textiles fashioned into garments that increasingly were a woman's skirt, blouse, and shawl, a man's tunic or a shirt and breeches, but signaled poverty and the tributary burden rather than affluence. For this reason, the emerging middle sectors of urban Indian communities chose to wear at least some goods that indicated affluence and upward mobility but still differentiated them from poorer Europeans and castas.

Conclusion: Dressing Like a Colonial Subject

Given our sources, it is difficult to provide an internal interpretation of the acquisition of new types of clothing from the perspective of non-Europeans in the colonial world. It is unlikely (though not impossible) that a silk mantellina held the same meaning for a woman born in Seville and one born in Huarochirí. And even if we could establish a framework for interpreting the meaning of individual items or styles, it would be a giant leap to argue that donning one garment indicated resistance to colonial rule or rejection or celebration of one's heritage. But we can draw certain important new conclusions from the various patterns of transculturation we see in these documents.

First, men and women of European descent did not demonstrate much willingness to adopt indigenous fashions, though they eagerly purchased home furnishings made of cumbe, which was said to compete favorably with European and Asian textiles. They did not, on the other hand, object to buying cheaper, obraje-made cloth for their clothing, nor to having indigenous tailors create these fashions, as long as they remained consistent with the forms that were perceived as being "European" in style. We may well correlate this with an ingrained notion of European cultural superiority that is evident in many other aspects of colonial life and does not need rehearsal here.

Many indigenous men and women, likewise, continued to wear the types of dresses, shawls, and tunics that their ancestors wore and were also comfortable with acquiring new fabrics, like ruán, silk, and paño, made in the New World or imported from Europe and Asia. The majority of the urban Indian population, we can be certain, did not look all that different from their rural kin, though over a long period of time men did shift away from the long tunic to pants, and women moved from the wrapped dress to the skirt.

But for the middling and elite sectors that were emerging in vibrant urban spaces such as Lima and Trujillo, which were deeply rooted in multiethnic social networks, there were choices to be made, and these came to have "ethnic" overtones. On the one hand, men and women of elite ancestry, descendants or purported descendants of Incas and other ruling groups, created a hybrid wardrobe that drew upon the now-symbiotic symbols of European and Andean nobility. These men and women clearly saw their dress as a public performance of their status, most importantly in community public events, religious processions, and court appearances, but presumably too in everyday life. Their elegant wardrobes indicate the range of these performances, not to mention the expense that must have supported them.

At another extreme we see men and women who did not claim noble ancestry, but had achieved economic success and now defined themselves without reference to rural communities or ayllus. Women like Francisca Ramírez seem to have made a conscious effort to rid themselves of the garments and occupations that defined them as poor in their pasts, not necessarily refusing their heritage, but perhaps seeing themselves as simply a part of an urban colonial elite that required no marking adjective like "india." These men and women are mirrored by the small group of testators identified as mestizos, usually illegitimate children of Spanish fathers and Indian mothers, who dressed entirely in a European style and demonstrated no visual connection to indigenous communities. Rather than see this as a rejection of their indigenous heritage, we could interpret it as an attempt to produce a new status for themselves, in light of the barriers to their social status erected by their birth.

But the majority of this urban middle sector made more ambivalent use of new fashions and old. In a move that reminds us that the seventeenth century was also the beginning of a larger movement to claim "Indianness" not as a term of opprobrium but as a source of political power or legal identity, these men and women crafted a creolized language of appearance that drew upon the similarities between European and Andean dress styles while also preserving the markers of difference, like Quechua names and stylistic flourishes. These consumers were drawn by novelty and extravagance, as evidence of their new status, but saw these as additive elements rather than something that negated their past or disrupted their present. These wardrobes demonstrate that men and women did not perceive their ethnic identities as static or already fashioned, but as malleable and creative.

In this sense, "dressing like an Indian" was far more complicated than colonial bureaucrats let on. Wearing the anaco and lliclla rather than a saya and camisa was not necessarily a permanent decision; wardrobes could and did draw on all these styles. As fabrics and tailors proliferated in urban centers, it would have been simple for Andeans with income and without caciques to imitate the styles of their social superiors, and indeed many did. But many more produced a new "traditional" wardrobe, forged out of the fabric of Spanish colonialism—the loss of agrarian ways of life, the introduction of wage labor and cash markets, the increased access to global products, and a hierarchy based upon ethnicity and class that became hegemonic as subalterns interpreted its rules for themselves.

CHAPTER 5

"Use and Custom":
Cacicas and the Invention of
Political Tradition in Colonial Peru

Introduction: The Cacica of Narigualá

A remarkable legal case was brought to the colonial high court, the
Real Audiencia, by indigenous litigants in 1610 in Piura, a small city
on the far northern coast of Peru. This case raised some then-startling
questions about prehispanic and early colonial political processes in
the region. Testimony given at the trial established that, in a number of
communities around Piura and possibly in Trujillo to its south, women
had succeeded to political office under certain circumstances, and that
they had probably exercised office rather than acted as figureheads or
placeholders for the male line. The outcome of the trial reinstated doña
Francisca Canapaynina in the cacicazgo or chieftainship of Narigualá
(Catacaos) over her paternal uncle, who had seized the office at the
death of his father and doña Francisca's grandfather, the cacique Diego
Mesocoñera, taking advantage of "the tender age of his niece."[1]

The history of the cacicazgo of Narigualá raises many legal issues,
as it was contested at various times specifically over the use of "prehispanic" versus "Spanish" succession rules, but the case of doña
Francisca was exceptional for setting precedent about the rights of indigenous women to inherit cacicazgos based upon the establishment
of regional prehispanic *uso y costumbre* (use and custom), in the legal
language of the time. As Rostworowski noted in her 1961 analysis of
the case, doña Francisca's succession was not exactly supported by
either prehispanic custom or colonial law, since she was still a minor at
the time of the trial and not legally eligible for the cacicazgo under

most known interpretations.[2] Rather than present this case as a triumph of indigenous custom over Spanish colonial law, we will therefore use it here to recognize the ways in which indigenous elites also participated in the production of their own history, in dialogue with the colonial power structure.

Seven male witnesses—four Indians and three Spaniards—gave testimony on behalf of doña Francisca. Three Indians spoke as elders: one claimed to have been seven or eight at the time the Spaniards entered Peru (or well over eighty when he testified), another was said to be about sixty, and a third, fifty-two. The remaining Indian witness was don Cristóbal, the cacique of nearby Mecomo. The Spanish witnesses were all vecinos or property owning citizens, including the local encomendero Capitán Bartolomé Carreño. They were asked specifically to address the question of whether, by their own personal recollections or through their understanding of the past, "it has been and is the accepted and kept custom in said repartimiento of Narigualá and in all the provinces of the valley since antiquity, before the Spanish entered in this kingdom, and after, that the *Capullanas* [female chiefs] inherited cacicazgos."[3]

Six of the seven witnesses agreed that it was indeed customary, in the absence of male heirs, that female children would succeed and would even exercise office (the seventh had no knowledge), "that the capullanas succeed in cacicazgos as if they were male and they serve and govern the said cacicazgos."[4]

Each man also stated that he was an eyewitness to this ongoing practice, mentioning other capullanas or cacicas who held the office within their memories: doña Luisa, who had ruled Colán; doña Leonor, once the capullana of Menon; doña Latacina, once the *cacica segunda persona* or secondary authority of Colán; and doña Isabel Socola, who governed and received the cacique's salary in Narigualá. The final witness was the encomendero Capitán Bartolomé Carreño, who stated that not only did he personally know of many such situations, but that he had heard "said that in this said repartimiento of Narigualá women were governing when the Spaniards entered this kingdom."[5] The encomendero's motivations may have been more political than historical, of course; he might have assumed that a young woman would be more easily manipulated than her adult uncle, he might have had a dislike for the usurping cacique, or he might have been aware of brewing discontent among the cacique's subjects which could have affected their ability or willingness to produce tribute and hence his livelihood. In any case, by concurring with their testimony and by establishing a

precedent at the moment of the conquest, the encomendero contributed to a reformulation of colonial political policy as well as of prehispanic history.

Doña Francisca won her case and became the cacica of Narigualá.
Within a few years she had married don Juan Temoche, who took the
title of cacique and apparently carried out the tasks of the office himself, predominantly organizing indigenous labor for tribute and otherwise mediating between the community and the colonial authorities. If
indeed women had ruled over their communities in the past, they were
not to be imagined doing it again under Spanish policy, though they
might act as figureheads.[6]

This legal case set important precedents for indigenous women.
Rather than a triumph of "traditional" society over colonialism, it is
part of a pattern of reinvention that indigenous elites participated in
throughout the colonial period. Across Spanish America, indigenous
elites joined with the incipient colonial state in constructing themselves
and their communities, juggling to produce legitimate succession both
from the perspective of the Spanish regime and of their own subjects.[7]
The legalistic hegemony of the Spanish conquest (imperfectly) colonized Andean memory, transforming Andean social forms but also
providing communities with new tools with which to defend themselves from colonial predations.[8] "Use and custom" was not the invocation of an objective past, but a construct that met the political needs
of present-day parties, Spaniards and Indians alike.

We have seen in earlier chapters how individuals wielded colonial
tools—from wills and other legal documents to discourses about wage
labor to clothing—to make a place for themselves in colonial settings.
In this chapter we will take the vantage point of the displaced indigenous elite, fighting to produce and maintain legitimacy in the tight
space between their own laboring subjects and colonial officials. In the
case of the cacicazgos of the north coast, unique political machinations
led to the establishment of female succession if not female rule, a model
that was then adopted in many other regions of the viceroyalty as
generalized "use and custom." By analyzing the cacicazgo as a colonial
artifact, reflecting contemporary power struggles, rather than a prehispanic remnant, we can see how indigenous women and men manipulated the narratives of their own history to claim legitimacy within the
new boundaries of colonial institutions.

The proliferation of cacicas in the seventeenth century was produced
by a number of intertwined premises. There were historic, literary, and

folkloric sources for European beliefs that women could inherit political office, and conquerors might well have encountered female rulers when they arrived in the New World. Europeans also brought with them a legal tradition, as we have seen, which enabled female inheritance, and which was key in creating the possibilities for succession by indigenous as well as Spanish women in the colonies. Indigenous elites utilized their own pasts as well as their new knowledges of what would be most convincing to their colonizers to carve out their space. The new institutions of the colonial era, encomiendas and cacicazgos, although they both claimed lineage in institutions that predated the conquest, were shaped by the interactions of elites, male and female, within the increasingly centralizing impetus of the colonial state.

Amazons of the New World

The chronicles of the Spanish conquest are replete with tales of memorable female overlords and tribes of Amazon warriors, creative composites of actual encounters and European imaginations. Works such as Oviedo's compendious *Corónica de las Yndias y la conquista del Peru* typify the literature of the "marvelous," intertwining eyewitness accounts (by Oviedo and others) with mythological interjections and discourses on natural history.[9] Oviedo's chronicle contains numerous tales of women rulers, and more particularly, *señoríos* or kingdoms of women who live "by themselves without men, and fight in wars, and are powerful and rich and possess great provinces," according to the stories he has heard. Some of these señoríos he explicitly compared to the Amazons of Greek legend. The women of Ciguatán, for example, generally lived apart from men, who were allowed to come into the women's territory and their beds for four months of the year to perform necessary sexual and labor services. According to Oviedo's informant, resultant male children were sent immediately to live with the other men, while female children were raised within the women's realm.[10] These mythical women had to do with the fantastic, the interrelations between fear and desire played out in the exoticized space of the Americas.

Although these fantastic accounts owe much to a Western mythic tradition, they also reflected an actual encounter with differently organized indigenous societies. Conquistadors with no knowledge of local languages or customs invented ways to describe their experiences; these necessarily drew upon their own European discourses of the possible. The "marvelous" is a response to that line between knowability and self-conscious uncertainty; the historian's problem lies in teasing out some aspects of ethnography from rhetorical devices.

It is likely that in South America, as in Europe, women periodically took on important political roles, including, occasionally, the highest offices. Within the central highlands of the Inca empire, the evidence is thin for female succession on any regular basis. Few chroniclers of Cuzco and the Incas mentioned female rulers, although stories of exceptional women surface from Inca mythology rather than eyewitness accounts. The Spanish chronicler Sarmiento de Gamboa and the indigenous chronicler Santa Cruz Pachacuti Yamqui both recounted the great military effort led by an Inca woman, apparently not a kuraka, in Cuzco to defeat the Chanca army long before the Spanish conquest. Chañan Cury Coca fought "valorously, like a manly woman," and "she did so much with her own hands against the Chancas who had assaulted them there, that she made them retreat."[11] In general, there is, as yet, no evidence that there was any possibility of female succession in the prehispanic central Andes while the Incas were dominant.

It remains provocative, though, that gender parallelism was a key component of Inca empire building, religion, and social organization. Certainly, it is the case that almost all the mythological-historical accounts that come to us from indigenous informants regarding the Inca era emphasize gender parallelisms, although we cannot know how to interpret these in terms of power balances and should not idealize parallelisms into material equality. The origin stories of the Incas center on four men and four women, the myths of the *Huarochirí Manuscript* speak to the importance and prominence of female deities, and most colonial-era Inca histories include parallel information on the *coyas* or queens (and sometimes sisters) of the Incas.[12] For these reasons we cannot discount the important roles played by elite women and wives in Inca society.

And, more concretely, the late prehispanic and early colonial periods provide us with evidence of women holding at least symbolic power. Huayna Capac, the last ruling Inca before the Spanish conquest, gave the title of kuraka of Ananguaylas to his secondary wife Contarhuacho, and presented the cacicazgo of the rest of Huaylas to another secondary wife, Añas Colque. We cannot know what this meant in terms of the exercise of office, since the Incas regularly used women to forge political relations through marriage, without necessarily granting them any individual power.[13]

But by far the most celebrated and well-substantiated female rulers of the prehispanic period were the women, called capullanas in the chronicles, of the far northern Piura region, a region not well integrated into the ambit of Cuzco due to the late and bitterly contested conquest of the Chimú kingdom by the Incas only decades before the Spanish invasion.[14] The term *capullana* already raises questions for our historical analysis, for it comes to us through colonial documents, and we do not know what these women called themselves. Many chroniclers asserted that the name came from *capuz*, the long cloak of Arab origin worn by women in Spain, which indigenous women's dress was said to resemble. For example, Cieza de León wrote "the dress of the women was long and wide like a capuz open on both sides, through which they stick their arms."[15] If so, the term was then a Spanish import, imposed by the conquistadors.

Rostworowski argues instead that the word *capullana* comes from a now-lost indigenous language spoken in Catacaos and Piura. According to her analysis, the word *capuc* referred to female gender (as in *icuchin capuc* or female child) and the suffixes *lla* and *na* indicated, respectively, status and gender.[16] Unfortunately we have no corroborating evidence for this suggestive analysis, which, if true, would substantiate that there was at least a distinct analytic category for elite women in that language.

The capullanas were colorful characters in the chronicles of northern Peru, reminiscent of the Amazons of other regions. Cieza de León, who traveled through the north in the 1540s, wrote of a capullana encountered by Francisco Pizarro and his army while sailing near Túmbez. Neither the capullana nor Pizarro trusted the other, and Pizarro hesitated to come ashore to meet her. Eventually, after many gifts and imprecations, she agreed to board his ship as evidence of her good faith; four Spaniards in return disembarked and were fed and welcomed by the Indians on land. The capullana challenged Pizarro's masculinity as she boarded, stating that "she, being a woman, had dared to enter his ship; thus he, being a man and captain, should not fear to tread on the land." The next day Pizarro finally decided to land, to a festive reception. When taking his leave, he told the Indians that he would be back to convert them and make them sworn subjects of the King of Spain, a statement rejected by the Indians who had only recently been defeated by the Inca Huayna Capac. Immediately upon setting sail, one of the conquistadors went berserk with love for the capullana, and had to be placed in chains.[17] Such tales clearly tantalized

European audiences demanding exotic locales and characters and re-inforced stereotypes of weak Indian men and strong Indian women.[18]

Reginaldo de Lizárraga, a Dominican priest who traveled around the continent from the 1550s until his death in 1615, like Cieza spent a great deal of time on the north coast. His chronicle also mentioned the capullanas but as a phenomenon of the past. He recounted, "Passing down the coast and coming a bit inland, because the coast is very rough, we come twenty leagues, more or less, to the great river Mo-tape [Motupe], where there is a town of the same name. This province, which extends for but a few leagues, was governed in ancient times by women, whom we call capullanas for the clothing they wore."[19] Lizár-raga did not mention any other regions that had female governors and, most interesting, did not suggest that the practice of female governor-ship continued during his time there.

Accounts such as these are difficult to interpret. On the one hand, they were clearly part of a mythic creation of prehispanic history by European conquerors. The chroniclers cast aspersions on the virility of Indian men by suggesting that women ruled them, establishing an ex-oticism that also entailed an inverted hierarchy. But it is probably the case that in certain American regions women did periodically take of-fice in the absence of males, as had Queen Isabella not long before in Castille. And these oft-repeated tales also served to create a shared mythology that could be invoked for present-day needs.

Succession in Prehispanic Cacicazgos

Ethnohistorical research has dispelled the colonial belief that the pre-hispanic provinces of Peru were unsophisticated *behetrías* or discon-nected towns subject to their own tenuous rule, a position held, for example, by Padre Calancha in the 17th century, who wrote: "*Behetría* was the government of those [northern coastal] valleys in ancient times; the eldest of the family was the lord of each *parcialidad*; there were few towns, and their inhabitants were without political order."[20]

Andean society was instead composed of various interlocking lev-els of political and social structure: smaller communities that may have functioned relatively independently at times, larger networks created by intermarriages between elites of these communities, and more provincial or "imperial" structures such as those forged by the Chimú and the Inca. The complexity of these various nexuses and the paucity of verifiable information make it difficult to generalize about the pre-hispanic north coast. Inca conquest and rule may have created some homogeneity, but this is not easy to establish either. This section will review some of what we know about local succession practices on the prehispanic north coast, prior to turning to the colonial cacicazgo. This also necessitates a brief examination of Inca practices in Cuzco and the question of whether these were imposed upon conquered polities.

Cacique is a word taken from the Arawak language, not a term indigenous to South America. It was applied by Europeans indiscriminately to leaders of various ethnic groups across the Americas. In the Mochica-Lambayeque language, spoken in some north coastal regions, the term for chief was *filca*, but this appears in no colonial documentation, replaced by the universalized "cacique." (It is nearly impossible to ascertain linguistic practice outside extant documentation, as most of these languages have disappeared.)[21] In the Quechua-speaking central and south Andes, local lords were called *kurakas*; this term was generalized over much of Peru either by the Spaniards or the Inca, as the Nahuatl *naboría* was generalized through New Spain.[22] Even kuraka did not refer to a single hierarchical level or function; there was a clear and complex hierarchy of sociopolitical groups (*pachacas* and *guarangas*) and local lords (*hatun* kurakas, kurakas, and *principales*), which adjusted when these groups were made dependent upon external authorities. Such complex power nexuses were generally obscured by the colonial terminology that mixed Spanish and indigenous concepts in an ad-hoc manner.

The question of cacicazgo succession in the prehispanic Andes is thus extremely knotty, because of the heterogeneity of local practices and the lack of clear and verifiable historical evidence. It is virtually impossible to trace colonial practices back to "traditional" society, because those societies were complex and nonstatic, and because the colonial language through which they are known to us incorporated its own biases. The north coast regions in particular were conquered at least twice within some forty years, by the Incas and the Spaniards, and reconstituted each time according to political necessity and opportunity. Colonial litigants over cacicazgos often claimed "traditional" social relations to favor their candidates, utilizing strategies that they knew would be received well by the courts, yielding contradictory narratives about these practices.

In fact, succession practices might not have been precisely fixed at all. Ethnohistorical studies of coastal Peru and Quito indicate that succession in the immediate prehispanic period in these regions was probably "designed for optimal flexibility" in order to prefer more able candidates within the lineage over structural rigor.[23] Thus, office could pass equally through male siblings or through male issue, and the like-lihood of regular political challenge could be thought of as a benefit of the system, ensuring that the best of the candidates might generally triumph. This flexibility also created the possibility of lengthy turmoil and malicious interventions. Cabello Balboa noted in the sixteenth cen-tury that, within the memory of his informants, the cacique of Lam-bayeque had put his own brothers to death in order to eliminate them preemptively as political rivals.[24] The celebrated litigiousness of colo-nial caciques might thus be attributed as much to prehispanic con-tentiousness as to colonial stresses and opportunities.

These studies have found no evidence whatsoever of cacicas or female chiefs, but, on the contrary, suggest that parallel inheritance patterns might have made succession *less* likely to go through the fe-male side, preferring nephews over wives and daughters.[25] These mod-ern arguments for flexibility within structure were indeed prefigured in the sixteenth century investigations of Hernando de Santillán, who noted that although Andean kurakas might have the ability to choose anyone to succeed them, they generally followed fairly strict genera-tional sequences, preferring brothers, then their own sons or nephews.[26]

The issue of succession on the north coast immediately before the Spanish conquest raises the question of the relationship between the Incas of Cuzco and their conquered polities. Political legitimacy was not an uncomplicated question for the Incas either, and what we think of as Inca tradition was of relatively recent invention. Pachacuti, the great Inca empire builder and the grandfather of the last ruling Inca, Huayna Capac, established most of what came to be regarded as Inca custom only a few generations before the Spanish conquest.[27] He insti-tuted, for example, the custom of brother-sister marriage for the Inca, although he himself chose as his successor the son (Topa Inca) of his marriage with a woman from the nobility of a neighboring town. The two generations after Pachacuti did marry their sisters to produce suc-cessors, although the dying Huayna Capac either changed his mind or was otherwise influenced in his choice of a successor, leading to the civil war between his two sons that brought down their rule before the Spanish conquest. At any rate, Inca succession was certainly not auto-matic or even a particularly ancient institution.[28]

Given the flexibility of Inca practice, and the realistic limitations of Cuzco's ability to intervene in the affairs of all its tributary regions, the Inca presumably exercised little direct control over local caciques. Only in limited cases, as when there might be fear of insurrection, would they have been chosen or imposed.[29] Instead there was presumably a ratification process by which the Inca confirmed local decisions. More important, the highland requirement of reciprocity between the kuraka and his subjects meant that possession of the cacicazgo was contingent upon the proper provision of services to the community and could not therefore be a purely hereditary office, such that an incompetent or bad kuraka could be removed.[30]

In summary, prehispanic polities such as those on the north coast displayed a variety of mechanisms for succession, some linked to Inca rule and others not. Inca practice itself was not static and evolved in interaction with the regions being integrated into its sphere. Evidence from the north coast points to a flexible system whereby candidates could be chosen from among a group of relatives, creating both legitimacy and the possibility of conflict. In none of these cases do we find a preference for female rule, and it is likely that, when it happened, it was the response to a specific problem rather than a guiding principle.

The Colonial Cacicazgo

The colonial cacicazgo, an institution for which we do have substantial documentation, was no less complicated and heterogeneous than its prehispanic predecessor. As Andean ethnohistorians have described it, colonial society was conflictual and contestatory and favored those individuals best able to adapt to the new legal system. The colonial cacique, who might have questionable or no elite lineage, was a particularly political animal. As Karen Powers puts it, success in the early colonial years

lies in a cacique's personal ability to resolve the leadership dilemma of the period. The successful colonial cacique legitimized his authority in both the Spanish and Indian spheres by simultaneously satisfying two sets of criteria. A cacique's power rested on his ability to fulfill contracts with both the colonial regime and the community by promptly provisioning tribute and labor, on the one hand, and by efficiently administering his people's work and resources and ensuring their good treatment, on the other. His subjects depended on him not only to prevent their exploitation but to show them great generosity, which in turn depended on his accumulating and maintaining wealth.[31]

Legitimacy thus depended on actual as well as perceived abilities, in both the indigenous and Spanish spheres, and was therefore subject to contestation on many fronts.

Not only was elite standing challenged by colonialism, but the actual structure of indigenous communities became a colonial product as well. The conquistadors were not given outright land grants in the New World, but rather authority over populations headed by a cacique, thus encomienda grants were overtly political interventions into ethnic communities. In fact, the encomienda system fragmented and reconstituted existing populations, grouping them under a *cacique principal* chosen from what might have been a number of local headmen, establishing from the latter group *segundas personas* or "secondary caciques" subservient to the principal. In many cases, small or dispersed ethnic groups were physically moved to a new site, called a *reducción*, where they could be merged with other groups for pedagogical and economic efficiency.[32]

On the north coast as elsewhere, colonial cacicazgos were often constructed by this combining or dividing up of previous political structures. Given the evidence of prehispanic strife over cacicazgos, compounded by the imposition of a new and somewhat random imperial system, it is no surprise that local communities quickly adapted to Spanish legal culture, becoming in fact rather successful at litigation. The multiple and often conflictual levels of jurisdiction—encomenderos, corregidores, viceroy, not to mention representatives of the Catholic Church—led to competing claims and lines of legitimation. A brief example from the north coast in the 1560s and 1570s will be illustrative of the contentiousness. Two encomiendas were created out of the prehispanic settlement of Callanca: Callanca (with its original cacique, Quico Chumbi) and Reque (headed by Xancol Chumbi, chosen by the encomendero for his service to Spaniards during the conquest). The new cacique Xancol Chumbi was hated by his subjects, who considered him illegitimate and too aggressive in tribute collection, and they assassinated him. He was succeeded briefly by his brother, then his son, and then someone "elected by the Indians by order of the encomendero" probably to reinstate a sense of legitimacy.[33]

These reducciones ostensibly served to facilitate religious indoctrination and tribute collection. But clearly they were also intended to make political administration easier, and (intentionally or not) they created peculiarly colonial cacicazgos, legitimated and overseen by the colonial state, out of the mosaic of prehispanic structures. The colonial political district most strongly reflects the machinations of the early colonial state and various strata of the indigenous elite.

The importance of this ethnic and geographic discontinuity for a discussion of succession patterns is obvious. On the north coast, where demographic collapse was profound, the remoldings of populations for the sake of "efficiency" were constant.[34] In the 1530s, Francisco Pizarro divided up the señoríos of the Lambayeque region among eleven Spanish men, granting each the labor of a community of Indians through the mediation of their caciques. As Indian populations dwindled over the next centuries, these repartimientos were redrawn and recombined to facilitate tribute collection and religious instruction and to create large enough labor forces for encomenderos, even if it meant placing communities beneath a "foreign" cacique.

Thus, the colonial cacicazgo was the result of at least two forces in tension with already-existing practices: the economic and political demands of colonial authorities and the creativity and adaptation to colonial legal procedures of indigenous elites. As Powers notes in her study of the Duchisela cacicazgo in Quito, "chiefly legitimacy" was invented through the creative manipulation of genealogies, notarial documents, and an ambivalent "prehispanic tradition." The ancient history of the colonized would also become a tool that Indians could use against the colonial regime.[35]

"Use and Custom": The Creation of Succession in Indigenous Communities

Finally, we should examine the bureaucratic system that produced a single notion of legitimate succession to apply to all indigenous communities, as part of what the Spanish Crown referred to as the "use and custom" of the Republic of Indians, the aspects of local political organization theoretically not imposed, although always overseen, by the Crown. This process was set in motion by a series of viceroys who asked their administrators to collect information about prehispanic social organization to aid in their governance of the region.

Thus sixteenth-century reports, often based upon substantial interviews with indigenous elites, repeatedly proposed that while local practice might have been heterogeneous, an omnipotent and tyrannical Inca Empire had imposed its own mandate across the provinces. Juan Polo de Ondegardo, on behalf of Viceroy Conde de Nieva in 1561, and Juan de Matienzo, under Viceroy Marqués de Cañete in 1567, both argued that central to Inca hegemony was the schooling of the sons of far-flung caciques in Cuzco, where they would learn Quechua and become indoctrinated in the ways of the Incas. This was, of course, an attractive proposition to the colonial state, which was attempting to ladinize and acculturate the caciques and their sons in order to create legitimate successors with strong loyalties to the colonial order.[36]

Viceroy Francisco de Toledo carried out even more extensive reviews during his long tenure (1569–82) and left more of a mark than his predecessors, because he also contributed to the establishment of legal formulas and procedures that continued to have effect long after his departure from office. Toledo's great concern was to institutionalize a stable indigenous elite that would "be the instruments of execution, in the spiritual as well as temporal," providing for colonial religious as well as political leadership.[37] Thus he had to legitimate indigenous successions that also supported colonial rule. In his instructions to the administrators carrying out the first general census of the population of the colony, in 1569, Toledo asked that they ascertain who had held the cacicazgo at the time when Spaniards first entered into the land, whether they had legitimate issue still alive, and

what order they had in the time of the Inca of succession in cacicazgos and *principalazgos*; whether the sons succeeded the fathers by way of succession, and which of the sons succeeded, if it was the eldest or the most able or he who was named by the Inca; or if, when the cacique was dead, the Inca himself according to his own will named a successor for such offices who might not be a son or descendent of the dead man, even if he left children.[38]

These instructions reveal that Toledo was aware of the existence of nonbloodline succession, in particular of the possibility of the succession of the "most able," though he clearly favored the patrilineal bloodline. His information gathering created conflict, as inspectors found themselves in a position to intervene in clashes between claimants to office and Spanish officials. In 1571 he clarified his instructions in the face of more activist visitadores, demanding that in the case of conflicts, they should simply write reports regarding the cacique and his children, so that the viceroy himself could decide on succession.[39] The supposed objectivity of fact finding took a backseat to the political necessity of defining succession such that those acceptable to the colonial administration would be placed in office, with the problem of native practice reduced to an issue of legitimacy and hegemony.

Similarly, political questions tended to overrule even notions of bloodline inheritance. In a case regarding succession in Carabuco in 1575, Toledo ordered that, in accordance with his own reading of Inca practice, the most intelligent or able son, or the most sufficient candidate among all his relatives, was to be chosen by the Viceroy (standing in for the Inca), rather than simply the eldest son of the late cacique. "Sufficiency" was herein defined so as to depend upon two characteristics, competence and Christianity, to discourage idolatry and witchcraft among the caciques.[40] Bloodline succession—the centerpiece of Spanish inheritance law—had now been shunted aside in favor of the ability of the colonial government to micromanage cacicazgos, now packaged as a reinterpretation or reinvigoration of Inca policy, with "ability" subsumed to "malleability" to the aims of the colonial state. This and subsequent orders established the new boundaries for debate over succession, demanding that bloodline inheritance within cacicazgos be largely respected, but with the right of refusal retained for the Crown and the Viceroy, based upon some criterion of aptitude for colonial office. This policy was flexible and ambiguous, leaving the state with the final say, but also creating a space for interpretations of prehispanic history by all those who had the ability to speak in the public realm.

Women and Succession in Peruvian Encomiendas

But there was one other source of influence on indigenous succession practices, not always fully considered by colonial historians. This was the constant interaction, within increasingly intimate spaces, between members of different ethnic groups, both within and across classes.

The encomienda system placed the new Iberian elites within the ambit of Indian towns, at least as figureheads and visitors (for encomenderos rarely lived outside the larger cities and their mayordomos oversaw daily matters). Caciques and tributaries alike viewed these families as sources of stress and authorities to be challenged, to be sure, but also as figures to emulate or network with, as can be seen by the common requests that they serve as godparents or eponyms. And as we have seen, an important minority of indigenous men and women were able to succeed economically in colonial cities, deploying new and old knowledges to secure themselves some financial stability and, in some cases, purchasing central residential sites, solares, in Lima and Trujillo. Some of the old indigenous nobility also parleyed their positions into colonial power; these were perhaps the first to move into "Spanish" neighborhoods.[41] These groups—the "old money" and "new money," so to speak, of the Andes and Iberia—enjoyed close contact, economically if not socially, as notarial records demonstrate. Thus it is more than likely that these groups knew well each other's business. Fights over succession within encomendero families were surely gossip among Indians held in encomienda as well as in urban kitchens.

And succession practices among the colonizers, and importantly, encomenderos, would be an obvious source for caciques' own presentation of their rights to succession. Although we cannot, with the documents presently available, prove such a direct connection, the parallels are too strong to be ignored. In other realms, we have seen that Indians borrowed European practices that suited them and that seemed likely to encourage legitimacy in the eyes of their rulers, from legal forms to coats of arms to clothing. It is likely, then, that the production of indigenous succession law was not simply a top-down matter, but also was affected by Indian men's and women's knowledge of their new overlords.

The initial encomiendas—there were some five hundred in Peru in the 1540s—were granted almost exclusively to Spanish men, usually soldiers who had fought either in the conquest or who had taken the Crown's side in the Peruvian civil wars that followed immediately after.[42] However this generation of soldiers was already ageing or ailing by the time they received their grants, and within a few decades the question of succession was prominent. The encomienda system was expected to populate the New World with legitimate children and to produce a steady stream of wealth; thus its stability was of primary importance to early administrations. Grants were generally made for a number of "lives," usually one to three, referring to the successive generations entitled to reap the estate's benefit.[43] The second generation of encomenderos included, in addition to the sons of the conquistadors, their wives and daughters. A listing of the individuals holding encomiendas in 1561—less than thirty years after the conquest began—includes not only women but a great number of men who obtained their title by marrying the widows of encomenderos.[44]

This flexibility came in contrast to medieval Iberian law regarding primogeniture (*mayorazgo*). Women could succeed their husbands in New World encomiendas, unlike medieval *feudos*, which were restricted to male issue. This special dispensation was made in order to attract more men (and families) as stable settlers, as well as to avoid impoverishing widows.[45] Succession to the daughter was preferred over the widow, but in the absence of heirs, or with underage children, the Crown preferred to name widows encomenderas rather than end a lineage's access to this most productive institution.[46]

Of twenty-four encomiendas in Trujillo in 1561, three were directly administered either by a woman or by a couple where the succession went through the woman.[47] By the turn of the seventeenth century the situation was more dramatic, as vacant encomiendas were turned over to the Crown's jurisdiction, and a larger number of women made up the diminishing population of encomenderos, although women always remained a small minority.

Women were not automatically granted the next life of the encomienda, an application had to be made, usually emphasizing the woman's poverty and her late husband's selfless service to the Crown. In 1601, doña Ana de Velasco y Avendaño successfully sued for the encomienda of Jayanca, near Trujillo, when her father, don Miguel de Avendaño, died just a year after being awarded an annual income in remuneration for his military service in Peru and Chile. Doña Ana, left "very poor" by her father's death, was thus granted the encomienda recently left vacant by the death of doña Ysabel Palomino, who had herself inherited it from her late husband don Manuel Criado de Castilla. The provision explicitly gave the right of succession to the eldest legitimate son or daughter of doña Ana (and of her husband, Juan de Calderón, who made the application in doña Ana's name).[48]

In many cases, widows (or daughters) acted as a placeholder until an appropriate male could exercise office.[49] Widows found themselves under enormous pressure to remarry quickly, and those holding an encomienda grant were extremely desirable partners in a colonial marriage market that lacked Spanish women in general and propertied women in particular. Nonetheless, a number of elite women acquired renown for their business acumen and the wielding of power through their encomiendas. The Trujillo region was home to no small number of these: Ana Pizarro, Florencia de Mora, and Beatriz de los Ríos all succeeded their husbands and, despite remarriages, notoriously retained active control over their own business interests. Doña Florencia ran an obraje, a cattle ranch, and her own encomienda, all in highland Huamachuco, and was known for her charitable works as well as her iron will.[50] In nearby Cajamarca, doña Beatriz de Ysásaga and doña Jordana Mexia, widows of two conquistadors, were regularly in the courts in the 1570s, suing each other over the possession of particular

Indian pueblos as part of their own encomiendas.[51] These women joined the ranks of other prominent businesswomen, forming a visible and voluble core of women involved in the social, economic, and political life of the region. But the encomenderas, in particular, modeled the successful maneuvering through the courts by women who could articulate their rights to succession based upon both law and personal histories.

The success of encomenderas in arguing their cases normalized female succession both for indigenous pretenders to office and for the Spanish officials who would judge their cases. It is particularly interesting in this context that Cajamarca, with no known record of prehispanic cacicas, was home during the colonial period to a number of highly activist cacicas. It is reasonable to believe that the Spanish women holding Cajamarca's encomiendas served as models for some politically ambitious indigenous women, and, at the very least, they made female succession part of the colonial legal discourse.

From Capullanas to Cacicas: Creating Female Succession

In the sixteenth century, litigation over cacicazgos was silent on the subject of gender. Successful applications for cacicazgos in that period tended to invoke an opportunistic mixture of prehispanic practices and contemporary political struggles. But this very mix opened the possibility of female succession by creating the space for contestatory histories and interventions. The confluence of these forces in the seventeenth century—the colonial government's desire to codify "traditional" practice while maintaining control over succession, the examples of women in power or as placeholders for power from the prehispanic past and in the colonial present—with an increasingly common demand from the part of the bureaucracy to limit contestations over succession led to the formal codification of the female right to succession, in the absence of male heirs. This process was stated most clearly in *Política indiana*, a critical commentary on the history of colonial law written by Juan de Solórzano y Pereyra in 1647.

According to Solórzano's reading of history, the colonial legal system faced the question of maintaining the hierarchical relationship that had previously existed between Indian subjects, their local cacique, representatives of the Inca, and the Inca himself. Structurally, the geometric relationship was to endure under colonial rule, although the autonomy of the cacique was to be greatly curtailed. The Inca and his representatives were replaced by the Crown, Viceroy, and corregidores, who "govern, protect and collect tribute," and the responsibility of the cacique was then "only to collect their subjects' tributary portion and carry it to the corregidor, to search for and bring together their subjects so that they go on their mitas and other personal services which they must attend to and to take care of other minor occupations." As compensation, caciques were entitled to a salary and some service from their subjects, shifting the community relationship of reciprocity to one of employment.[52]

As we have noted, some colonial administrators saw firsthand the dangers that could arise from delegitimizing local governance, from plummeting tribute revenues to uprisings and other violent destabilizations. In part to avoid this, the law explicitly repudiated direct colonial control of cacicazgos and the selection process, so that encomenderos and corregidores would not name candidates who might be unpopular with their erstwhile subjects. Given the desire to incorporate the cacicazgo structure into colonial administration, it was necessary to translate the cacicazgo into something more familiar that could then be subsumed. This was done primarily by adapting the definition of inheritance while insisting upon the preeminence of "prehispanic customs." The *Política indiana* accomplished this by denying corregidores and encomenderos the right to intervene in the selection of a cacique, but simultaneously asserting that the Indians have the right to determine "succession by right of blood in imitation of mayorazgos." That is, the right to administer succession was left in Indian hands, but the method of determining succession was now to be limited to bloodline: "succession derived from fathers to sons."[53]

Once "most able" was replaced by the mayorazgo, the problem of female inheritance became prominent. If there were no males to inherit office, there arose the possibility of counternarratives (of ability or election, for example) reestablishing themselves, creating power vacuums that could be manipulated by local players. In this case, the ability for office to pass through female lines could resolve many crises, and as we have seen, already enjoyed some status both in European and indigenous imaginations. Solórzano noted the unwillingness of Viceroy Toledo to allow women to exclude any male kin, even of more remote descent. But because of the tendency in the coastal lowlands of the north to allow women, especially when married, to hold office, he argued, "this custom ought to be observed where it is proven and is accompanied by acts that suffice to introduce it, because we do not find a lack of examples of offices, duties and dignities of much greater import in which females succeed although they have mixed jurisdiction; so we see that they are competent to inherit Kingdoms, States and Lordships, feudos and mayorazgos."[54] In this case, offering daughters as successors, but only in the absence of sons, decreased the likelihood of contested succession and provided the Viceroy with a wider range of potential candidates when intervention proved necessary.

Cacicas, Genealogies, and the Exercise of Power in the Seventeenth Century

Clearly, by the seventeenth century, it was already common for Indian women or their male relatives to invoke narratives of past practice and tradition from "time immemorial" to establish their own claims to office. We have already seen this done in the case of Narigualá in 1610 and subsequently in numerous north coast polities where women took office "because capullanas succeeded in cacicazgos as if they were male."[55] This practice was accompanied by the assimilation of another common Spanish tool, the family tree or genealogy, to prove direct bloodlines. The results of litigation could turn on the presentation of a "proper" genealogy supported by credible witnesses.

In sixteenth-century America, as in Iberia, genealogies played a number of critical legal roles, most particularly in *pruebas de hidalguía* (proofs of noble status) and *pruebas de limpieza de sangre* (proofs of the absence of Muslim, Jewish, or heretic ancestry).[56] Inherent to both of these forms was the centrality of Catholic marriage and legitimate birth. Indigenous men and women adapted this form for their own purposes. Given that Christianity was a recent import to the New World, indigenous genealogies took creative license with prehispanic marital and sexual relationships, and the genealogy took a form particular to this moment of contact between these highly hierarchical societies.[57]

A particularly powerful example comes from the 1692 will of doña María Chumbi Guaman, the cacica principal of Santiago de Huamán, outside Trujillo. Doña María opened her will in a remarkably unconventional manner. While most testaments identified the speaker in a line or two and went on to invoke the glory of God and his intercessors, doña María spent more than a folio listing her own antecedents on both her father's and mother's sides before even mentioning her religion. She is, she said, legitimate daughter of don Pedro Oja Guaman and legitimate granddaughter of don Antonio Phelipe Chumbi Guaman and legitimate great-great granddaughter of don Diego Phelipe Chancon and great-great-great granddaughter of don Lorenço Chancon, who was the natural son of don Alonço Chancon, and great-great-great-great granddaughter of Guamanchumo, cacique principal and lord who was of all these valleys in their heathendom; as well I am the legitimate daughter of doña María Bacus, casica principal along with my sister doña María Binsur, we are the granddaughters of doña Ysabel Sui Sui, we are also legitimate granddaughters of don Antonio Ambrosio Chayhuac and legitimate great granddaughters of don Juan Sep Chayhuac, also we are great-great granddaughters of don Antonio Yspichi Guaman and great-great-great-granddaughters of don Antonio Chayhuac, all caciques principales who were of these towns of Mansiche, Guaman and Guanchaco.[58]

Here doña María invoked every strategy available to her: a direct and linear elite genealogy on both sides, the "legitimacy" of most of the inheritors, and a direct connection to Guamanchumo, or the great Chimú, lord of the north coast prior to the Inca and Spanish conquests. The genealogy presented in her will provides an illuminating example of the way hybrid strategies solidified into colonial narratives of the past.

However, two decades earlier, when she was presented by her husband, don Manuel Fernández Asmat Inga, as a candidate for the cacicazgo, her genealogy was quite different: "and she was legitimate daughter of don Alonso Suy Suy Chimo, late cacique principal and governor of the said town, and as such she was the legitimate successor of said cacicazgo, given that he had no sons who might be favored."[59] Their application was successful and don Manuel—himself a lesser cacique—thus became the governor of Huamán. How to explain the inconsistency? One possibility is that her earlier genealogy was faked by herself or by her husband in her name. Don Pedro Oja Guaman, whom she calls her father in her will, did indeed have an illustrious pedigree and was a principal or member of the nobility, but had failed in his own attempt to be made governor of Huamán by virtue of his marriage to a woman publicly known as the cacica yet denied that title by the Real Audiencia. Don Alonso Suy Suy Chimo, doña María's father in her application for the cacicazgo, was indeed named cacique and governor, though more of his story is unknown.

We lack the documentation that might fill in some of these gaps: if her ascendance to the cacicazgo was fraudulent, we have no records of complaints by other candidates that might clarify the situation. But doña María's expertise in adapting colonial rules to her particulars was evident. In her will, she named her only daughter as her successor in the *cacicazgo*, her son not being of age, with the provision that her son would succeed only after her daughter's death. In this way she protected her line immediately but shifted inheritance to the male side of her issue in the future.

Throughout the seventeenth century many more north coast women called themselves cacicas, sometimes in order to claim office or benefits, other times simply as a title of respect or an honorific. In 1679, an extremely long and contentious litigation over the cacicazgo of Túcume and Mochumi ended in favor of doña María Josepha Mincha. This case was particularly notable because two other women had claimed the office at one time or another; testimony established that in cacicazgos, "women only entered in the absence of legitimate males." The case thus ostensibly centered on questions of legitimacy, genealogy, and gender, and if any male relatives proved to be legitimate, a choice would have to be made between these criteria; doña María Josepha eventually won because she was the sister of the late cacique. Another claimant, doña Catalina, was dismissed by witnesses because "if she were [the cacica] . . . the Indians of the repartimiento would treat her as their *señora* and they didn't, they view her like any other individual Indian." Another stated that "he knows her as a woman and an yndia like all the rest, that although she knows how to speak Spanish in the end she is an yndia."[60] The question of chiefly legitimacy, both from the perspective of the state and the community, remained a concern in colonial cacicazgos.

The question of who would actually govern when a cacica was allowed to succeed in the cacicazgo merited some debate. The job of the cacique was, in the blunt words of one document, "dispatching mitayos . . . and collecting tribute with punctuality" in exchange for "salary and services and care for fields as established by the tasa."[61] This necessitated the respect of both the Indian community and the Spanish powerbrokers. Because of the problem of legitimacy and the threat of corruption, the colonial administration preferred not to allow Spaniards to adjudicate between indigenous middlemen and ordered that the husband of the cacica would carry out the office (often receiving the title "governor"). This was clarified in a royal provision regarding the cacicazgo of Huamán in 1673 as follows, "because when succession and the right of cacicazgos are deferred to females who are married, it is convenient that the government reside with the husbands, if they are competent, because the Indians obey them and respect them as husbands of their cacicas."[62]

A succession crisis in Chicama demonstrated the problems faced by many female lords in the colonial world. After the cacique don Alonso de Mora was assassinated in 1598, his only daughter, doña María de Mora Caxahuamán, should have inherited his office, but she was too young to marry, and her uncle took possession in her stead. Her mother, doña María Ispacoch, was appointed her daughter's tutor or guardian, but soon requested that her brother exercise the office "because she speaks no Spanish, she cannot attend to the cultivation of her daughter's possessions and lands nor collect her inheritance."[63]

Such a statement raises the question of whether elite indigenous women were any more or less qualified than male counterparts to rule in the colonial setting. The sons and daughters of caciques and other nobility may indeed have received differential treatment that gave them different sets of skills. Although the education of noble native girls had been a pet project of Queen Isabella, and a school (*colegio*) for them was founded in Mexico in the 1530s, this experiment ended with the epidemic of 1545, and no such institutions were founded in Peru in this period.[64] Convents did accept indigenous noblewomen in some places, like Cuzco, usually as lower status nuns of the "white veil," and it is likely that some girls received a convent education without taking orders.[65] And the daughters of caciques might be brought up in the homes of their encomenderos.[66] But boys, on the other hand, might be sent to a school like the Jesuit order's Colegio de San Francisco de Borja, or might be instructed by a local priest or schoolmaster. The sons of caciques had more opportunities to learn to speak Spanish, to become literate, and to have the working knowledge of Spanish society necessary to act as a leader to their own communities within the context of colonial rule.

But such a statement assumes that the lives of men and women were separate and that rural elites were—unless sent off to school—isolated within their indigenous villages. On the contrary, as our analysis of urban notarial archives has demonstrated, indigenous elites of both genders maintained residences in cities and presumably traveled regularly between locations in order to have access to the luxuries of urban life that befit their status while maintaining a close connection to the kin networks and tributary populations that gave them that social position. What can be said, then, is that in some cases elite women might well be disadvantaged—as might some elite men—by their lack of Spanish or their illiteracy, but for the most part comments such as those of doña María Ispacoch above were likely part of a common rhetorical strategy (such as we have seen before) that drew upon standing beliefs about women's inadequacies. It is clear from the litigation record that many elite Indian women were savvy and politic leaders.

Although it is not surprising that cacicas began to proliferate on the north coast, an unexpected number of them arose in places as unlikely as the central and northern sierra, strongholds of the Inca before the conquest. Cajamarca had an extremely lively tradition of colonial cacicas, who appear with great frequency in the archival record, carrying out the duties of their office. These included the two youthful cacicas doña Feliciana and doña María de Barrionuevo, who won back doña Feliciana's cacicazgo after attaining majority in 1681; and doña María Collquisilles, the cacica of Otusco, who died in 1636, leaving a vast estate of personal goods, animals, and family lands. Doña María left her estate to three "orphan mestizos" (also referred to as her children) she had raised, as well as to her brother; she made only fleeting mention of her husband in her first will and never identified him as her husband in the second. She appears to have served as the cacica; all the legal documents following her death identify her as such. That her use of the office may have been contested is suggested, however, by her statement that "by provision of the Lord Viceroys, my parents were granted two mitayos to guard their livestock, and I have been robbed of the said provisions, I order my executors to search for them so that my inheriting children can take advantage of them for the guarding of the livestock of the ranch for which they were given."[67] As noted above, the proliferation of cacicas may have had to do both with Cajamarca's proximity to Trujillo, with its tradition of cacicas, and with the powerful Spanish encomenderas who held labor grants in both regions.

In other regions, women calling themselves cacica also flourished, though they were less likely to hold the office. In Chincha, in 1616, doña Juana Carilla, "cacica principal of the Valley of Chincha, as legitimate daughter and heir of doña Ysabel Canchilla" sued the corregidor's lieutenant over some lands that were taken from her, which she claimed to have inherited from her ancestors. The lawyer for the corregidor's lieutenant referred to her as "Juana Curilla yndia" rather than cacica and based his defense on witnesses who testified as to how stupid, corrupt, and immoral Indians were.[68] No documentation in that file supports her claim to be cacica, which was not relevant to her suit but the title apparently afforded her some status when battling the bureaucracy.

On the other hand, in Jauja in 1629, doña María Llaxachumbi sued for possession of the cacicazgo of her ayllu, which came to her "by direct male line." She applied for the title for herself and the governor-ship for her husband don Diego Clemente Tisi Guaman, who spoke on their behalf. Don Diego had been acting as cacique since their marriage, although a male relative of doña María's had temporarily obtained the title via his mother's line. The title was restored to doña María and don Diego. The question of gender was never raised in the litigation, and it may be relevant that this cacicazgo was a colonial creation and thus there was no ability to invoke a long tradition (which would probably not have included female succession).[69]

The will of Ysauel Caja y Yapa "cacica" was made before a notary public in 1701 and was preserved because she left a small capellanía from her estate. However, nothing in her will indicates that the title "cacica" was more than an honorific: she was the daughter of don Francisco Yapa and Catalina Josepha of San Juan de Coyata, neither of whom were titled, and was married to Bartolomé Rosales, a native of Guacho. She made no mention of a cacicazgo within the will, and it is possible that "cacica" (like *palla* in the previous century) simply became a strong honorific of the period for those with some connection to cacical or elite lineage.[70]

These and other cases illustrate the ways in which the title "cacica" came to be used with growing frequency by elite indigenous women over the seventeenth century, departing from its geographic ambit and occupational specificity to have broader and more ambiguous significance. The dilution of the meaning of the term, which accompanied the declining significance of the rural indigenous elite overall, allowed it eventually to become a romanticized marker of past status and indigenist identity. But it also provided a space for elite women to promote their own interests, within the bounds of colonial society.

In a concluding section, I examine in close detail a single case that illustrates one process by which this proliferation took place. The fact that the intricate absurdities of some of its arguments were considered seriously in court indicates the ways in which narratives of family genealogies and intrigues came to dominate the legal discourse over status. And the location of the litigation, in a highland region that had no known prehispanic tradition of women in power, demonstrates the power of this gendered narrative

Conclusion: Magdalena Mallao and the Child Cacica

By the middle of the seventeenth century, the cacica was firmly established as a type. No longer confined to her geographic origins near

Piura, she was invoked whenever it seemed strategic and practicable to those seeking power. In conclusion to this chapter, I look at a litigation over a piece of land that invoked the "tradition" of female inheritance; in this case, however, there was no tradition to speak of, and the fact that the lawsuit went on as it did indicates that female succession had become part of a generalized "traditional past" that could be invoked whenever convenient. The suit was brought before the Real Audiencia, the highest colonial court, in 1643; the land in question was in Huánuco, in the central sierra. In many ways the trajectory of the story encapsulates many of the arguments of this study, illustrating the ways by which Indians and Spaniards invoked prehispanic and Spanish law and custom in the hybrid language of the colonial state. Notions of legitimacy and illegitimacy, tradition and law all intermingle in a story that is ultimately only about the struggle over power in the guise of resources in a world where indigenous men and women were truly at a disadvantage unless they could invoke colonial justice in their favor.

The suit began when don Pedro Ayra and his niece doña Francisca Ayra (married at the time to the cacique don Juan Bautista Curicaya) tried to throw Magdalena Mallao, an elderly Indian woman, out of a house and two lots they owned in the city of León de Huánuco. Mallao had lived in the house and made use of the surrounding farmland for some years prior to the complaint. Don Pedro and doña Francisca had recently returned to the city after a two-year absence and found themselves unable to remove Mallao from their property. Although they initially stated that Mallao had "invaded" their house, in their interrogatories they clarified that they had indeed, "from the pity they had for the said doña Madalena Mallao, being poor and having no house to live in, consented to her living in a chamber on the lot of land, sowing for her food on a piece of land."[71]

Don Pedro and doña Francisca's ownership of the two lots stemmed from a legal donation made by doña Francisca Ruray after the death of her husband don Francisco Ayra, the cacique of Ychuc. Doña Francisca and don Francisco had only one child who survived don Francisco, named Leonor, and she passed away within six months of her father's death. In 1601 doña Francisca Ruray, aging and with no living children of her own, decided to transfer her property to some of her late husband's illegitimate children, of which there were at least five. That donation recognized don Pedro Ayra, the legitimate son of don Francisco's illegitimate son don Andrés, and three other *hijos naturales*: don Santiago Ayra, don Tomás Ayra and don Domingo Ayra. Doña Francisca Ayra, the co-petitioner with don Pedro, was the legitimate daughter of don Santiago Ayra, granddaughter of the cacique, and heir to her father's share of the property.

The confusion over the property had to do with the vagaries of law regarding children born outside of wedlock. It is by no means clear from the documentary record exactly which of don Francisco's children were "bastards" (born while he was married to another woman) and which "natural" (born while both parents were single), and much of the testimony argues heartily over this issue. As we have seen, natural children could be legally recognized by a parent and could thus inherit, but bastards could not. The second issue was whether they had been legally recognized by don Francisco and doña Francisca; therefore the outcome hinged in great part on the donation and subsequent wills leaving the property to future generations. In the midst of this wrangling, Magdalena Mallao claimed to be yet another of don Francisco's illegitimate children, who should share equally in the property and live peaceably alongside them.[72]

The question of legitimacy and inheritance had long been on the minds of all the participants; Don Santiago Ayra in his own will of 1606 stated that only he, the eldest of the illegitimate children of the cacique, was "natural" and all the others were bastards.[73] However, another will, supporting Magdalena Mallao's claim, was introduced during the appeal to the high court. It belonged to doña Leonor Lliuyac Mallo, the daughter of the late cacique don Francisco, who had died in 1586. Doña Leonor in this will called herself "cacica principal" and named Magdalena Mallao as her "sister." Doña Leonor left a small amount of cash and some sheep to her mother doña Francisca Ruray, but left the great majority of her estate including the house and lands in question to her sister Magdalena, "because I have raised her since she was small." And she left this parting shot for the other future claimants:

and all the rest of my relatives and bastard brothers have done great injuries to my father and to me in taking away many houses and haciendas that were my father's, and the title that my father left me to the cacicazgo; they have insulted me and their parents without any right whatsoever . . . and thus they do not deserve to inherit my goods for being such bad Christians . . . and to the said doña Madalena Mallao . . . I leave her the said lot with the consent of my mother and may none of my relatives interfere in this, let her enjoy it freely, and it is my will and may she plead with God for my soul.[74]

Don Pedro and doña Francisca immediately declared the will a fake, and not without reason: doña Leonor was only eight or nine years old when she died and hardly able to construct such a document. And if it was authentic, why did Magdalena Mallao wait so long to produce it? Their witnesses, mainly elderly Indian men, continued to argue over the marital status of don Francisco and doña Francisca Ruray at the birth of various children, all agreeing that Magdalena's status as bastard entirely disqualified her from inheritance. On the other hand, Magdalena Mallao's witnesses, Spanish and mestiza women and a handful of Indians, testified as to their knowledge of the existence of the will and its validity. Friends and relatives of the late priest whose signature was on the document verified his handwriting and the fact that they had heard him speak of it or had even seen it.

In the end, the high court failed to overturn the findings of the lower, and awarded possession of the house to Magdalena Mallao. The frankly unbelievable story of a will made by a nine-year-old girl and secreted for forty years triumphed over the machinations of the local indigenous elite. While it is impossible to say with certainty why some strategies succeeded and others did not, the documentation offers some interesting possibilities to us. What seems to have been a familial conflict actually spilled out beyond those boundaries, and it is likely that it was the interventions of Spanish society that won Magdalena Mallao her house.

While local Indian officials had recognized doña Francisca Ayra as the possessor of the land and house, and she clearly had the weight of her husband's and uncle's status in indigenous society behind her, either she failed to involve the non-Indian power structure in her case or she received no support from it. On the other hand, Magdalena Mallao had a mestiza daughter with whom she was sharing the disputed house. Her witnesses included a "mestiza dressed like an Indian," the niece of the Spanish priest who witnessed doña Leonor's will, a master blacksmith, and the town councilman and his sister. Their testimony centered on gossip heard in Spanish households, which established public knowledge of the will and inheritance. Although the legal character of the will of a child (girls under the age of twelve were explicitly prohibited from testating)[75] should have been questionable, and the particulars of its rhetorical style and its sudden appearance strongly suggest it was faked, the authorization of a Spanish priest and the public discourse of the Spanish community validated it. The attempt to invoke indigenous authority at the same time, Leonor's claim to be cacica upon her father's death, was never challenged and only served to underscore the role of the successful narrative in supporting this rather political agenda.

Magdalena Mallao's story is not, of course, the triumph of prehispanic gender parallelism over European law, but neither is it clearly the converse. Instead, her victory stemmed from her (and her lawyer's) ability to manage multiple discourses in the colonial arena, appealing to beliefs about indigenous tradition within a legal context that supported particular types of narratives. Her situation seems to have hinged in great part on her own navigation of mestizo and Spanish urban societies, rather than within her own ethnic community. In the end, the meaning of these victories is that individuals—male, female, Spaniard, Indian—were rapidly becoming adept at managing the new rules, and in fact were participating in their creation. The success of someone like doña Francisca Canapaynina in Nariguala in 1610 led indirectly to the ability of future generations of women and men to claim that "indigenous tradition" supported their own accession to power.

Conclusion:
Gender, Ethnicity, and Other Identities in Early Colonial Peru

IN THE PRECEDING CHAPTERS, each introduced by vignettes culled from colonial archives, we have seen the development of colonial Andean society through the eyes of a diverse group of Indian women, rural and urban, elite and plebeian, successful and more marginal. Rather than begin with a fixed definition and associated expectations—of gender, ethnicity, or class—I have chosen to think through these women's particular choices in their rapidly changing environments. Choices are not always deliberate, but they do represent individual interactions within an institutional environment and the process by which subjects learn the rules of the game, in this case, of life under Spanish occupation and colonization.

Raymond Williams has called "structures of feeling" those "characteristic elements of impulse, restraint, and tone; specifically, affective elements of unconsciousness and relationships; not feeling against thought, but thought as felt and feeling as thought; practical consciousness of a present kind, in a living and interrelated continuity." These elements reflect individuals' interactions with their institutional and natural environments and represent the particular experience of living in a certain time and place. Williams's goal, with this phrase, is to open up the process of history rather than analyze a set of already-formed institutions, the "reduction of the social to fixed forms."[1]

In that vein, in these chapters I have tried to accomplish two tasks. First, I have sought to understand that process of institutional formation that became "colonial society." From the tributary economy to colonial law to religious organizations, I have charted these institutions as they emerged from contact and conquest and came to be the bulwarks of everyday life, the "fixed forms." But I have also tried to elucidate some of the experience of daily existence within these forming institutions, Williams's "structures of feelings," by thinking through how Andean men and especially women experienced shifts in labor and culture over the first century of colonial rule.

For the indigenous peoples who "encountered" Spanish colonialism beginning in the sixteenth century, life was to be characterized by a series of important changes, though these were not necessarily experienced as total breaks with the past. These changes took place on all levels—they were certainly political, as new governing elites emerged and older ones had to fight to retain their legitimacy; they were economic, as transatlantic and regional markets penetrated even small, rural communities with new demands for production and new consumer commodities for purchase. Although political economy and labor have been at the center of analysis in this study, other aspects of colonial life have also come into focus. We have seen slow changes in the religio-political sphere, as the Catholic Church first attempted to legislate conversion and then acquiesced to the particularities of an Andean Church, which gained wealth and power as it slowly picked up converts. And there were extensive cultural transformations, not the least of which was the creation of the new category of *Indian* and the centuries of debate over what that meant to the various ethnic groups and classes elided by this term.

As we have seen, indigenous communities responded to the challenges of colonialism with vigor and invention, despite the terrible collapse of populations due to war, disease, and overwork. Residents of rural communities who found themselves confronted by a quota-based tribute (rather than the Inca labor-time system) adapted their practices to meet two or three annual demands for new and common products, and the gender division of labor shifted as widows became the major producers in many communities. Andean men and women quickly learned the new language of markets and wage labor, and, sometimes led by their caciques and sometimes not, used these to make demands upon their new rulers.

Monetization was another side effect of colonial rule. Not only did the growing demand of encomenderos and corregidores for tribute in cash, toward the end of the sixteenth century, teach Andeans that silver and gold were to be the major concerns of colonial rule, but the availability of a whole new range of consumer goods, with status-enhancing properties, led them to seek wage labor or putting-out arrangements. The privatization of property also had serious ramifications for rural as well as urban life. As Spaniards encroached upon rural property, and as caciques sold off community lands or had them removed from their power by bureaucrats "recomposing" property regimes, nonelite Andeans also learned of the value of staking personal claims to land, even in regions where property had not been fixed in individuals prior to the conquest. This marketization and monetization were also part of the circumstances that led individuals and families to migrate to urban centers, where wages beckoned and where it was more difficult to round up tributaries for their regular contributions. And though they fled their tributary status, many men and women retained ties to their natal communities and some even continued to own property there, still lessening the hold of caciques on the integrity of their communities.

Given the scarcity of circulating coin in the early years, credit also became an important aspect of colonial life. The most elite were able to arrange loans from larger institutions, like the few private banks that sprang up and the many convents and religious organizations that were rapidly becoming the colony's major propertyholders. But nonelites also needed funds, albeit smaller amounts, and they turned to each other, and to their own religious organizations, the cofradías, which aided in the construction of new communities with colonial identities: Andean, Christian, and increasingly urban.

Although the vast majority of the indigenous population remained in rural regions (though not always within their natal communities, since migration between rural areas was also common), rural elites experienced a diminution of their power. Colonization meant that ultimate power was theoretically vested in the Spanish Crown and its representatives, and local circumstances often meant that corrupt Spaniards inserted themselves even in the aspects of political rule that were legally reserved for indigenous communities. The rise of the Catholic Church and the waves of extirpation of "idolatry," as the Church called non-Christian religious and spiritual practices, meant that religious leaders—often also caciques—lost their public standing and would have to change their practices to survive, moving rituals underground, camouflaging them through syncretism, or converting. Communities recognized this too, sometimes banding with their elites to contest exploitation and corruption in the courts. But in many situations, Andean peasants learned to bypass their own elites, who were increasingly beholden to Spanish officials and merchants and therefore powerless to defend their subjects. Instead, as in the case of the unpaid women weavers of the Lupaqa, they appealed directly to corregidores, judges and visitadores, sometimes to their advantage but other times to little avail. But many more simply saw the new routes to (limited) power—migration, wage labor, the legal system, the Catholic Church— and tried their fortunes. The wills analyzed in this study are evidence that a small but significant group succeeded by these standards. But they do not tell us that older practices and beliefs were wiped out, only that Andeans adapted culturally to meet their new environment and thus transformed colonial culture overall.

These particular forms of colonization had deep effects on gender relations and identities. As we have seen, men and women sometimes experienced colonization differently. Different types of demands were made upon them, resulting from the conjunction of Iberian-Christian ideologies, the organization of the societies in which they lived prior to the conquest, tragic demographic patterns that left women as majorities in many rural communities but minorities as immigrants to urban centers, and miscommunications and misperceptions on the part of those in power. For these reasons, gender identities also developed differentially across regions. Colonial law saw plebeian Indian women as a homogeneous category (elites always enjoyed their own privileges) but local conditions meant that women might have vastly divergent experiences.

Women who migrated to cities, in search of better circumstances or under less voluntary conditions, also found themselves with gender-specific challenges. Our sources indicate that few women found a single occupation that would serve them over a lifetime; instead their weeks were filled with multiple activities: serving a master for wages while selling market goods on the side; selling in the market and renting rooms from their house; or acting as farmer, marketeer, and manager of a family agricultural operation. Men, through apprenticeships, might be channeled into a career; women had less access to these more steady employments and instead cobbled together a living from many sources. And there are many sources of income that we cannot learn much about from wills, informal and often illegal activities, such as healing, petty theft, and prostitution, which men and women certainly engaged in as main or side employments.

Men and women both learned to utilize the legal system to serve their particular needs and expectations. The remarkable fact that so many plebeian men and women left wills tells us that a large number found solace in the Catholic Church, purchasing its comforting rituals with alms, but they also utilized these documents to define and protect their perceived rights within the colonial order. Women in particular seem to have found wills helpful in resolving familial conflicts, especially when they were widowed or had illegitimate children. Men, at least in the two cities studied here, were more likely to use their wills to provide for "official" families; if they had illegitimate children, we are less likely to learn it from these documents. Women also overwhelmingly used their resources to provide for their own and their families' passage out of purgatory; this difference in the form of religious participation (for men were no less active in cofradías or Catholicism in general) may be the basis for the popular, if misplaced, sense that indigenous women were faster and better converts to Christianity.

But the similarities between the experiences of Indian men and women under colonial rule were also striking. The rapid acquiescence to and even embrace of the wage-labor system by a small minority (those who saw it as a relief from the encomienda system and its unrelenting demands) was common to men and women, even if their routes to the city were somewhat different. Men and women alike claimed the new labels of "criollo" and "solarero," consciously enjoying their relative prestige in this emerging society. And their use of the courts to create social roles, here illustrated by the machinations of elite women to hold cacicazgos, showed no preference for men or women, though their tactics might have taken different forms depending upon gender.

Contestations over gender roles and their symbolic as well as productive value continue into the present. The roles that men and women acquired through historical contestation have often hardened to appear "traditional." Our access to the preconquest past is mainly through colonial-era documents, which are not easily read for precontact content, thus even if we wanted to freeze gender roles to a particular moment and place as "traditional," we would be hard-pressed to provide clear evidence.[2] But the period prior to the Spanish conquest remains symbolically powerful, and the ability to trace practices to a precontact moment carries a great deal of weight. In particular, the singular association of women with low-tech weaving, shown here to be a colonial construction, deepened to the point where a prominent feminist ethnohistorian can assert in a timeless way that "women were the weavers of Andean society . . . Andean gender norms [designated] weaving as the quintessential female activity."[3] Of course, where such weaving was well remunerated, it was (and remains) likely to be performed by men.[4]

What has, perhaps, been most novel in this journey through the first century of colonialism is a glimpse into the invention of new identities, or modes of relating, on the part of subalterns. Iberian policy congregated the innumerable ayllus and political communities under the rubric of "Indians," producing a juridical identity that was deployed not only by the Spanish Crown but by those who saw its legal benefits, including indigenous men and women themselves. But "Indian" did not fulfill all the needs of colonized indigenous peoples. They retained (and still do, in many places) their prehispanic group affiliations, including historic rivalries and alliances.[5] But they also invented new ways to distinguish themselves: they became caciques and cacicas, under colonial definitions; pallas and Incas, reaching into the Cuzqueño past; don and doñas, utilizing the terms of the Spanish nobility; solareros or even vecinos, property owners in urban centers; ladinos, whose command of the Spanish language afforded them an intermediary role; indios criollos, or men and women whose natal ties were to cities and colonial culture rather than to rural communities.

This vocabulary was heteroglossic; words shifted meanings depending upon who was speaking. As we have seen, "criollo" is perhaps the most concrete example of this, where it could refer to an African born into slavery in the Americas or one who had acquired the language and religious practices of his or her master; a man or woman of Spanish descent born in the colonies rather than in more prestigious Iberia; or it could mean an indigenous subject exempt from tribute, raised in a city, brought up speaking Spanish, attending the Catholic Church, and dressing in an identifiably urban style. "Indianness," in all these highly particular senses, was an idea worked out by indigenous peoples in cities as well as in rural communities; it may be the case that urban centers, with many immigrant groups in close proximity, were the places where producing and determining identity was most compelling. But our evidence for the ongoing communications between rural and urban communities—through kin networks as well as the encroachment of Spanish institutions and peoples, including notaries, the Church, and the visitas—means that changes in one region probably bled rapidly into others. The vitality of this language of belonging, its permutations in the documentary record, suggests that many groups of people needed to articulate their perceived places in this new society.

These terminologies apparently had much more power for colonial subjects than the "ethnic" categories that were basic to colonial administration: Spaniards, Indians, blacks, mestizos, and the various permutations that eventually resulted. The fluidity and ambiguity of ethnic designations were a source of irritation to governors, "misdressed" subjects or those who otherwise rejected or ignored their juridical place posed problems for tribute collection, the imposition of justice, and the simple attempts of bureaucrats to describe and count their populations. But neither did the Crown settle upon a simple way to distinguish its subjects. Elites and plebeians received differential treatment, confusing the social order, and mixed groups, the castas and especially mestizos, were the topic of constant legal revisionism. Rather than a postenlightenment scientific racism, based upon supposed biological characteristics, as would be seen in the nineteenth and twentieth centuries in Peru, ethnicity was a slippery concept, defined culturally for the most part, but with deep suspicion that visual cues were not always revelatory of the truth. In this sense, ethnic identity in colonial Latin America shared its basis with notions of religious difference exercised in Iberia in the centuries before Columbus's expeditions. There, conversion from Islam and Judaism was encouraged (or required, depending upon the period and place), but the converted were also subject to suspicion of reversion, even generations after the initial conversion. The complicated mixture of discourses of blood with those of culture produced ambiguity, fluidity, and distrust.

Later in the colonial period, and even more so in the nineteenth and twentieth centuries, intellectuals and politicians would argue over the meaning of these suspect categories: was phenotype a marker of intelligence and thus the possibility of progress and modernity? Was culture rather the source of group traits, such that a certain form of education could "breed out" the embarrassing aspects of poverty and "backwardness"? Was "purity" preferable to *mestizaje*, or vice versa?[6] But the interrelatedness of blood and culture were already being questioned in the sixteenth century, and the political dangers of ambiguity led policy makers to urge more fixed and eventually racialist definitions.

Symbols of modernity and "Indianness" thus remain part of a continuing political and cultural dialogue in the Andes. During the colonial period, indigenous elites would fight for the right to use the insignias of Inca power, like the *mascapaicha*, in public representations of elite legitimacy, including religious processions and literary works. In the twentieth century, *indigenista* intellectuals donned "Indian" *ojota* sandals and

chullo knit caps, opposing the elite project of turning Indians into mestizos through educational projects in favor of maintaining their "Indianness" while empowering them with literacy.[7] These were part of an
ongoing dialogue over the meaning of modernity in a postcolonial society where the majority remained impoverished and disempowered.

In conclusion, this study contributes to our knowledge of both the
past and the present by demonstrating that the early colonial period was
a fluid and ambiguous place, not easily divided into separable resisting
and accommodating factions. Clearly the radical demographic changes—
the importation of African slaves as well as the migratory patterns of
diverse groups of Iberians and indigenous men and women—contributed to that flexibility. Lima and Trujillo, because they were coastal
settlements and thus did not have the indigenous majorities enjoyed by
Cuzco and Potosí, had exceptional patterns of coexistence and dependence. Examining their histories through the lens of gender has enabled
us to place the aspirations and choices of indigenous men and women at
the center of the construction of colonial society.

REFERENCE MATTER

Notes

1. "Testamento de Francisca Ramírez," Archivo Regional de La Libertad (hereafter ARLL) Protocolos Notariales (hereafter PN) Alvarez 84 (1653) f. 144.

2. "Testamento de Francisca Ramírez," ARLL PN Escobar 136 (1633); ARLL PN Salina 238 (1686) f. 201.

3. Archivo General de la Nación, Lima (hereafter AGN) Real Hacienda—Trujillo, leg. 1295 c. 2 (1637–1641).

4. The Catholic Church allowed divorce in certain cases, for example serious physical abuse or the mismanagement of dowry funds. Such a divorce is better termed a permanent separation; the partners could live apart but neither could remarry while the other lived. The archives do not inform us whether Ramírez's petition succeeded, but few did. See Arrom, *Women of Mexico City*, chapter 5.

5. Rostworowski de Diez Canseco, *Curacas y sucesiones*. For an appraisal of her contributions, see van Deusen, "An Interview with María Rostworowski."

6. An ethnohistoric approach has been more popular with historians of early Mexico, as seen in the contributions to the volume *Indian Women of Early Mexico*, ed. Schroeder, Wood, and Haskett. This may reflect the larger number of early colonial indigenous texts, like the codices, that appear to offer more of an indigenous perspective (although this too is a controversial position). Prehispanic gender studies can, of course, run to stereotypes and gendered assumptions; in contrast see the excellent collection edited by Klein, *Gender in Pre-Hispanic America*.

7. Silverblatt's recent work takes a more poststructuralist approach to questions of gender and ethnicity that still argues for the connection between social structures and cultural constructions; see, for example, her "Lessons of Gender and Ethnohistory in Mesoamerica."

8. Burkett, "Indian Women and White Society," and also her dissertation, "Early Colonial Peru."

9. For critiques, see Zulawski, "Social Differentiation, Gender, and Ethnicity"; and Glave, "Mujer indígena," 305–62.

10. Powers, "Conquering Discourses of 'Sexual Conquest.'"

11. Zulawski, "Social Differentiation," 95.

12. For example, Mangan, *Trading Roles*; Gauderman, *Women's Lives in Colonial Quito*.

13. Lewis, *Hall of Mirrors*.

14. Few, *Women Who Live Evil Lives*.

15. For example, Sabean, *Power in the Blood*; Giles, ed., *Women in the Inquisition*; and Ginzburg, *The Cheese and the Worms*.

16. On these multiethnic social networks, see Osorio, "El callejón de la soledad."

17. Burns, *Colonial Habits*.

18. Cope, *The Limits of Racial Domination*. See also Lewis, *Hall of Mirrors*; Gauderman, *Women's Lives in Colonial Quito*; Few, *Women Who Live Evil Lives*; Seed, *To Love, Honor and Obey in Colonial Mexico*; and Cahill's critique of the determinist discussion of race in his "Colour by Numbers."

19. "Ethnicity" is clearly a problematic term, since there were (and continue to be) ethnic divisions and allegiances within the juridical category of "Indians" imposed by Spanish colonists, which were flattened by this term. But it remains preferable to "race," which carries too much postenlightenment, biological determinist baggage to be useful in this analysis of the early years of colonization. See the critiques by the authors listed in note 18 above; also see Silverblatt, "Becoming Indian."

20. Gauderman, *Women's Lives in Colonial Quito*, 4.

21. For example, Few, *Women Who Live Evil Lives*.

22. See Harvey, *Islamic Spain, 1250 to 1500*; García-Arenal, "Moriscos and Indians: A Comparative Approach"; Phillips and Phillips, "Spain in the Fifteenth Century."

23. See, for example, the 1518 "Real Poder para dar entera libertad a los indios que hubieren capacidad de vivir por si ordenadamente" published in Konetzske, *Colección de documentos* I, 69–70.

24. Conniff and Davis, *Africans in the Americas*, 114–6.

25. Important studies of the early viceroyalty of Peru (encompassing modern Bolivia and Ecuador) include Larson, *Cochabamba*; Powers, *Andean Journeys*; Spalding, *Huarochirí*; Stern, *Peru's Indian Peoples*; Trelles Aréstegui, *Lucas Martínez Vegazo*; Varón Gabai, *Curacas y encomenderos*; Zulawski, *They Eat from Their Labor*.

26. Andrien, *Crisis and Decline*.

27. On the prehispanic form of the mita, see Spalding, *Huarochirí*, 82–91, and Pease, *Curacas, reciprocidad y riqueza*. The colonial reformulation of the Inca mita and its effects on local labor are described by Wightman, *Indigenous Migration and Social Change*.

28. See, for example, the essays in Larson and Harris, eds., *Ethnicity, Markets and Migration in the Andes.*

29. Konetzske, *Colección de documentos* I, 184, 187.

30. Fraser, *The Architecture of Conquest*, 74–75; Rostworowski, *Señoríos indígenas de Lima y Canta*, 49–55; Cabero, "El corregimiento de Saña," 345. The residents of Trujillo in 1575, according to Cabero, were classified as Spanish (1,017), *mestizos* (925), Indians (1,094) and Africans (1,073).

31. On the development of the gridded plan, see Fraser, *The Architecture of Conquest*, especially 1–20, 36–40. Phillip II's 1573 *ordenanzas*, promulgated much later than these foundings, but perhaps a representation of the idealized city plan, are published in Torres de Mendoza, *Colección de documentos inéditos relativos al descubrimiento*, tomo VIII: 484–537. On the public role of the plaza in Lima, see Osorio, "The King in Lima," 452–8. On the segregation of Lima's Indian population, to be discussed later in this chapter, see Lowry, "Forging an Indian Nation."

32. Fraser, *Architecture of Conquest*, 50.

33. Quoted in Saignes, "Indian Migration and Social Change in Seventeenth-Century Charcas," in Larson and Harris, eds., *Ethnicity, Markets and Migration in the Andes*, 167. At roughly the same time, the King of Spain called for an opinion from the *Real Audiencia* of New Spain as to whether it might be suitable for Indians and Spaniards to live together. The answer was presumably "no," since orders continued to rule against this, e.g., in 1581. Konetzske, *Colección de documentos* I, 425, 535–6.

34. Zevallos Quiñones, *Los fundadores y primeros pobladores de Trujillo*, Tomo I, 11.

35. Lowry, "Forging an Indian Nation," chapter 3 describes the foundation and settlement of Lima at length. On Lima's founding see also Cobo, "Historia de la fundación de Lima"; Charney, "A Sense of Belonging"; and Fraser, *Architecture of Conquest*, 63. Bromley and Barbagelata describe the physical development of the city in their *Evolución urbana de la Ciudad de Lima*. On Trujillo, see Castañeda Murga, "Notas para una historia de la Ciudad de Trujillo"; Cabero, "El corregimiento de Saña"; and on Trujillo's early economy, Coleman, "Provincial Urban Problems: Trujillo, Peru, 1600–1784."

36. Rostworowski, *Señoríos indígenas de Lima y Canta*, 49–55, 84–86. Fraser, *Architecture of Conquest*, 74–75. The Lima Valley encomienda of Pizarro's mestiza daughter, doña Francisca Pizarro, had only ninety Indians according to a 1549 census. Rostworowski, "La tasa ordenada por el Licenciado Pedro de la Gasca (1549)," 331.

37. Population movement is now thought of as more strategic and less permanent in the colonial Andes. Wightman, *Indigenous Migration and Social Change*, discusses the relationship between migration and contract labor in Cuzco; Zulawski, *They Eat from Their Labor*, in Oruro. See also the distinction between Indians noted as absent on census records either with "whereabouts known" by the cacique, or "lost," in Powers, *Andean Journeys*, 11.

38. A detailed census of the Indian population of Lima was carried out in 1613 and part has been published as Contreras, *Padrón de los indios de Lima en*

1613; Charney, "El indio urbano"; Durán Montero, "Lima en 1613"; and Lowry, "Forging an Indian Nation." The entire population of Lima was also counted at this time; I have used here the numbers from Fray Buenaventura Salinas y Córdova's [1630] publication, *Memorial de las historias del nuevo mundo Peru.* Colonial Trujillo has no comparable documentary record, but Romero, "Fragmento de una historia de Trujillo," is a piece of a summary report on the population and socioeconomic life of that city in the first decade of the seventeenth century; Castañeda Murga, "Notas para una historia de la Ciudad de Trujillo," brings together various archival sources in his brief history. Ironically, demographic data is easier to come by (although it is just as untrustworthy) for rural areas, where the Indian population was constantly counted and recounted in order to justify and contest tribute and labor demands. See Guevara-Gil and Salomon, "A 'Personal Visit.'"

39. Lowry, "Forging an Indian Nation," and Bromley and Barbagelata, *Evolución urbana de la Ciudad de Lima* have reconstructed the spatial plans of colonial Lima in marvelous detail.

40. See Charney, "El indio urbano"; Durán, "Lima en 1613"; Vergara Ormeño, "Migración y trabajo femenino"; and Osorio, "El callejón de la soledad." Durán's analysis of the census provides us with an example of an Indian apprenticed to a silversmith, an occupation supposedly reserved for Spaniards. Durán, "Lima en 1613," 13. On the multiethnic convents of Cuzco, where there were even mestiza nuns, see Burns, *Colonial Habits*, chapter 1.

41. *Actas del Cabildo de Trujillo*, Tomo I, 127–8, 150. This appears not to be a sole exception in the early colonial period, though achieving citizenship was uncommon for all ethnic groups. Nearly a century later, in 1631, Sebastian Rodriguez, the illegitimate son of a free black man and an Indian woman, called himself vecino in his will. "Testamento de Sebastián Rodriguez," ARLL PN Paz 199 (1631) f. 325. See also Chapter 2 of this study.

42. Ramírez, *Provincial Patriarchs*, 63–64; Huertas, "Fundación de la Villa de Santiago de Miraflores de Zaña; Cabero, "El corregimiento de Saña."

43. Mannarelli, *Pecados públicos*; Osorio, "El callejón de la soledad"; and Lowry, "Forging an Indian Nation," 125–8, 199.

44. By the late sixteenth century, political citizens in Trujillo were either *vecinos-feudatorios* (encomenderos) or *vecinos-ciudadanos* (property owners who were not encomenderos). The remaining individuals, who could not serve in political office, were *residentes* or *moradores*, nonowning residents (Ramírez, *Provincial Patriarchs*, 410).

45. Noack, "La diversidad cultural de la ciudad colonial"; Castañeda Murga, "Organización espacial y socioétnica de la ciudad de Trujillo."

46. Quoted in Castañeda Murga, "Notas para una historia de la Ciudad de Trujillo," 165.

47. ARLL Cabildo Causas Criminales (hereafter CCr) leg. 77 exp. 1281 (1606).

48. Contreras, *Padrón de los indios de Lima*, 251–3. Osorio, "El callejón de la soledad," looks at the multiethnic *callejones*.

49. Durán, "Lima en 1613."

50. On hybridity and the problems of this term for colonial history, see Young, *Colonial Desire* and García Canclini, *Hybrid Cultures*.

51. Ortíz, *Contrapunteo cubano del tabaco y el azúcar*. See also Pratt, *Imperial Eyes*.

52. See Dean and Leibsohn, "Hybridity and Its Discontents."

53. For an overview, see the essays in Buisseret and Reinhardt, eds., *Creolization in the Americas*, especially the introduction by Buisseret and the essay by Rath.

54. "Criollo," *Diccionario Real de la Lengua Española*.

55. *Criollo* may have been a word used by the African community itself, to differentiate between the generations marked by slavery, or it may have been imposed by slave traders exploiting stereotypes about the dispositions of their human chattel. See Burns, "Unfixing 'Race.'"

56. O'Toole, "Inventing Difference," 28.

57. My use of "creole" here partly parallels Barragán's "cultural mestizos," individuals who were at least partially estranged from corporate Indian society and by their appearance and activities participated in the hybrid urban world. However, attaching the adjective "cultural" to a supposedly biological term like *mestizo* puts us in the position of determining "real" and "false" *mestizajes*; for this reason I prefer transculturation and creolization. Barragán, "Entre polleras, lliqllas y ñañacas."

58. See, on this question, the essays in Kellogg and Restall, eds., *Dead Giveaways*, especially the essay by Cline on model testaments; and also Burns, "Notaries, Truth, and Consequences."

59. On population decline and gender in rural Peru, see Cook, *Demographic Collapse* and Wachtel, *The Vision of the Vanquished*.

CHAPTER 1

1. According to the local notary, there were contracts with nine Spaniards over a twenty-month period, accounting for over 4,000 sets of clothing, for which the caciques received two pesos per set. Currency during this period is notoriously difficult to evaluate, since there were at least three concurrent conceptual systems: the peso of eight reales (also called a *patacón*), the peso *corriente* of nine reales, and the peso *ensayado* of twelve or thirteen reales. The *tomín* either equalled one real or a half a real (Ramírez, *Provincial Patriarchs*, appendix 1).

2. Díez, *Visita hecha a la provincia de Chucuito*, 62, 217.

3. On reciprocity in the prehispanic Andes, and the production of cloth in particular, see Pease, *Curacas, reciprocidad y riqueza*; and Murra, "Cloth and its Function in the Inka State."

4. See, for example, Lockhart, "Trunk Lines and Feeder Lines," and Assadourian, *El sistema de la economía colonial*.

5. Zevallos Quiñones, "La ropa tributo."

6. Wachtel, *The Vision of the Vanquished*; Stern, *Peru's Indian Peoples*; Spalding, *Huarochirí*; Larson, *Cochabamba*; Varón, *Curacas y encomenderos*; Trelles, *Lucas Martínez Vegazo*.

7. Ramírez, *The World Upside Down*; Spalding, "Kurakas and Commerce"; Powers, *Andean Journeys*.

8. The introduction of credit among the Indians was much decried both by Lupaqas and Spaniards. According to informants, local European merchants were making coca, wine, and Spanish clothing easily available on credit at inflated prices, and when the Indians (especially nobles) could not pay, they collected in cattle or labor. See Díez, *Visita hecha a la provincia de Chucuito*, 48–49, 59, 83–84, and the discussion in Assadourian, *Transiciones hacia el sistema colonial andina*.

9. Adult women greatly outnumbered adult men in many of the tribute censuses; see the tables in Cook, "Population Data for Indian Peru." This could reflect any of a number of phenomena: higher mortality rates for men due to differential patterns of disease, work, and warfare; migration patterns; but also the successful hiding of male tributaries by communities in the hopes of reducing tribute payments.

10. Tribute was assessed upon married males, thus presumably encompassing the labor of wives and children, but tributary rolls often registered only male "heads of household."

11. For rural Mexico, see especially the articles in Schroeder, Wood, and Haskett, eds., *Indian Women of Early Mexico*; Kellogg, *Law and the Transformation of Aztec Culture*; and Cline, *Colonial Culhuacán*. On weaving and gender specifically, see Villanueva, "From Calpixqui to Corregidor."

12. Zulawski, "Social Differentiation, Gender, and Ethnicity," 95.

13. Honeyman and Goodman, "Women's work, gender conflict, and labour markets." Seville's silk-weavers guild admitted both male and female members—women often entered as widows of an artisan; after a year's grace period she had to submit her work to the guild in order to gain permanent admission; even so, women generally were prevented from becoming master weavers. Perry, *Gender and Disorder*, 16–17.

14. Cobo, *History of the Inca Empire*, 30.

15. On the "feminization" of the Indian, see Lewis, *Hall of Mirrors*, chapters 2 and 5. On gender complementarity in the Andes see Silverblatt, *Moon, Sun, and Witches*.

16. Díez, *Visita hecha a la provincia de Chucuito*, 70; Ortiz de Zúñiga, *Visita de la provincia de León de Huánuco*.

17. For example, Morris and Thompson, *Huánuco Pampa*, 70, 91.

18. On Inca textiles see Murra, "Cloth and Its Function in the Inka State"; Vanstan, "Did Inca Weavers Use an Upright Loom?"; Rowe, "Inca Culture at the Time of the Spanish Conquest."

19. Much writing on the acllas depends too literally on Spanish chroniclers and their assumptions about virginity, convents, and Roman vestal virgins. For an overview, see two articles by Alberti Manzanares, "Una insti-

tución exclusivamente femenina en la época incaica: las acllacuna," and "Mujer y religión: Vestales y Acllacuna, dos instituciones religiosas de mujeres." See also Graubart, "Indecent Living"; Rostworowski, "La mujer en el Perú prehispánico"; Silverblatt, *Moon, Sun, and Witches*; and an important argument from textile evidence in Gisbert, Arze, and Cajías, *Arte textil y mundo andino*, 300.

20. Donnan, *Moche Art of Peru*, 65. This pot has sometimes been described as showing only women weavers, but the iconography appears to indicate men as well as women.

21. Paul, "Paracas Necrópolis Bundle 89," 218.

22. I use here the common Quechua names, which appear most often in records in Lima and Trujillo. The masterful work on Andean textiles is Gisbert et al., *Arte textil y mundo andino*. See Chapter Four below for more discussion of the forms and names of tributary clothing.

23. Ortiz de Zúñiga, *Visita a la provincia de León de Huánuco*, 38.

24. Díez, *Visita hecha a la provincia de Chucuito*, 46. Paul estimates the labor time for embroidered Paracas funerary garments of varying qualities as ranging from about 168 hours per square meter to 628 hours per square meter. These garments, woven approximately 1,500 years before the Spanish conquest, were far more ceremonial and labor intensive than tributary cloth was likely to be. Paul, "Paracas Necrópolis Bundle 89," 176.

25. Niles, "Artist and Empire in Inca and Colonial Textiles," 52.

26. Rostworowski, "Algunos comentarios hechos a las ordenanzas del Doctor Cuenca," 149; Espinoza Soriano, "El valle de Jayanca," 262.

27. Díez, *Visita hecha a la provincia de Chucuito*, 70, 216.

28. Díez, *Visita hecha a la provincia de Chucuito*, 199.

29. This was likewise true in Mexico, where women were the main weaving specialists prior to the Spanish conquest. However, women were already the primary weavers in Aztec Mexico, and they were also accustomed to weaving both for tribute and for markets. Villanueva, "From Calpixqui to Corregidor," 21.

30. Rostworowski, "Algunos comentarios," 141, 153.

31. Estete, *El descubrimiento y la conquista del Perú*, 31–32.

32. *Relación de la religión y ritos del Perú hecha por los padres agustinos*, 11.

33. Pizarro, *Relación del descubrimiento*, 112.

34. Montesinos, *Memorias antiguas historiales del Perú*, 32.

35. Cobo, *History of the Inca Empire*, 206.

36. Dean, *Inka Bodies and the Body of Christ*, chapter 6.

37. Guaman Poma de Ayala, *El primer nueva corónica*, 692.

38. Guaman Poma de Ayala, *El primer nueva corónica*, 707.

39. Colón, *Los cuatro viajes*, 62, 125.

40. See, for example, Bartra, *The Wildman in the Looking Glass*; Greenblatt, *Marvellous Possessions*; and Pagden, *The Fall of Natural Man*.

41. Rostworowski, "Algunos comentarios," 147.

42. Matienzo, *Gobierno del Perú*, 68–71.

43. Matienzo, *Gobierno del Perú*, 69–70.

44. "Testamento de don Pedro Anco Guaman," ARLL PN 41 Obregón, reg. 6 [1594] f. 259; Zevallos Quiñones, *Los cacicazgos de Trujillo*, 17–18.

45. Guaman Poma de Ayala, *El primer nueva corónica*, 873.

46. Garcilaso de la Vega, *Royal Commentaries of the Incas*, 38.

47. Spalding, *Huarochirí*, 134.

48. Zevallos Quiñones, "La ropa tributo," 108.

49. Quoted in Zevallos Quiñones, "La ropa tributo," 109.

50. See particularly Matienzo, *Gobierno del Perú*, 42–43.

51. Rostworowski, *Ensayos de historia andina*, 438–9.

52. Spalding, *Huarochirí*, chapters 5 and 6, for perhaps the best example. See also Ramírez, *The World Upside Down*.

53. Ramírez, *The World Upside Down*, 105. On the political background to La Gasca's reforms, see Assadourian, *Transiciones hacia el sistema colonial andina*.

54. Ramírez, *The World Upside Down*, 109–10.

55. On Toledo's reforms, see Spalding, *Huarochirí*, 162.

56. Romero, "Fragmento de una historia de Trujillo," 89.

57. ARLL Corr CO leg 148 exp 69 [1566].

58. Ramírez, *The World Upside Down*, 35.

59. AGN DI leg 3 c 37 [1594].

60. "Compañía," ARLL PN 33 Muñoz [1575].

61. ARLL PN Mata 8 reg 5 [1565] f 233v; reg 2 [1565] f. 66.

62. ARLL CO leg 149 exp 90 [1569].

63. Cabero, "El corregimiento de Saña," 497.

64. Zevallos Quiñones, "La ropa tributo," 112–13.

65. Ramírez, *Provincial Patriarchs*, 82–83.

66. ARLL PN Mata 11 [1570] f. 402.

67. ARLL PN Mata 16 [1582] f. 45.

68. Matienzo, *Gobierno del Perú*, 94–95.

69. Anónimo Judío Portugués [Pedro León Portocarrero], *Descripción del virreinato del Perú*, 58.

70. On the development of obrajes, see Escandell-Tur, *Producción y comercio de tejidos coloniales*.

71. Quoted in Málaga Medina, "El Virrey Don Francisco de Toledo y la reglamentación del tributo," 613–14.

72. On changes in *cacicazgos* on the northern coast in this period, see Ramírez, *The World Upside Down* as well as Chapter 5 below.

73. Spalding, "*Kurakas* and Commerce," 587.

74. Rostworowski, "Algunos comentarios," 141.

75. Zevallos Quiñones, "La ropa tributo," 115.

76. ARLL PN Muñoz Ternero 32 reg 2 [1574] f.106.

77. Lisson Chaves, ed., *La iglesia de España en el Perú*, Vol II, 357; AGI Justicia 455–7.

78. Díez, *Visita hecha a la provincia de Chucuito*, 197–8. It was common for churches to be decorated with expensive, imported goods, donated by the community or wealthy individuals. According to a document from 1600, the

church of Santa María de la Parilla on the north coast contained ornamental curtains, habits, and coverings made of damasks from the Far East and Spain, brocades, silks, French *ruán*, taffetas, and other luxurious textiles (AAL Papeles Importantes 19A:1A [1600]).

79. Díez, *Visita hecha a la provincia de Chucuito*, 198, 121.

80. AGN JR leg 2 c 5 [1582].

81. ARLL PN Vega 75 [1583] f. 39v.

82. AGN JR leg 2 c 5 [1582] f. 220.

83. ARLL PN Mata 12 [1571] f.113v.

84. The resale of tributed or expropriated goods to their original indigenous owners was common. The Indians of Lucas Martínez Vegazo's encomienda bought back 35 percent of the llamas they paid in tribute, at a price higher than market value in nearby Potosí (Trelles, *Lucas Martínez Vegazo*, 207–8); the resale of expropriated lands to Indians at inflated prices is detailed by Spalding, *Huarochirí*, 179–81 and Ramírez, *Provincial Patriarchs*, 79.

85. Small, informal contracts were not uncommon, nor necessarily coerced. In her 1574 will, Isabel Pacho, the wife of encomendero Melchior de Osorno, left small bequests to the Indians of the repartimiento of Ferriñafe because they "had given me some gifts of clothing . . . and thread . . . apart from that which they are obligated to give us" (ARLL PN Muñoz Ternero 32 [1574] f. 105). The word *gifts* may reflect doña Isabel's sense of noblesse oblige rather than the absence of coercion.

86. AGN JR leg 22 c 57 [1611] f. 175.

87. AGN JR leg 22 c 57 [1611].

88. Hampe Martínez, "Sobre encomenderos y repartimientos de la diócesis de Lima," 127–30. Female ownership was not associated with low rents, as three of the highest-rent encomiendas in 1601 belonged to Jordana Mejía (Cajamarca), Lucía de Montenegro (Andajes y Atavillos), and Beatriz Marriquí (Huarochirí).

89. Romero, "Libro de la visita general," 159–60.

90. Romero, "Fragmento de una historia de Trujillo," 97–99.

91. Ramírez, *Provincial Patriarchs*, 44.

92. Assadourian, *El sistema de la economía colonial*.

CHAPTER 2

1. "Testamento de Catalina Carua," AGN PN Tamayo 1856 [1635] f. 84v. Enslaved Africans were usually given a Christian baptismal name but also identified by a place name, often referring to the market where they were originally purchased by Europeans ("Sebastiana Folupa"). I use both "names" to identify enslaved persons in this study, reproducing the style of the archive for clarity.

2. No Quechua or Aymara wills have been found for this period, although native-language wills were made in colonial Mesoamerica. See Cline and León-Portilla, *The Testaments of Culhuacan*; Kellogg, *Law and the Transformation of Aztec Culture*; Terraciano, "Native Expressions of Piety in Mixtec Testaments."

3. Cline, "Fray Alonso de Molina's Model Testament."

4. A small number of wills take the form of any other notarial document ("Let all those who see this letter know that I Costanza Ticlla, wife of Pedro Payante yndio, native of Santiago de Surco of the ayllu Taulli, being ill in body but healthy of mind . . ." ["Testamento de Costanza Ticlla," AGN TI leg 1 (1596)]), but there were also gradients of religiosity in between, though urban Indian wills did not differ substantially from those of urban Africans or Spaniards. Mixtec-language wills in Oaxaca, in contrast, expressed Catholic piety in a more transculturated way. See Terraciano, "Native Expressions of Piety."

5. See Ramos, "Death, Conversion, and Identity in the Peruvian Andes." We must make room, of course, for syncretic beliefs as well as popular inter-pretations of Christian doctrine, although these are not easily discerned in Lima's and Trujillo's wills. See Burkhart, *The Slippery Earth*; MacCormack, *Religion in the Andes*; and Klor de Alva, "'Telling Lives.'"

6. Calculated from Charney, "El indio urbano," cuadro 4.

7. Wightman, *Indigenous Migration and Social Change*, 49–51.

8. Vergara Ormeño, "Migración y trabajo femenino," 136–7.

9. "Asiento de María Sanchez yndia," AGN PN Tamayo 1854 [1631] f. 253; "Asiento de Beatriz yndia," ARLL PN Jimeno 94 [1620] f. 206.

10. "Testamento de Catalina Chumbi," ARLL PN Muñoz Ternero 32 reg. 7 [1574] f. 355; "Testamento de Ysabel Yauri Saco," BNP A391 [1594].

11. And not all servants wanted a contract. Gaspar Zuazo, a lawyer in Tru-jillo, complained in 1576 of his servant, an *yndio yanacona*, that is, not a tribu-tary, who refused to sign an employment contract, "because he was not under anyone's control but very free, as he had always been." While some saw a legal contract as an enforceable protection, others might have seen it as an undesir-able bond. "Testamento de Gaspar Zuazo," ARLL PN folios sueltos [1576].

12. "Asiento de Juana María yndia," AGN PN Tamayo 1853 [1630] f. 99.

13. Monsalve, *Reducion de todo el Piru*, 7v.

14. In particular, see Zulawski, "Social Differentiation, Gender, and Ethnic-ity"; Burkett, "Indian Women and White Society"; and Glave, "Mujer indígena."

15. "Testamento de Catalina de Agüero," ARLL PN Mata 11 [1570] f. 42.

16. ARLL Corr CO leg 181 exp 968 [1633]. The wage demands appear exag-gerated next to extant labor contracts, which stipulated between ten and twenty patacones per year.

17. Glave, "Mujer indígena," 311.

18. Zulawski, "Social Differentiation."

19. "Testamento de Elvira Carua," ARLL PN Vega 80 [1588] f 146v.

20. "Testamento de Secilia de Abila," AGN PN Rodriguez de Torquemada 141 [1589].

21. "Testamento de Ysabel de Montenegro," AGN PN Rodríguez de Torque-mada 141 [1589] f. 714.

22. Glave, "Mujer indígena," 354–7.

23. "Donación," AGN PN de la Cueva 29 [1579] f. 193.

24. "Testamento de Ana Velazquez," AGN PN Pérez 131 [1579] f. 68.
25. Glave, "Mujer indígena," 338, see also Burkett, "Indian Women and White Society."
26. See Osorio, "El callejón de la soledad."
27. Saignes has argued that migration in the colonial Andes did not always entail rupture with natal communities: *Caciques, Tribute and Migration*, 16.
28. "Testamento de Catalina de Agüero," ARLL PN Mata 11 [1570] f. 42.
29. "Testamento de doña Mencia Balyde biuda," ARLL PN Mata 17[1584] f. 233.
30. "Testamento de María Henrriquez yndia": ARLL PN Paz 204 [1642]f 248v, ARLL PN Viera Gutiérrez 252 [1643] f 128, ARLL PN Viera Gutiérrez 257 [1650] f 47; "Testamento de Doña Gerónima de Bustamante," ARLL PN Paz 204 [1643] f 107; "Testamento de Juan de Castañeda Bustamante vezino," ARLL PN Paz 204 [1643] f 30.
31. "Testamento de Ana Velázquez," AGN PN Pérez 131 reg 2 [1579] ff 68-72v; "Testamento de Catalina," AGN PN Pérez 131 reg 10 [1579] f 470. On Indians owning slaves, see below.
32. Glave, "Mujer indígena," 338.
33. See the discussions in Garofalo, "The Ethno-Economy of Food, Drink, and Stimulants," and Mangan, *Trading Roles*.
34. Cited and translated in Lowry, "Forging an Indian Nation," 191.
35. "Testamento de Ynes Quispi," AGN PN Tamayo 1851 [1623] f.143.
36. Mangan, *Trading Roles*; Gauderman, *Women's Lives in Colonial Quito*; Garofalo, "The Ethno-Economy of Food, Drink, and Stimulants"; and Vergara Ormeño, "Migración y trabajo femenino."
37. For example, "Testamento de Barbola Guacha," AGN TI leg 1A [1616]; "Testamento de Francisca Yllay," AGN PN 1854 Tamayo 1854 [1631] f. 736.
38. Very few men's wills list a chichero; one exception is the will of Luis Mateo, who listed a complete apparatus except the bottles necessary to sell it; he did not list any outstanding debts for chicha. AGN PN Tamayo 1850 [1622] f. 939.
39. Garofalo, "Bebidas del Inca en copas coloniales," 175–7.
40. See Garofalo, "The Ethno-Economy of Food, Drink, and Stimulants," 115 for a description of the chicha-making process.
41. "Testamento de Lucía Holguín," AGN PN Gómez de Baeza 735 [1601] f. 502.
42. "Testamento de María Pazña," AGN TI leg 1A [1633].
43. "Testamento de Ysabel Carua Chumbi," AGN TI 1A [1628].
44. "Testamento de Juana Gómez," AGN PN Tamayo 1852 [1625] f. 478.
45. "Testamento de Francisca Yllay," AGN PN Tamayo 1843 [1631] f. 736.
46. "Testamento de Francisca Ramírez," ARLL PN Escobar 136 [1633]; ARLL PN Alvarez 84 esc. 81, f. 144 [1653]; ARLL PN Rentero 207 [1677] f. 119.
47. "Testamento de Juana López," ARLL PN Obregón 50 reg. 8 [1616] f. 264.
48. On curing and midwifery, see Osorio, "El callejón de la soledad"; Silverblatt, *Moon, Sun, and Witches*; and the articles in Millones and Lemlij, eds.,

En el nombre del Señor. Evidence for these discussions tends to come from idolatry trials; there are no extant records of idolatry trials in sixteenth-century
Trujillo at present except the case analyzed by Noack, "Hechicería y la negociación de una nueva sociedad urbana."

49. "Testamento de María Magdalena," AGN TI leg 1 [1639]; "Testamento
de Doña Juana de la Crus," AGN TI leg 1A [1684].

50. "Testamento de Ana Esteban," AAL Testamentos 47:5 [1645].

51. "Compañía," AGN PN de la Cueva 28 [1577] f 285.

52. "Testamento de Baltasar de los Reyes," AGN PN Tamayo 1850 [1620]
f. 183.

53. See also Mangan, *Trading Roles,* chapter 4.

54. "Testamento de Juliana de Mendoza," AGN PN Tamayo 1853[1630]
f. 324.

55. "Testamento de Catalina Chumbi," ARLL PN Obregon 44 [1574] f. 195.

56. "Testamento de Francisca Ana de la Magdalena," AGN TI leg 1A [1600];
"Testamento de Angelina de Albarado," ARLL PN Obregón 54 [1627] f 54v;
"Testamento de Juana," ARLL PN Mata 11 [1573] f 5v.

57. "Testamento de Diego Guaman," AGN PN Tamayo 1851 [1624] f 500;
"Declaración," AGN PN Tamayo 1854 [1631] f 250v. On colonial banking, see
Suárez, *Desafíos transatlánticos,* chapter 2 and her study of Juan de la Cueva,
Comercio y fraude en el Perú colonial.

58. Burns, *Colonial Habits.*

59. "Testamento de Luis Pérez," AGN PN Tamayo 1851 [1623] f. 75v.

60. "Testamento de Francisca Ramírez," ARLL PN Alvarez leg 84 esc 81
[1653] ff. 144–50.

61. This is especially contentious for the north coast, where some ethnohistorians and archaeologists have found what they consider to be evidence of
long-standing commercial activity. Rostworowski and Espinoza Soriano have
interpreted certain early colonial documents as expressing a prehispanic lineage for commercial trade in Chincha and on the north coast; Ramírez surveys
these and other materials and concludes that markets were a colonial artifact
but that prehispanic exchange took place in a number of modes, primarily as
long-distance trade overseen by ethnic lords. Rostworowski, *Costa peruana prehispánica;* Espinoza Soriano, *Artesanos, transacciones, monedas y formas de pago;*
Ramírez, "Un mercader . . . es un pescador," and her "Exchange and Markets
in the Sixteenth Century."

62. Spalding describes the mutual responsibilities inherent in ayllu membership in *Huarochirí,* 28–34. See also the discussion in Salomon's "Introduction" to Salomon and Urioste, eds., *The Huarochirí Manuscript,* 21–23.

63. This may have been a fiction repeated by chroniclers; certainly the notion that the Inca himself did such annual distributions was entirely fictive; at
most his role was to confirm communal order performatively. (Personal communication, Susan Ramírez, March 2005.)

64. Kellogg, *Law and the Transformation of Aztec Culture,* chapter 4; Cline,
Colonial Culhuacán, chapter 5.

65. On this, see Salles-Reese, "Las divergencias semióticas," 62.
66. *Actas del Cabildo de Trujillo*, vol. I, 150.
67. "Testamento de Magdalena Jiquil," ARLL PN Obregón 41 reg. 3 [1594] f. 89.
68. "Venta," ARLL PN Obregón 41 reg. 3 [1594] f. 84; "Testamento de Catalina Roman," ARLL PN Obregón 44 [1607] f. 145.
69. Ramírez, *Provincial Patriarchs*, 64–66.
70. ARLL Cabildo CO leg. 15, c. 299 [1607].
71. "Testamento de Lucia Cusi," AGN PN Tamayo 1851 [1624] f. 396.
72. "Testamento de María Magdalena de Urraco," ARLL PN Paz 198 [1627] f. 4v.
73. "Testamento de Francisca Chani," AGN TI leg 1 [1652].
74. Although don Hernando's name does not appear in the text, see Rostworowski, *Señoríos indígenas de Lima y Canta*, chapter 2, for similar stories of dispossessed caciques.
75. "Obligación de Juan de Castro a Luissa de Osorno yndia," ARLL PN Escobar 135 [1633] f 135.
76. "Testamento de Barbola," ARLL PN Juárez 82 reg 4 [1608] f. 4.
77. "Testamento de Ynes Tamayo," AGN PN Gómez Baeza 738 [1604] f. 560; "Declaración de Catalina Gualcum," AGN PN Arias Cortez 10 [1582] f. 267.
78. "Testamento de Ana Alli," AGN TI leg 1 [1616]. This was also the pattern followed by some cacicas, for example, the cacica of Huamán, in Trujillo, spoke of twelve *fanegadas* (the land needed to produce a fanega or bushel and a half of a crop) of land "which belonged to my parents and grandparents" that she left to her daughter, as "eldest and female" (ARLL PN Aguilar 284 [1692] f 581). See Chapter 5 for discussion of these special cases.
79. "Testamento de Barbola Guacha," AGN TI leg 1A [1616].
80. "Testamento de María Cayn," AGN TI leg 1A [1638].
81. "Testamento de Magdalena Picona," AGN PN Tamayo 1853 [1630] f. 833.
82. Foreign "Indians"—generally from other Spanish colonies—could under certain conditions be enslaved, and Chilean Indian slaves were fairly common in Peru. In 1630 Beatriz Magdalena, an Indian woman married to a master tailor, sold a female Indian slave, aged thirty and captured in a "just war" in Chile, to the Spanish bookkeeper Martín de Mayorga for 260 pesos in cash, through the Lima bank of Juan de la Cueva. Beatriz Magdalena had bought the Indian slave two years earlier from the merchant Pedro Ruiz de Aguila (AGN PN Tamayo 1853 [1630] f. 420v).
83. Barbagelata, "Desarrollo urbano de Lima," 65. Most, though not all, would have been slaves.
84. Bowser, *The African Slave in Colonial Peru*, 90–91. As Bowser notes, the attempt to end the agricultural mita (in expectation that Indians would freely contract for wage labor) was unsuccessful.
85. Bowser, *The African Slave*, 95.
86. Bowser, *The African Slave*, 80.
87. Bowser, *The African Slave*, 70.

88. "Testamento de Francisca Yllay," AGN PN Tamayo 1854 [1631] f. 736.
89. AGN DI leg 7 cuad 93 [1636] f. 151.
90. Published in Rostworowski, *Costa peruana prehispánica*, 194.
91. "Testamento de Juana Gómez," AGN PN Tamayo 1852 [1625] f. 478.
92. "Testamento de Ana Velazquez," AGN PN Pérez 130 reg 2 [1579] f. 68.
93. "Testamento de Catalina Payco," AGN PN Esquivel 33 [1575] f. 509; "Testamento de María de Jesús," AGN PN Jiménez 102 [1598] f 842.
94. "Testamento de doña Catalina Llacla," AGN PN Barrientos 181 [1606] f. 166; "Testamento de Mencia López," AGN PN Pérez 130 reg. 9 [1578] f. 439.
95. See Lowry, "Forging an Indian Nation," 151.
96. "Testamento de Juana López," ARLL PN Obregón 50 reg. 8 [1616] f. 264.
97. It is also possible that there were simply shortages of slaves on the north coast: Ramírez finds this to be true in the later seventeenth and early eighteenth centuries, *Provincial Patriarchs*, 161.
98. "Resivo de Don Carlos Chamo Chumbi," ARLL PN Obregon 64 [1617] f. 858v; "Testamento de Luissa Madalena," ARLL PN Obregon 64 [1617] f. 858v and ARLL PN Obregon 53 [1626] f. 63v.
99. O'Toole, "Inventing Difference," chapter 6.
100. "Testamento de Ynes Quispi," AGN PN Tamayo 1851 [1623] f. 143.
101. "Testamento de María Pazña," AGN TI leg 1A [1633].
102. "Testamento de Pedro Biafara," AGN PN Gómez de Baeza 738 [1604] f. 147.
103. "Testamento de Mencia Lopez," AGN PN Pérez 130 reg 9 [1578] f 439.
104. "Testamento de Catalina de Ysásaga," AGN PN Gutiérrez 73 [1578] f 378v.

CHAPTER 3

1. "Declaración," AGN PN Arias Cortez 10 [1582] f. 267.
2. This was the case in many Andean regions. Stern, *Peru's Indian Peoples*, 173. See also the contemporary statement by Fray Monsalve, *Reducion de todo el Piru*, 15–15v.
3. However, the conversion of Indians in general was limited, especially in rural areas. See Mills, *Idolatry and its Enemies*. On the development of the Church's economic positions because of inheritance decisions such as the one described here, see Burns, *Colonial Habits*, especially chapter 2; and Bauer, "The Church in the Economy of Spanish America."
4. In particular, Cline, *Colonial Culhuacán*; Kellogg, *Law and the Transformation of Aztec Culture*; and articles by Kellogg, Restall, and Terraciano in Kellogg and Restall, *Dead Giveaways*.
5. Silverblatt, *Moon, Sun, and Witches*, 120. However, if Stern's findings that highland kurakas absorbed rural properties in the absence of heirs can be generalized to Cuzco, Chimbo also appears to have been rejecting "traditional" custom as well by invoking colonial law. Stern, *Peru's Indian People*, 173.
6. In much the same way that indigenous elites in the Andes used colonial law to invent and shore up their own legitimacy. See Powers, "A Battle of Wills," in Kellogg and Restall, *Dead Giveaways*; see also Chapter 5 below.

7. *Recopilación de leyes*, Título 32.

8. "Testamento de don Diego Cossanosan," ARLL PN Paz 198 [1627] f. 285.

9. ARLL PN Obregon 44 [1607] f. 145v; ARLL PN Obregon 47 [1611] ff. 8-9, 12v, 13v, 134, 223.

10. For example, see *Siete Partidas*, Partida IV, título xi on dowries, donations and marriage gifts.

11. For law and custom in Spain, see Dillard, *Daughters of the Reconquest*, chapters 2 and 3. For colonial Latin America, see Lavrin and Couturier, "Dowries and Wills"; Arrom, *The Women of Mexico City*, chapter 2; Kellogg, *Law and the Transformation of Aztec Culture*, 104–11; Ots y Capdequí, *Historia del derecho español en América*.

12. Arrom, *The Women of Mexico City*. See also Kellogg, *Law and the Transformation of Aztec Culture*, chapter 3.

13. ARLL PN 4 López de Córdova reg 1 [1563].

14. Kellogg found the same pattern in the Valley of Mexico, *Law and the Transformation of Aztec Culture*, chapter 4; as did Cline in Culhuacán, *Colonial Culhuacán*, 11–12.

15. "Testamento de Catalina," ARLL PN Mata 8 reg 12 [1565] f. 549v.

16. "Testamento de Miguel de Paz," ARLL PN Mata 8 reg 12 [1590] f. 549v.

17. "Testamento de María Sacha Chumbi,"ARLL PN Mata 21 [1632] f. 38v.

18. "Testamento de Ines Guamguam," AGN TI leg 1A [1614].

19. "Testamento de Francisca Ramirez,"ARLL PN Escobar 136 [1633].

20. "Testamento de Francisca Ramirez,"ARLL PN Alvarez leg 84 esc 81 [1653] ff. 144–50.

21. "Testamento de Juliana de Mendoza," AGN PN Tamayo 1853 [1630] f. 324.

22. "Declaración," ARLL PN Bernal Jimeno 96 [1624] f. 78v.

23. *Siete Partidas*, vol. 5, partida VI. See also Arrom, *The Women of Mexico City*, chapter 2.

24. Kellogg, *Law and the Transformation of Aztec Culture*, 325.

25. Which could generally not be more than one-fifth of the value of the estate. Ots y Capdequí, *Historia del derecho español en América*, 63.

26. Bastards, one or both of whose parents were married to someone else when they were born, were excluded from inheritance entirely. Twinam, *Public Lives, Private Secrets*, 174–5.

27. "Testamento de Catalina de Agüero," ARLL PN Mata 11 [1570] f. 42; "Testamento de Elvira," ARLL PN Muñoz 31 reg 10 [1573] f. 506 and reg 13 [1573] f. 680.

28. Twinam, *Public Lives, Private Secrets*, 128–30. See also the studies of honor in various classes and *castas* in Johnson and Lipsett-Rivera, *The Faces of Honor*.

29. "Testamento de María de la O," ARLL PN García Durand 165 [1660] f. 374.

30. For another clear case, see the will of Catalina de Agüero, ARLL PN 11 [1570] f. 42r.

31. Van Deusen, *Between the Sacred and the Worldly*, 39–50; Burns, *Colonial Habits*, 20–22; Lockhart, *Spanish Peru*, 163–70. Other provocative and important studies include Kuznesof, "Ethnic and Gender Influences on 'Spanish' Creole

Society"; Schwartz, "Spaniards, *Pardos* and the Missing Mestizos"; and his response to Kuznesof, "Colonial Identities and the *Sociedad de Castas."*

32. Lowry, "Forging an Indian Nation," 36.

33. For example, Cope found that individuals in crossethnic marriages tended to assimilate into a spouse's category in colonial Mexico City. *The Limits of Racial Domination*, 67. See also Graubart, "Hybrid Thinking."

34. Mannarelli, *Pecados públicos*, cuadros v.1, v.2.

35. Rostworowski, *Doña Francisca Pizarro*, 30.

36. AGN PN de la Cueva 28 [1577] f. 237.

37. ARLL PN Obregon 50 reg 4 [1616] f. 39.

38. Lockhart, *Spanish Peru*, 164. See also Burns, *Colonial Habits*, chapter 1.

39. It was common practice in Peru as in Spain to use names to express strategic linkages; while *hatun kurakas* generally maintained their names to preserve ancestral connections (and hence their legitimacy), lesser elites often took the surname of their encomendero as well as a Christian name at baptism (such as the numerous indigenous nobles named Mora after the powerful Mora family of Trujillo; or the many Indian Pizarros), and young girls sent into service were given the surname of their mistress. Cope finds that in plebeian Mexico City, Spaniards maintained their surnames as indications of heritage while castas treated them as a "bureaucratic necessity," supporting my contention that they might have perceived them as juridical strategies as well. *The Limits of Racial Domination*, 62.

40. "Testamento de Jerónima Martines," ARLL PN Morales Melgarejo 179 reg 7 [1605] f. 143; "Testamento de Doña Melchora Marañón,"ARLL PN Rentero 207 [1676–8] f. 196v; "Testamento de Doña María de la Oliva y de los Santos," ARLL PN Espino y Alvarado 148 [1683].

41. Lockhart, *Spanish Peru*, 155. This practice was also common among some Nahua Indians after the conquest; parents sometimes used the patronym of a baptismal sponsor or a prominent Spaniard. Horn, "Gender and Social Identity," 117.

42. "Testamento de Catalina Guisado," ARLL PN Toledo 248 [1626] f. 283v; "Testamento de Barbola Guay," ARLL PN Muñoz Ternero 36 [1578] f. 422v.

43. Kellogg similarly found that Nahua women were unlikely to leave property to their husbands, although Nahua husbands were more likely to leave property to wives.

44. A price schedule for funerals and masses appears in "Memoria de los derechos que a de lleuar el cura y sacristan desta parroquia ansi de los entierros como de belaciones," AAL Papeles Importantes 19A:1A [1597/1605].

45. Bauer demystifies the complex financial arrangements that these terms encompassed in "The Church in the Economy of Spanish America." See also the discussions in Burns, *Colonial Habits*, 61–67, and Quiroz, "Reassessing the Role of Credit in Late Colonial Peru."

46. There is no evidence that urban Indian men were less active in the Church than women were, only that they did not use their wills to provide income for the Church to the same extent. Forty-nine percent of men in the Lima

sample and 54 percent in the Trujillo sample were members of cofradías, a slightly higher rate than among women testators.

47. On religion and death in early modern Spain, see Eire, *From Madrid to Purgatory*. Salles-Reese in "Las divergencias semióticas" argues that the trend toward more opulent funerals, which she analyzes among caciques, could indicate a desire to emulate Spaniards, or conversely a way of making the new religion one's own, by linking new socioreligious practices with older Andean ones. However, the fact that such acts were also common to poorer people and particularly women suggests that they also were important to urban community formation.

48. AAL Testamentos 47:5 [1645].

49. ARLL PN Alvarez 84 [1653] ff. 144–150.

50. "Testamento de Elvira,"ARLL PN Muñoz 31 reg 10 [1573] f. 506 and reg 13 [1573] f. 680.

51. On spousal abuse, law, and the Church, see Boyer, "Women, *La Mala Vida*, and the Politics of Marriage."

52. "Testamento de Mencia Mayuay," AGN PN Tamayo 1854 [1631] f. 309.

53. AGN TI leg 1 [1615].

54. AGN PN Tamayo 1852 [1625–26] ff. 198, 234, 242.

55. Burns, *Colonial Habits*.

56. "Memoria de los derechos que a de lleuar el cura y sacristan desta parroquia ansi de los entierros como de belaciones," AAL Papeles Importantes 19A:1A [1597/1605].

57. Ramos, "Death, Conversion, and Identity in the Peruvian Andes,"179–81 and 205–6.

58. "Memorial de Elena de Ffaria yndia solarera," ARLL PN 44 Obregón [1600] f. 216v.

59. AGN PN Tamayo 1853 [1630] f. 1023.

60. Castañeda Murga, "Notas para una historia de la Ciudad de Trujillo," 175–6.

61. AGN RA CC leg 82 cuad 310 [1631].

62. Padre Alvaro Pinto shows up in numerous documents from the Cercado over this decade, demonstrating either his activist concern for his flock or a more malevolent preoccupation.

63. Charney argues that leaving property to the cofradía was also a strategy against "the worst scenario of Spanish intrusion onto indigenous turf," i.e., the purchase of Indian lands by Spaniards. I find no evidence that individual Indians conceived of their bequests in this fashion, and, as Charney himself notes, the cofradías often rented or sold the lands to Spaniards. Charney, "A Sense of Belonging," 397, 399.

64. "Testamento de Ysabel Yauri Saco," BNP A391 [1594]; "Testamento de Ysabel de Ayala," ARLL PN Paz 204 [1643].

65. Lowry, "Forging an Indian Nation," 149.

66. ARLL PN Vega 80 [1588] f. 428.

67. AGN TI leg 1A [1649].

CHAPTER 4

1. Contreras, *Padrón de los indios de Lima,* 416.

2. De la Cadena illustrates the continued anxiety over classification with a more recent case when the director of the 1912 census of the city of Cuzco "corrected" his results because "the tendency both of the interviewer and of the interviewed, is and always will be to prefer the superior classification. This means that the mestizo will try to be included as white, and many Indians [will choose] to be [considered] mestizos." Here a biological definition of "race" was at stake rather than classification as legal tributaries, but the same assumption of "uplift" for the purpose of evasion is at work. De la Cadena, *Indigenous Mestizos,* 44.

3. For one fascinating example, see Cook, "The Mysterious Catalina."

4. Konetzke, ed., *Colección de documentos,* vol. I, 436–37.

5. Various scholars have approached the relationship between the formation of ethnic identity and appearance from different directions. Two treatments of "race," ethnicity, and appearance in the modern world are notable for historicizing a Latin American notion of biological race: de la Cadena, *Indigenous Mestizos,* and Poole, *Vision, Race, and Modernity.* Powers addresses the political aspect of how identity and clothing might come to converge in her essay, "The Battle for Bodies and Souls." See also Silverblatt, "Becoming Indian" for a discussion of the construction of "Indianness" critical to this question.

6. My theoretical discussion of the symbolic role of clothing and fashion draws upon Barthes, *The Fashion System,* and Hollander, *Seeing Through Clothes.*

7. See, in this respect, the literature concerning literacy and visual material culture under colonial rule, especially Boone and Mignolo, eds., *Writing Without Words,* and Boone and Cummins, eds., *Native Traditions in the Postconquest World.*

8. According to Niles, in the sixteenth century cumbicamayos "were recruited to make household goods rather than clothing for Iberian tastes," including carpets, furniture coverings, and bedspreads that we shall see inventoried in wills. Niles, "Artist and Empire," 52.

9. For an overview of European and Spanish American fashions of the colonial period, see Ribeiro, *Dress in Eighteenth-Century Europe;* Duarte, *Historia del traje durante la época colonial Venezolana;* Cruz de Amenábar, *El traje;* and Money, *Los obrajes, el traje y el comercio de ropa en la audiencia de Charcas.*

10. Cruz de Amenábar, *El traje,* 45.

11. AGN RA CC leg 17, cuad 84 [1577].

12. *Siete Partidas,* volume 5, partida 7, título XXIV, law xi.

13. "Real pragmática sobre el vestir y gastar seda en las Indias," in Konetzke, *Colección de documentos,* vol. I, pp. 23–24.

14. An example of these sumptuary laws from 1612 appears in Konetzke, *Colección de documentos,* vol. II, part I, 182–23. For a critical discussion of the tapadas, see Poole, *Vision, Race, and Modernity,* chapter 4.

15. Money, *Los obrajes, el traje y el comercio de ropa;* Duarte, *Historia del traje durante la época colonial venezolana;* Cummins, "Let Me See!"; and Niles, "Artist and Empire."

16. These items, or similar ones, were known by different names depending upon region and language spoken. In Lima and Trujillo, mainly these names and styles continued to appear in colonial wills; in more indigenous-dominated regions like Potosí and Cuzco, a broader variety of garments were common (personal communications, Ana María Presta and Jean-Jacques Decoster, July 2003).

17. Cummins, "Let Me See!," 104.

18. Zárate, *Historia del descrubrimiento y conquista del Perú*, 33; Cobo, *Inca Religion and Customs*, 188.

19. An analysis of changes in weaving techniques and iconography within Andean clothing is beyond the scope of this work, but see Niles, "Artist and Empire"; Desrosiers, "Las técnicas de tejido ¿tienen un sentido?"; and Iriarte, "Tapices con escenas bíblicas del Perú colonial."

20. Parry, *The Age of Reconnaissance*, 178.

21. AGN RA CC leg 17 c. 84 [1577] f.2. See also Cruz de Amenábar, *El traje*, 105–6.

22. Castillian bayeta was usually so identified. "Testamento de María Daça,"AGN PN Gutiérrez 71 [1573] f. 69.

23. "Testamento de Ynes Diez," AGN PN Esquivel 33 [1577] f. 891.

24. "Testamento de Ysabel Lopez," AGN PN Jimenez 102 [1597] f. 388.

25. "Testamento de Andres Gomez," AGN PN Esquivel 33 [1570] f. 221.

26. "Testamento de Juan de Ayala," ARLL PN Mata 17 [1584] f. 108.

27. For a description of some extant examples of these furnishings, possibly made by cumbicamayos, see Niles, "Artist and Empire," 52–53 and plates; Iriarte, "Tapices con escenas bíblicas"; and Gisbert et al., *Arte textil*, 299–315 and plates 361–89.

28. On this topic, in addition to studies mentioned previously, see Graubart, "Hybrid Thinking"; Schwartz, "Colonial Identities and the *Sociedad de Castas*."

29. Cummins, "Let Me See!," 114.

30. Salomon, "Indian Women of Early Colonial Quito," 336.

31. Burns, *Colonial Habits*, 32. On the growing marginalization of mestizos, see van Deusen, *Between the Sacred and the Worldly*, chapter 2.

32. Powers, "The Battle for Bodies and Souls," 39–40.

33. The fact that no women's ethnicities were challenged in this document is further support for this thesis, since women were not nominal tributaries and would not incur the skepticism of the census taker. Graubart, "Hybrid Thinking," 226.

34. Murra, "Cloth and its Function in the Inka State." This was also the case in many other colonial situations. See, for one example from British North America, Shannon, "Dressing for Success on the Mohawk Frontier."

35. *Actas del Cabildo de Trujillo*, Tomo I, 150.

36. "Testamento de Domingo Fino," AGN PN de la Cueva 29 [1579] f. 170.

37. ARLL Cabildo CO leg 12, c 237 [1604]; Sarabia Viejo, *Francisco de Toledo*, Tomo I, 228. Indians were not legally minors but because of their "Indian condition" were subject to different jurisdictions and penalties than were Spaniards and mestizos (as were minors—those under twenty-five years of

age—of all ethnicities). Don Pedro was participating in a long-standing rhetorical strategy to exploit the ambiguous status of Indians in colonial laws. See Premo, "Minor Offenses," 126–7 on the "double minority" of Indian youths in the criminal justice system and Kellogg, *Law and the Transformation of Aztec Culture*, 5–8 on the competing strategies of indigenous litigants.

38. Garcilaso de la Vega, *Royal Commentaries*, vol. I, p. 375.

39. Dean, *Inka Bodies and the Body of Christ*, chapter 5; Burga, "El Corpus Christi y la nobleza inca colonial"; Cahill, "The Virgin and the Inca."

40. "Testamento de Angelina Palla," ARLL Contratos Privados, Diego de Sequiera, legajo 2307 [1571].

41. Guaman Poma, *El Primer nueva corónica*, 732–34 [folios 787/801].

42. Parry and Keith, *New Iberian World*, vol I, 342.

43. "Testamento de Martín Taco," AGN PN Esquivel 33 [1569–77] f. 819.

44. "Testamento de doña Beatriz de Escobar," ARLL PN Muñoz 31 reg. 3 [1573] f. 114.

45. Spalding, "Exploitation as an Economic System," 333; Escandell-Tur, *Producción y comercio de tejidos coloniales*, 326.

46. AGN RA CC leg 17, c. 84 [1577].

47. Cook, "Introducción," in Contreras, *Padrón*, p. xii.

48. "Testamento de Domingo Hernandez," AGN PN Esquivel 33 [1569–77] f. 182.

49. "Testamento de Diego Lastara," AGN Testamentos de Indios 1A [1606].

50. "Testamento de Francisca Ramírez," ARLL PN Escobar 136 [1633]; Alvarez 84 esc 81 [1653]; Rentero 207 [1677].

51. "Testamento de Ysabel," AGN PN 33 Esquivel [1569–77] f. 215; "Testamento de Juana," AGN PN 33 Esquivel [1569–77] f. 189.

52. "Testamento de María Cura," AGN PN Esquivel 33 [1569–77]. Or this might refer to a prehispanic style, as seen in the illustration by Guaman Poma above.

53. "Testamento de Elbira," AGN PN Esquivel 33 [1569–77] f. 303.

54. "Testamento de Beatriz Utca," AGN PN Esquivel 33 [1569–77] f. 72.

55. "Testamento de Ana," AGN PN Esquivel 33 [1569–77] f. 582.

56. "Testamento de Madalena Carua Sisue," AGN PN Rodríguez de Torquemada 141 [1589] f. 890v.

57. "Testamento de Ysabel," ARLL PN Mata 11 [1589] f. 5v.

58. "Testamento de Juana," ARLL PN Muñoz 31 reg. 7 [1573] f. 336.

59. "Testamento de Beatriz Guanca," AGN PN Esquivel 33 [1569–77] f. 72.

60. "Testamento de Costança Ticlla," AGN TI leg 1 [1596].

61. "Testamento de Elvira Coyti," AGN TI leg 1 [1596].

62. "Testamento de Martín Cungo," AGN PN Esquivel 33 [1572] f. 356.

63. The prehispanic man's tunic, called unku in Quechua, was immediately translated into the Spanish camiseta, and the mantle was known as a manta, so that the indigenous unit of clothing was known by a Spanish name at least as early as the middle of the sixteenth century. "Testamento de Alonso Julca,"

ARLL PN Mata 17 [1584] f. 112 and "Testamento de Juan Quispe," ARLL PN Vega 76, doc. 67 [1584]. This was not always the case in other cities, including Cuzco and Potosí (personal communications, Ana María Presta and Jean-Jacques Decoster, July 2003).

64. "Testamento de don Melchior Carorayco yndio cacique," ARLL PN Mata 8 reg. 7 [1565] f. 308.

65. As suggested by the will of the widow of a Trujillo merchant, who asked that an Indian named Francisco Anton pay her for the men's breeches and shirts he brought to the highlands to sell on her behalf. "Testamento de Juana Lopez," ARLL PN Obregón 50 reg, 8 [1616] f. 265.

66. "Testamento de Catalina de Agüero," ARLL PN Mata 11 [1570] f. 42.

67. Escandell-Tur, *Producción y comercio de tejidos coloniales*, 31–32.

68. Here I disagree with Bernard Lavallé, who states that "indio criollo" referred in a more general way to any birth place, as equivalent to "natural." Documents do not describe an Indian as criollo of a rural town or ayllu, but only of cities. Other words already existed to describe aspects of the acculturation process: *ladino* for speakers of Spanish, *infiel* or *gentil* for those not converted to the Christian faith. Thus *criollo* must have arisen to describe cases not entirely explained by these other common terms. Lavallé, *Las Promesas ambiguas*, 15–21.

69. "Testamento de Diego Sedeño," AGN TI leg 1 [1609], and "Testamento de Alonso de Paz," AGN TI leg 1 [1617].

70. "Testamento de Catalina Sacsa Nurma," AGN PN Jiménez 103 [1600] f. 666.

71. "Testamento de Catalina Carguay Chumbi," AGN PN TI legajo 1A [1608].

72. "Testamento de Melchor Payta," AGN PN Tamayo 1854 [1631] f. 506.

73. "Testamento de doña María de Saavedra," AGN PN Rodriguez de Torquemada 141 [1589].

74. "Almoneda de bienes de Ynes Lopes," AGN PN Tamayo 1853 [1630] f. 516; "Ymbentario de bienes de Ynes Descobar yndia y almoneda dellos," AGN PN Tamayo 1853 [1630] f. 587.

75. "Testamento de Juliana de Mendoza," AGN PN Tamayo 1853 [1630] f. 324.

76. "Carta de pago," AGN PN Tamayo 1853 [1630] f. 434.

77. "Testamento de Lucia Cusi," AGN PN Tamayo 1851 [1624] f. 396.

78. "Testamento de Mencia Mayuay," AGN PN Tamayo 1854 [1631] f. 309.

79. "Testamento de Luis Perez," AGN PN Tamayo 1851 [1623] f. 75v.

80. "Testamento de Catalina Carua," AGN PN Tamayo 1856 [1635] f. 84v. For the ñañaca see Money, *Los obrajes, el traje y el comercio de ropa*, 219.

81. Lowry, *Forging an Indian Nation*, 156–9.

82. "Testamento de Joan Magdalena," AGN TI leg 1A [1631].

83. "Testamento de María Magdalena de Urraco," ARLL PN Paz 198 [1627] f. 4v. The Trujillo Valley was among the last regions to convert from tribute in goods to tribute in silver, and thus ropa de la tierra remained easily available there throughout the first half of the seventeenth century.

84. "Testamento de Angelina de Albarado," ARLL PN Obregón 54 [1627] f. 54v.

85. "Testamento de Luisa Gregoria mulata," ARLL PN Bernal 96 [1624] f. 640.

86. "Testamento de Ysabel Gutierrez," AGN PN Esquivel 33 [1569-77] f. 80.

87. "Carta de aprendiz," AGN PN Gutiérrez 171 [1573] f. 97.

88. "Concierto de yndio," AGN PN Rodríguez de Torquemada 141 [1589] f. 851.

89. "Testamento de Maria Carauajal," AGN PN Esquivel 33 [1569–77] f. 298.

90. "Testamento de Maria Madalena," AGN PN Gómez de Baeza 35 [1601] f. 1088.

CHAPTER 5

1. María Rostworowski first analyzed and published the records of this case in her *Curacas y sucesiones*, 28. The original document is AGN DI c 627 [1610].

2. Rostworowski, *Curacas y sucesiones*, 29. Minors seem not to have been legitimate successors in most of these regions prior to the Spanish conquest, although another relative might have served as interim cacique until the minor came of age. For such a case in Cajamarca see Pilar Remy, "La visita a Cajamarca de 1571–2/1578," 77.

3. Rostworowski, *Curacas y sucesiones*, 29–30. I have translated from her published transcription.

4. Rostworowski, *Curacas y sucesiones*, 30.

5. Rostworowski, *Curacas y sucesiones*, 30–32.

6. Rostworowski, *Curacas y sucesiones*, 33–34; Silverblatt, *Moon, Sun, and Witches*, 150–51.

7. The most dramatic example comes from Powers, "A Battle of Wills." See also Karoline Noack, "Caciques, escribanos y las construcciones de historias."

8. On this topic, see Abercrombie, *Pathways of Memory and Power*, part 2.

9. On this literature, see especially Greenblatt, *Marvellous Possessions* and Pagden, *The Fall of Natural Man*.

10. Oviedo y Valdés, *Corónica de las Yndias*, 388.

11. Santa Cruz Pachacuti Yamqui Salcamayga, *Relación de antiguedades deste reyno del Pirú*, 19v; Sarmiento de Gamboa, *Histórica Indica* in Levillier, ed., *Don Francisco de Toledo*, 73. Rostworowski calls Chañana Cury Coca a "female kuraka" but the two chronicles she cites only refer to her as a woman and a widow. Rostworowski, "La mujer en el Perú prehispánico," 9.

12. The *Huarochirí Manuscript* (ed. Salomon and Urioste) is a colonial compilation of Andean religious traditions, produced by Andean informants under the influence of Father Francisco de Avila, a notorious extirpator in the Andes. Guaman Poma's *Primer nueva corónica y buen gobierno* includes parallel chapters on male Incas and female Coyas, as it does on male and female principales or lesser lords, and on male and female age-based occupations for tributary Indians. Silverblatt, *Moon, Sun, and Witches*, discusses these, although her argument for gender parallelism suffers from some idealism.

13. Rostworowski, "La mujer en el Perú prehispánico," 10. The Inca institution referred to here is the *acllahuasi*, the collection of young girls chosen by Inca administrators from provinces within the empire, some of whom were distributed as wives to those with whom the Inca wanted to forge relations.

14. Piura is separated by distance and deserts from the twelve river valleys which stretch from present-day Lambayeque to Huarmey, the colonial province of Trujillo. While this entire coastal region was part of the Chimú kingdom prior to the Inca and then Spanish conquests, there are distinctive historical and archaeological traditions linked to smaller regions within the Chimú culture, which suggest multiple political and ethnic groups. Lumbreras, *The Peoples and Cultures of Ancient Peru*, 179–90.

15. Cieza de León, *Crónica del Perú, Primera Parte*, 192.

16. Rostworowski, "La mujer en el Perú prehispánico," 12.

17. Cieza de León, *Crónica del Perú, Tercera Parte*, 62–69.

18. Lewis, *Hall of Mirrors*.

19. Lizárraga, *Descripción del Perú, Tucumán*, 69–70.

20. Calancha, *Chronica moralizada*, I, 237.

21. Zevallos Quiñones, *Los cacicazgos de Lambayeque*, 2. Susan Ramírez has found the word *siec* for *señor* in north-coast colonial documents (personal communication, 2005). I have encountered only one colonial use of the word *kuraka* on the north coast, in a 1562 document (cited in Zevallos Quiñones, *Los cacicazgos de Trujillo*, 217), and its source is the viceroy rather than local informants.

22. Lockhart and Schwartz, *Early Latin America*, 51. See Hulme, *Colonial Encounters*, 73–78 for a discussion of the use of such politically loaded terms.

23. Netherly, "Local Level Lords on the North Coast of Peru," 202. See also Salomon, *Native Lords of Quito*.

24. Cabello Balboa, *Miscelánea antártica*, 468.

25. Salomon, *Native Lords of Quito*, 133.

26. Santillán, "Relación del orígen y gobierno de los Incas," 109.

27. Rostworowski proposes that various Incas progressively tightened the rules for designating a successor in order to limit the squabbles that regularly broke out. "Succession, Cooptation to Kingship, and Royal Incest among the Inca," 417–27.

28. On brother-sister marriages and the successors to Huayna Capac, see Niles, *The Shape of Inca History*, 302, 305–6. See also MacCormack, *Religion in the Andes*, 118–37 on Inca chronology and history.

29. Pease, *Curacas, reciprocidad, y riqueza*, 20.

30. Pease, *Curacas, reciprocidad, y riqueza*, 21.

31. Powers, *Andean Journeys*, 108. For regional studies, see Stern, *Peru's Indian Peoples*; Spalding, *Huarochirí*; Powers, "A Battle of Wills"; Varón Gabai, *Curacas y encomenderos*.

32. Of particular importance to this discussion of colonial restructuring of Andean communities are Rostworowski, *Señoríos indígenas de Lima y Canta*; Burga, *De la encomienda a la hacienda capitalista*; Powers, *Andean Journeys*; Spalding, *Huarochirí*; Wightman, *Indigenous Migration and Social Change*; and Assadourian, *Transiciones hacia el sistema colonial andino*.

33. Rostworowski, *Curacas y sucesiones*, 14–15. See also Zevallos Quiñones, *Los cacicazgos de Lambayeque*, 113–15.

34. Netherly, "Local Level Lords," chapter 5; Ramírez, *Provincial Patriarchs*, 17–18.

35. Powers, "A Battle of Wills."

36. Polo de Ondegardo, "Informe del Licenciado," 194; Matienzo, *Gobierno del Perú*, 8, 21. See Assadourian's excellent study, "Los señores étnicos" in *Transiciones hacia el sistema colonial andino*, 209–79.

37. Levillier, *Don Francisco de Toledo*, Tomo II, lxxi.

38. Sarabia Viejo, *Francisco de Toledo. Disposiciones gubernativas para el virreinato del Perú*, Tomo I, 19.

39. Sarabia Viejo, Francisco de Toledo. *Disposiciones gubernativas*, Tomo I, 139.

40. Sarabia Viejo, Francisco de Toledo. *Disposiciones gubernativas*, Tomo II, 113–14.

41. The caciques of Cajamarca were early inhabitants of Trujillo's traza, for example. Noack, "Caciques, escribanos y las construcciones de historias," 214.

42. Only one woman was directly granted an encomienda, and that was doña Francisca Pizarro, the mestiza daughter of the conquistador Francisco Pizarro (who granted her the title in 1540) and granddaughter of Huayna Capac. See Rostworowski, *Doña Francisca Pizarro*, 36–37, 69.

43. The "New Laws" of 1542 were intended to limit encomiendas to a single life in order to restrict the influence of encomenderos in the colonies, but the revolts that they inspired in Peru forced that colonial administration to treat succession as a privilege rather than a right, providing much more government control over encomiendas.

44. Hampe Martínez, "Relación de los encomenderos y repartimientos."

45. Solórzano y Pereyra, *Política indiana*, Tomo II, 246.

46. Presta, "Detrás de la mejor dote una encomienda"; Presta, "Portraits of Four Women," 251.

47. Hampe, "Relación de los encomenderos y repartimientos," 101–3.

48. BNP B137 (1601).

49. Lockhart is dismissive of the role of encomenderas in Peru, suggesting both that they simply acted as placeholders until they were married and that when they did act as officeholders they were ineffective or "heartless, avaricious and destructive." *Spanish Peru*, 157–8. Substantial evidence since Lockhart's investigation has shown that Spanish women did play important social, political, and economic roles in the colony, but perhaps most strongly after the period of his research (which ended in 1560). See especially Presta, "Detrás de la mejor dote." Burns, *Colonial Habits*, is a powerful illustration of another role played by Spanish (and some mestiza) women in the colony, through the Catholic Church and the convent.

50. ARLL PN Mata 25 f. 71, 187, 229v.

51. ARLL Corr CO leg 151 exp 126; AGN JR leg 2 c 5 [1582].

52. Solórzano y Pereyra, *Política indiana*, I, 407.
53. Solórzano y Pereyra, *Política indiana*, I, 408–9. This is, of course, the theory; in fact, the colonial authorities always reserved the right to confirm successors.
54. Solórzano y Pereyra, *Política indiana*, I, 410.
55. Rostworowski, *Curacas y sucesiones*, 30.
56. On the nobility—both those with ties to noble houses in Europe and those receiving titles in the New World—in the Americas, see Lohmann Villena, *Los Americanos en las órdenes nobiliarias*; on *limpieza de sangre* see Martínez López, "The Spanish Concept of *Limpieza de Sangre*."
57. Indigenous nobility were eventually granted parallel privileges to those of Iberian *hidalgos*, if they could prove their own legitimate descent, according to a 1697 royal decree, "Que se considere a los descendientes de caciques como nobles de su raça." Koneztke, *Colección de documentos*, vol. 3, book 1, 66–69.
58. "Testamento de Doña María Chumbi Guaman," ARLL PN Aguilar 284 [1692] ff. 581–82.
59. ARLL CO leg. 203 exp. 1407 [1677].
60. BNP B1486 [1679]. It is fascinating to note that Doña Catalina, although an "yndia like all the rest," knew how to write and sign her own name (f. 50), a very unusual ability in indigenous women.
61. BNP B1087 [1629] ff. 2, 6.
62. ARLL Corr CO leg 202 exp 1407 [1673].
63. Zevallos Quiñones, *Los cacicazgos de Trujillo*, 13–32; ARLL Corr CO leg 159 exp 348.
64. Van Deusen, *Between the Sacred and the Worldly*, chapter 1.
65. As well, *beaterios* would provide spaces, beginning in the late seventeenth century, where the daughters of indigenous elites might observe a religious life outside the convent and possibly also receive an education. Burns, *Colonial Habits*, 124 and personal communication, 2006.
66. Spalding, *Huarochirí*, 127.
67. BNP B1385 [1681]; ADC Corr CCr leg 2; ADC CO leg 25. Many thanks to Cecilia Barrantes and Tanja Christiansen for their help with these documents.
68. BNP B1051 [1616].
69. BNP B1087 [1689].
70. "Testamento de Ysauel Caja y Yapa cacica," AAL Testamentos 134:9 [1701].
71. AGN DI leg 103 [1639] f. 47.
72. Throughout the litigation Magdalena Mallao referred to herself as Magdalena Ayra, although no other participants did. She also cast aspersions on Don Pedro's claims by calling him "don Pedro Guaclla, aka Ayra" and the "so-called cacique of Singa." AGN DI c 101 [1643] ff. 40, 29
73. AGN DI c 101 [1643] f. 18.
74. AGN DI c 101 [1643] f. 33.
75. *Las Siete Partidas*, 522.

CONCLUSION

1. Williams, *Marxism and Literature*, 132.
2. Burkhart, "Gender in Nahuatl Texts of the Early Colonial Period," 87.
3. Silverblatt, *Moon, Sun, and Witches*, 9.
4. For a case from the nineteenth century where weaving was a male, salaried task, while spinning was the occupation of the majority of women, see Teruel and Gil Montero, "Trabajo familiar y producción de textiles," 206–7.
5. On modern rejections of "Indian" in favor of more localized labels, see de la Cadena, *Indigenous Mestizos*, 320. Of course, no ethnic label describes a heterogeneous people: "Spaniards" too had vastly different experiences elided by grouping them together.
6. See especially Poole, *Vision, Race, and Modernity*, and de la Cadena, *Indigenous Mestizos*, for these debates in the Andes.
7. de la Cadena, *Indigenous Mestizos*, 91–92.

Bibliography

ARCHIVAL SOURCES OF MATERIALS

Archivo General de la Nación, Lima, Perú (AGN):
  Derecho Indígena (DI)
  Juicios de Residencia (JR)
  Protocolos Notariales (PN)
  Real Audiencia: Causas Civiles (RA CC)
  Real Hacienda: Trujillo (RH)
  Testamentos de Indios (TI)
Archivo Arzobispal de Lima, Perú (AAL):
  Papeles Importantes
  Testamentos
Biblioteca Nacional del Perú, Lima (BNP):
  Manuscritos
Archivo Regional de La Libertad, Trujillo, Perú (ARLL):
  Cabildo: Causas Ordinarias (Cab CO)
    Causas Criminales (Cab CCr)
  Contrados Privados
  Corregimiento: Causas Ordinarias (Corr CO)
    Causas Criminales (Corr Cr)
  Protocolos Notariales (PN)
Archivo Arzobispal de Trujillo, Perú (AAT):
  Visitas Pastorales (VP)
Archivo Departamental de Cajamarca, Perú (ADC):
  Corregimiento: Causas Ordinarias (Corr CO)
    Causas Criminales (Corr CCr)
Archivo General de Indias, Seville, Spain (AGI):
  Justicia

PUBLISHED SOURCES

Abercrombie, Thomas. *Pathways of Memory and Power: Ethnography and History Among an Andean People* (Madison, University of Wisconsin Press, 1998).

Actas del Cabildo de Trujillo (Trujillo, Concejo Provincial de Trujillo, 1969).

Alberti Manzanares, Pilar. "Una institución exclusivamente femenina en la época incaica: las acllacuna," *Revista Española de Antropología Americana* XVI (1986): 153–90.

———. "Mujer y religión: Vestales y Acllacuna, dos instituciones religiosas de mujeres," *Revista Española de Antropología Americana* XVII (1987): 155–96.

Andrien, Kenneth. *Crisis and Decline: The Viceroyalty of Peru in the Seventeenth Century* (Albuquerque, University of New Mexico Press, 1985).

Anónimo Judío Portugués [Pedro León Portocarrero], *Descripción del virreinato del Perú: Crónica inédita de comienzos del siglo XVII,* ed. Boleslao Lewin (Rosario, Argentina, Instituto de Investigaciones Históricos, 1958).

Arrom, Silvia Marina. *Women of Mexico City, 1790–1857* (Stanford, Stanford University Press, 1985).

Assadourian, Carlos Sempat. *El sistema de la economía colonial: Mercado interno, regiones y espacio económico* (Lima, Instituto de Estudios Peruanos, 1982).

———. *Transiciones hacia el sistema colonial andino* (Lima, Instituto de Estudios Peruanos, 1995).

Barbagelata, José. "Desarrollo urbano de Lima (Apuntes históricos)," in Juan Bromley y José Barbagelata, eds., *Evolución urbana de la ciudad de Lima* (Lima, Peru, Concejo Provincial de Lima, 1945).

Barragán, Rossana. "Entre polleras, lliqllas y ñañacas. Los mestizos y la emergencia de la *tercera república,*" in *Etnicidad, economía y simbolismo en los Andes,* ed. Silvia Arze, Rossana Barragán, Laura Escobari, and Ximena Medinaceli (La Paz, Bolivia, HISBOL/IFEA/SBH-ASUR, 1992).

Barthes, Roland. *The Fashion System,* trans. Matthew Ward and Richard Howard (Berkeley, University of California Press, 1990).

Bartra, Roger. *The Wildman in the Looking Glass: The Mythic Origins of European Otherness* (Ann Arbor, University of Michigan Press, 1994).

Bauer, Arnold. "The Church in the Economy of Spanish America: *Censos* and *Depósitos* in the Eighteenth and Nineteenth Centuries," *Hispanic American Historical Review* 63 (1983), 707–33.

Boone, Elizabeth Hill and Walter D. Mignolo, eds. *Writing Without Words: Alternative Literacies in Mesoamerica and the Andes* (Chapel Hill, Duke University Press, 1994).

Boone, Elizabeth Hill and Tom Cummins, eds. *Native Traditions in the Postconquest World* (Washington, DC, Dumbarton Oaks, 1998).

Bowser, Frederick. *The African Slave in Colonial Peru, 1524–1650* (Stanford, Stanford University Press, 1974).

Boyer, Richard. "Women, *La Mala Vida,* and the Politics of Marriage," in *Sexuality and Marriage in Colonial Latin America,* ed. Asunción Lavrin (Lincoln, University of Nebraska Press, 1989), 252–86.

Bromley, Juan and José Barbagelata, *Evolución urbana de la Ciudad de Lima* (Lima, Concejo Provincial de Lima, 1945).

Buisseret, David and Steven G. Reinhardt, eds., *Creolization in the Americas* (Arlington: University of Texas Press, 2000).

Burga, Manuel. "El Corpus Christi y la nobleza inca colonial," in *Los conquistadores: 1492 y la población indígena de las Américas, ed. Heraclio Bonilla (Bogotá:* FLACSO, 1992).

———. *De la encomienda a la hacienda capitalista* (Lima, Instituto de Estudios Peruanos, 1976).

Burkett, Elinor. "Early Colonial Peru: The Urban Female Experience," Ph.D. dissertation, University of Pittsburgh, 1975.

———. "Indian Women and White Society: The Case of Sixteenth-Century Peru" in *Latin American Women: Historical Perspectives*, ed. Asunción Lavrin (Westport, CT, Greenwood Press, 1978), 101–28

Burkhart, Louise. *The Slippery Earth: Nahua-Christian Moral Dialogue in Sixteenth-Century Mexico* (Tucson, University of Arizona Press, 1989).

———. "Gender in Nahuatl Texts of the Early Colonial Period: Native 'Tradition' and the Dialogue with Christianity," in *Gender in Pre-Hispanic America*, ed. Cecilia Klein (Washington, DC, Dumbarton Oaks, 2001).

Burns, Kathryn. *Colonial Habits* (Durham, Duke University Press, 1999).

———. "Unfixing 'race,'" paper presented at the annual meeting of the American Historical Association, Chicago, IL, January 2003.

———, "Notaries, Truth, and Consequences," *American Historical Review* 110:2 (April 2005), 350-79.

Cabello Balboa, Miguel. *Miscelánea antártica: Una historia del Perú antiguo* (Lima, Universidad Nacional Mayor de San Marcos, 1951).

Cabero, Marco. "El corregimiento de Saña y el problema histórico de la fundación de Trujillo," *Revista Histórica* I:i–iii (1906).

Cahill, David. "Colour by Numbers: Racial and Ethnic Categories in the Viceroyalty of Peru, 1532–1824," *Journal of Latin American Studies* 26 (1994): 325-46.

———. "The Virgin and the Inca: An Incaic Procession in the City of Cuzco in 1692," *Ethnohistory* 49:3 (Summer 2002): 611–49.

Calancha, Padre Antonio de la. *Chronica moralizada del orden de San Agustin en el Peru, con sucesos exemplares vistos en esta Monarchia* (Barcelona, n.p., 1638).

Castañeda Murga, Juan. "Notas para una historia de la Ciudad de Trujillo del Perú en el siglo XVII," in Hiroyasu Tomoeda and Luis Millones, eds., *La tradición andina en tiempos modernos* (Osaka, National Museum of Ethnology, 1996).

———. "Organización espacial y socioétnica de la ciudad de Trujillo, 1534–1619," unpublished paper, 2003.

Charney, Paul. "El indio urbano: un análisis económico y social de la población india de Lima en 1613," *Histórica* XII:1 (julio 1988): 5–33.

———. "A Sense of Belonging: Colonial Indian *Cofradías* and Ethnicity in the Valley of Lima, Peru," *The Americas* 54:3 (January 1998), 379-407.

Cieza de León, Pedro de. *Crónica del Perú, Primera Parte* (Lima, Pontificia Universidad Católica del Perú, 1986).

——. *Crónica del Perú, Tercera Parte* (Lima, Pontificia Universidad Católica del Perú, 1989).

Cline, Sarah. *Colonial Culhuacán, 1580–1600: A Social History of an Aztec Town* (Albuquerque, University of New Mexico Press, 1986).

——. "Fray Alonso de Molina's Model Testament and Antecedents to Indigenous Wills in Spanish America," in Susan Kellogg and Matthew Restall, eds., *Dead Giveaways: Indigenous Testaments of Colonial Mesoamerica and the Andes* (Salt Lake City, University of Utah Press, 1998): 13–33.

—— and Miguel León-Portilla, *The Testaments of Culhuacan* (Los Angeles, University of California at Los Angeles, 1984).

Cobo, Fray Bernabé. "La historia de la fundación de Lima," in *Monografías históricas sobre la Ciudad de Lima, Tomo I* (Lima, Concejo Provincial de Lima, 1935).

——. *Inca Religion and Customs*, ed. Roland Hamilton (Austin, University of Texas Press, 1990).

——. *History of the Inca Empire*, trans. Roland Hamilton (Austin, University of Texas, 1991).

Coleman, Kathryn. "Provincial Urban Problems: Trujillo, Peru, 1600–1784," in David J. Robinson, ed., *Social Fabric and Spatial Structure in Colonial Latin America* (Michigan, University Microfilms International, 1979), 369–408.

Colón, Cristóbal. *Los cuatro viajes. Testamento*, ed. Consuelo Varela (Madrid, Alianza Editorial, 1992).

Conniff, Michael and Thomas Davis, *Africans in the Americas: A History of the Black Diaspora* (New York, St. Martin's Press, 1994)..

Contreras, Miguel de. *Padrón de los indios de Lima en 1613*, ed. Noble David Cook (Lima, Seminario de Historia Rural Andina, 1968).

Cook, Noble David. *Demographic Collapse: Indian Peru, 1520–1620* (New York, Cambridge University Press, 1981).

——. "Population Data for Indian Peru: Sixteenth and Seventeenth Centuries," *Hispanic American Historical Review* 62:1 (1982): 73–120.

——. "The Mysterious Catalina: Indian or Spaniard?" in *The Human Tradition in Colonial Latin America*, ed. Kenneth Andrien (Delaware, Scholarly Resources, 2002).

Cope, R. Douglas. *The Limits of Racial Domination: Plebeian Society in Colonial Mexico City, 1660–1720* (Madison, University of Wisconsin Press, 1994).

Cruz de Amenábar, Isabel. *El traje. Transformaciones de una segunda piel* (Santiago, Ediciones Universidad Católica de Chile, 1995).

Cummins, Tom. "Let Me See! Reading Is for Them: Colonial Andean Images and Objects 'como es costumbre tener los caciques Señores,'" in *Native Traditions in the Postconquest World*, ed. Elizabeth Hill Boone and Tom Cummins (Washington, DC, Dumbarton Oaks, 1998).

Dean, Carolyn. *Inka Bodies and the Body of Christ* (Durham, Duke University Press, 1999).

———— and Dana Liebsohn. "Hybridity and Its Discontents: Considering Visual Culture in Colonial Spanish America," *Colonial Latin American Review* 12:1 (2003): 5–35.

de la Cadena, Marisol. *Indigenous Mestizos: The Politics of Race and Culture in Cuzco, Peru, 1919–1991* (Durham, Duke University Press, 2000).

Desrosiers, Sophie. "Las técnicas de tejido ¿tienen un sentido? Una propuesta de lectura de los tejidos andinos," *Revista Andina* 19:1 (julio 1992), 7–34.

Díez de San Miguel, Garci. *Visita hecha a la provincia de Chucuito por Garci Díez de San Miguel en el año 1567*, ed. John V. Murra (Lima, Casa de la Cultura del Perú, 1964).

Dillard, Heath. *Daughters of the Reconquest: Women in Castilian Town Society* (Cambridge, Cambridge University Press, 1984).

Donnan, Christopher. *Moche Art of Peru: Pre-Columbian Symbolic Communication* (Los Angeles, Museum of Cultural History, UCLA, 1978).

Duarte, Carlos. *Historia del traje durante la época colonial venezolana* (Caracas, Armitano, 1984).

Durán Montero, María Antonia. "Lima en 1613. Aspectos urbanos," *Anuario de Estudios Americanos* XLIX (1992): 171–88.

Eire, Carlos. *From Madrid to Purgatory: The Art and Craft of Dying in Early Modern Spain* (Cambridge, Cambridge University Press, 1995).

Espinoza Soriano, Waldemar. "El Valle de Jayanca y el reino de los mochica siglos XV y XVI," *Bulletin de l'Institut français d'études andines* 4:3 (1975): 243–74.

————. *Artesanos, transacciones, monedas y formas de pago en el mundo andino. Siglos XV y XVI* (Lima, Banco Central de Reserva, 1987).

Escandell-Tur, Neus. *Producción y comercio de tejidos coloniales: Los obrajes y chorillos del Cusco, 1570–1820* (Cuzco, Centro de Estudios Andinos "Bartolomé de las Casas," 1997).

Estete, Miguel de. *El descubrimiento y la conquista del Perú* (Quito, Universidad Central de Ecuador, 1918).

Few, Martha. *Women Who Live Evil Lives. Gender, Religion, and the Politics of Power in Colonial Guatemala* (Austin, University of Texas Press, 2002).

Fraser, Valerie. *The Architecture of Conquest: Building in the Viceroyalty of Peru, 1535–1635* (New York, Cambridge University Press, 1990).

García-Arenal, Mercedes. "Moriscos and Indians: A Comparative Approach," *Orientations* I (1992), 39–55.

García Canclini, Néstor. *Hybrid Cultures: Strategies for Entering and Leaving Modernity* (Minneapolis, University of Minnesota Press, 1995).

Garcilaso de la Vega. *Royal Commentaries of the Incas and General History of Peru* (Austin, University of Texas Press, 1989).

Garofalo, Leo. "The Ethno-Economy of Food, Drink, and Stimulants: The Making of Race in Colonial Lima and Cuzco," Ph.D. dissertation, University of Wisconsin, 2001.

————. "La bebida del Inca en copas coloniales: Los curacas del mercado de chicha del Cuzco, 1640–1700," in David Cahill and Blanca Tovías, eds., *Élites indígenas en los Andes. Nobles, caciques y cabildantes bajo el yugo colonial* (Quito, Ecuador, Abya-Yala, 2003): 175–212.

Gauderman, Kimberly. *Women's Lives in Colonial Quito* (Albuquerque, University of New Mexico Press, 2003).

Giles, Mary E., ed., *Women in the Inquisition: Spain and the New World* (Baltimore, Johns Hopkins University Press, 1999).

Ginzburg, Carlo. *The Cheese and the Worms: The Cosmos of a Sixteenth-Century Miller* trans. John Tedeschi and Anne Tedeschi (Baltimore, Johns Hopkins University Press, 1980).

Gisbert, Teresa, Silvia Arze, and Martha Cajías, *Arte textil y mundo andino* (La Paz, Gisbert y Cia., 1987).

Glave, Luis Miguel. "Mujer indígena, trabajo doméstico y cambio social en el siglo XVII," in *Trajinantes: Caminos indígenas en la sociedad colonial siglos XVI/XVII* (Lima, Instituto de Apoyo Agrario, 1989).

Graubart, Karen B. "Indecent Living: Indigenous Women and the Politics of Representation in Early Colonial Peru," *Colonial Latin American Review* 9:2 (December 2000), 213–36.

———. "Hybrid Thinking: Bringing Postcolonial Theory to Colonial Latin American Economic History," in *Postcolonialism Meets Economics*, ed. S. Charusheela and Eiman Zein-Elabden (Routledge, 2003), 215–34.

Greenblatt, Stephen. *Marvelous Possessions: The Wonder of the New World* (Chicago, University of Chicago Press, 1991).

Guaman Poma de Ayala, don Felipe. *El Primer nueva corónica i buen gobierno*, ed. John V. Murra and Rolena Adorno (Mexico, Siglo Veintiuno, 1992).

Guevara-Gil, Armando and Frank Salomon. "A 'Personal Visit': Colonial Political Ritual and the Making of Indians in the Andes," *Colonial Latin American Review* 3:1–2 (1994), 3–36.

Hampe Martínez, Teodoro. "Relación de los encomenderos y repartimientos del Perú en 1561," *Historia y cultura* 12 (1979), 75–117.

———. "Sobre encomenderos y repartimientos de la diócesis de Lima a principios del siglo XVII," *Jahrbuch für Gesichte von Staat, Wirtschaft und Gesellschaft Lateinamerika* 23 (1989).

Harvey, L. P. *Islamic Spain, 1250 to 1500* (Chicago, University of Chicago Press, 1990).

Hollander, Anne. *Seeing Through Clothes* (Berkeley, University of California Press, 1993).

Honeyman, Katrina and Jordan Goodman, "Women's work, gender conflict, and labour markets in Europe, 1500–1900," *Economic History Review* XLIV:4 (1991): 608–28.

Horn, Rebecca. "Gender and Social Identity: Nahua Naming Patterns in Postconquest Central Mexico," in *Indian Women of Early Mexico*, ed. Susan Schroeder, Stephanie Wood, and Robert Haskett (Norman, University of Oklahoma Press, 1997), 105–22.

Huertas, Lorenzo. "Fundación de la Villa de Santiago de Miraflores de Zaña: Un modelo hispano de planificación urbana," *Historia y cultura* 22 (1993), 145–205.

Hulme, Peter. *Colonial Encounters. Europe and the Native Caribbean*, 1492–1797 (New York, Routledge, 1986).

Iriarte, Isabel. "Tapices con escenas bíblicas del Perú colonial," *Revista Andina* 10:1 (julio 1992), 1–105.

Johnson, Lyman and Sonya Lipsett-Rivera. *The Faces of Honor: Sex, Shame and Violence in Colonial Latin America* (Santa Fe, University of New Mexico Press, 1998).

Kellogg, Susan. *Law and the Transformation of Aztec Culture*, 1500–1700 (Norman, University of Oklahoma Press, 1995).

——— and Matthew Restall, eds. *Dead Giveaways: Indigenous Testaments of Colonial Mesoamerica and the Andes* (Salt Lake City, University of Utah Press, 1998).

Klein, Cecilia, ed., *Gender in Pre-Hispanic America* (Washington, DC, Dumbarton Oaks, 2001).

Klor de Alva, J. Jorge. "'Telling Lives': Confessional Autobiography and the Reconstruction of the Nahua Self," in *Spiritual Encounters: Interactions Between Christianity and Native Religions in Colonial America*, ed. Nicholas Griffiths and Fernando Cervantes (Lincoln, University of Nebraska Press, 1999), 136–62.

Konetzske, Richard. *Colección de documentos para la historia de la formación social de Hispanoamérica* (Madrid, Consejo Superior de Investigaciones Científicas, 1953).

Kuznesof, Elizabeth. "Ethnic and Gender Influences on 'Spanish' Creole Society in Colonial Spanish America," *Colonial Latin American Review* 4:1 (1995), 153–76.

Larson, Brooke. *Cochabamba, 1550–1900: Colonialism and Agrarian Transformation in Bolivia* (Durham, Duke University Press, 1999).

——— and Olivia Harris, eds. *Ethnicity, Markets, and Migration in the Andes: At the Crossroads of History and Anthropology* (Durham, Duke University Press, 1995).

Lavallé, Bernard. *Las Promesas ambiguas: Criollismo colonial en los Andes* (Lima, Pontificia Universidad Católica del Perú, Instituto Riva-Aguero, 1993).

Lavrin, Asunción and Edith Couturier. "Dowries and Wills: A View of Women's Socioeconomic Role in Colonial Guadalajara and Puebla, 1640–1790," *Hispanic American Historical Review* 59:2 (May 1979), 280–304.

Levillier, Roberto. *Don Francisco de Toledo, supremo organizador del Perú* (Buenos Aires, Espasa-Calpa, S.A., 1940–42).

Lewis, Laura. *Hall of Mirrors: Power, Witchcraft, and Caste in Colonial Mexico* (Durham, Duke University Press, 2003).

Lisson Chaves, Emile, ed. *La iglesia de España en el Perú: Sección Primera: Archivo General de Indias* (Sevilla, Editoria Católica Española, 1944).

Lizárraga, Reginaldo de. *Descripción del Perú, Tucumán, Río de la Plata y Chile* (Madrid, Historia 16, 1986).

Lockhart, James. *Spanish Peru* 1532–1560: A Colonial Society (Madison, University of Wisconsin Press, 1972).

———. "Trunk Lines and Feeder Lines: The Spanish Reaction to American Resources," in *Transatlantic Encounters: Europeans and Andeans in the Sixteenth*

Century, ed. Kenneth Andrien and Rolena Adorno (Berkeley, University of California, 1991).

—— and Stuart Schwartz. *Early Latin America. A History of Colonial Spanish America and Brazil* (Cambridge, Cambridge University Press, 1983).

Lohmann Villena, Guillermo. *Los Americanos en las órdenes nobiliarias* (Madrid, Consejo Superior de Investigaciones Científicas "Gonzalo Fernández de Oviedo," 1947).

Lowry, Lynn Brandon. "Forging an Indian Nation: Urban Indians Under Spanish Colonial Control, Lima, Peru 1535–1765," Ph.D. dissertation, University of California at Berkeley, 1991.

Lumbreras, Luis. *The Peoples and Cultures of Ancient Peru* (Washington, DC, Smithsonian Institute, 1974).

MacCormack, Sabine. *Religion in the Andes* (Princeton, Princeton University Press, 1991).

Málaga Medina, Alejandro. "El Virrey Don Francisco de Toledo y la reglamentación del tributo en el virreinato del Perú," *Anuario de Estudios Americanos* XXX (1972).

Mangan, Jane. *Trading Roles: Gender, Ethnicity and the Urban Economy in Potosí, Peru*, 1545–1570 (Durham, Duke University Press, 2005).

Mannarelli, María Emma. *Pecados públicos: La ilegitimidad en Lima, siglo XVII* (Lima, Ediciones Flora Tristán, 1993).

Martínez López, María Elena. "The Spanish Concept of *Limpieza de sangre* and the Emergence of the 'Race / Caste' System in the Viceroyalty of New Spain." Ph.D. dissertation, University of Chicago, 2002.

Matienzo, Juan de. *Gobierno del Perú* [1567], ed. Guillermo Lohmann Villena (Lima, Institut Français d'Etudes Andines, 1967).

Millones, Luis and Moises Lemlij, eds. *En el nombre del Señor: Shamanes, demonios y curanderos del norte del Perú* (Lima: Biblioteca Peruana de Psicoanálisis, 1994).

Mills, Kenneth R. *Idolatry and its Enemies: Colonial Andean Religion and Extirpation, 1640–1750* (Princeton, Princeton University Press, 1997).

Money, Mary. *Los obrajes, el traje y el comercio de ropa en la audiencia de Charcas* (La Paz, Instituto de Estudios Bolivianos, 1983).

Monsalve, Miguel de. *Reducion de todo el Piru* [1604] (photocopy of manuscript in The British Library), John Carter Brown Library, Providence, RI.

Montesinos, Fernando. *Memorias antiguas historiales del Perú* (London, Hakluyt Society, 1920).

Morris, Craig and Donald E. Thompson, *Huánuco Pampa: An Inca City and its Hinterland* (London, Thames and Hudson, 1985).

Murra, John V. "Cloth and its Function in the Inka State," in *Cloth and Human Experience*, ed. Annette B. Weiner and Jane Schneider (Washington, DC: Smithsonian, 1989).

Netherly, Patricia. "Local Level Lords on the North Coast of Peru," Ph.D. dissertation, Cornell University, 1977.

Niles, Susan. "Artist and Empire in Inca and Colonial Textiles," in *To Weave For the Sun: Ancient Andean Textiles*, ed. Rebecca Stone-Miller (Boston, Museum of Fine Arts, 1992), 50–66.

———. *The Shape of Inca History. Narrative and Archaeology in an Andean Empire* (Iowa, University of Iowa Press, 1999).

Noack, Karoline. "Caciques, escribanos y las construcciones de historias: Cajamarca, Perú, siglo XVI," in *Elites indígenas en los Andes: Nobles, caciques y cabildantes bajo el yugo colonial*, ed. David Cahill and Blanca Tovias (Quito: Abya-Yala, 2003), 213–28.

———. "La diversidad cultural de la ciudad colonial: Trujillo del Perú, s. XVI," unpublished paper, 2003.

———. "Hechicería y la negociación de una nueva sociedad urbana: Trujillo del Perú en el siglo XVI," unpublished paper, 2003.

Ortíz, Fernando. *Contrapunteo cubano del tabaco y el azúcar* (Havana, Editoria de Ciencias Sociales, 1983).

Ortíz de Zúñiga, Iñigo. *Visita de la provincia de León de Huánuco en 1562* (Huánuco, Perú, Universidad Nacional Hermilio Valdizán, 1967).

Osorio, Alejandra. "*El callejón de la soledad:* Vectors of Cultural Hybridity in Seventeenth-Century Lima" in *Spiritual Encounters: Interactions Between Christianity and Native Religions in Colonial America*, ed. Nicholas Griffiths and Fernando Cervantes (Lincoln, University of Nebraska Press, 1999), 198–229.

———. "The King in Lima: Simulacra, Ritual, and Rule in Seventeenth-Century Peru," *Hispanic American Historical Review* 84:3 (August 2004), 447–74.

O'Toole, Rachel Sarah. "Inventing Difference: Africans, Indians and the Antecedents of 'Race' in Colonial Peru (1580s–1720s), Ph.D. dissertation, University of North Carolina at Chapel Hill, 2001.

Ots y Capdequí, José María. *Historia del derecho español en América y del derecho indiano* (Madrid, Aguilar S.A., 1967).

Oviedo y Valdés, Gonzalo Fernández. *Corónica de las Yndias y la conquista del Peru. La hystoria general de las Yndias agora nueuamente impressa corregida y emendada.* (Salamanca, Juan de Junta, 1547).

Pagden, Anthony. *The Fall of Natural Man: The American Indian and the Origins of Comparative Ethnology* (Cambridge, Cambridge University Press, 1982).

Parry, John H. *The Age of Reconnaissance: Discovery, Exploration and Settlement 1450 to 1650* (Berkeley, University of California Press, 1981).

Parry, John H. and Robert Keith, *New Iberian World: A Documentary History of the Discovery and Settlement of Latin America to the Early* 17th *Century* (New York, Times Books, 1984).

Paul, Anne. "Paracas Necrópolis Bundle 89: A Description and Discussion of Its Contents," in *Paracas Art and Architecture: Object and Context in South Coastal Peru* (Iowa City, University of Iowa Press, 1991).

Pease G. Y., Franklin. *Curacas, reciprocidad y riqueza* (Lima, Pontificia Universidad Católica del Perú, 1992).

Perry, Mary Elizabeth. *Gender and Disorder in Early Modern Seville* (Princeton, Princeton University Press, 1990).

Phillips Jr., William and Carla Rahn Phillips, "Spain in the Fifteenth Century," in *Transatlantic Encounters: Europeans and Andeans in the Sixteenth Century*, ed. Kenneth Andrien and Rolena Adorno (Berkeley, University of California Press, 1991).

Pizarro, Pedro. *Relación del descubrimiento y conquista del Perú* (Lima, Pontificia Universidad Católica del Perú, 1978).

Polo de Ondegardo, Juan. "Informe del Licenciado Juan Polo de Ondegardo al Licenciado Briviesca de Muñatones sobre la perpetuidad de las encomiendas en el Perú," *Revista Histórica* XIII (1940), 125–96.

Poole, Deborah. *Vision, Race, and Modernity. A Visual Economy of the Andean Image World* (Princeton, Princeton University Press, 1997).

Powers, Karen Vieira. *Andean Journeys: Migration, Ethnogenesis and the State in Colonial Quito* (Albuquerque, University of New Mexico Press, 1995).

———. "The Battle for Bodies and Souls in the Colonial North Andes: Intra-ecclesiastical Struggles and the Politics of Migration," *Hispanic American Historical Review*, Vol. 75:1 (Feb. 1995), 31-56.

———. "A Battle of Wills: Inventing Chiefly Legitimacy in the Colonial North Andes," in *Dead Giveaways: Indigenous Testaments of Colonial Mesoamerica and the Andes*, ed. Susan Kellogg and Matthew Restall (Salt Lake City, University of Utah Press, 1998), 183–214.

———. "Conquering Discourses of 'Sexual Conquest': Of Women, Language, and *Mestizaje*," *Colonial Latin American Review* 11:1 (June 2002), 7–32.

Pratt, Mary Louise, *Imperial Eyes: Travel Writing and Transculturation* (London, Routledge, 1992).

Premo, Bianca. "Minor Offenses: Youth, Crime, and Law in Eighteenth-Century Lima," in Tobias Hecht, ed., *Minor Omissions: Children in Latin American History and Society* (Madison, University of Wisconsin Press, 2002), 114–64.

Presta, Ana María. "Detrás de la mejor dote una encomienda. Hijas y viudas de la primera generación de encomenderos en el mercado matrimonial de Charcas, 1534–1548," *Revista Andes* 8 (1997), 27–46

———. "Portraits of Four Women: Traditional Female Roles and Transgressions in Colonial Elite Families in Charcas, 1550–1600," *Colonial Latin American Review* 9:2 (December 2000), 237–62.

Quiroz, Alfonso. "Reassessing the Role of Credit in Late Colonial Peru: *Censos, Escrituras* and *Imposiciones*," *Hispanic American Historical Review* 74:2 (1994), 193–230.

Ramírez, Susan. *Provincial Patriarchs: Land Tenure and the Economics of Power in Colonial Peru* (Albuquerque, University of New Mexico Press, 1986).

———. "Exchange and Markets in the Sixteenth Century: A View From the North," in *Ethnicity, Markets, and Migration in the Andes: At the Crossroads of History and Anthropology*, ed. Brooke Larson and Olivia Harris (Durham, Duke University Press, 1995), 135–64.

————. *The World Upside Down: Cross-Cultural Contact and Conflict in Sixteenth-Century Peru* (Stanford, Stanford University Press, 1996).

————. "Un mercader . . . es un pescador: reflexiones sobre las relaciones económicas y los múltiples roles de los indios americanos en el Perú del siglo XVI," in *Homenaje a María Rostworowski*, ed. Rafael Varón Gabai and Javier Flores Espinoza (Lima, Instituto de Estudios Peruanos, 1997).

Ramos, Gabriela. "Death, Conversion, and Identity in the Peruvian Andes: Lima and Cuzco, 1532–1670," Ph.D. dissertation, University of Pennsylvania, 2001.

Recopilación de leyes de los Reynos de las Indias. Prólogo por Ramón Menéndez y Pidal. (Madrid, Ediciones Cultura Hispánica, 1973).

Relación de la religión y ritos del Perú hecha por los padres agustinos (Lima, Pontificia Universidad Católica del Perú, 1992).

Remy, Pilar. "La visita a Cajamarca de 1571–2/1578," in *Las visitas a Cajamarca 1571–2/1578*, eds. María Rostworowski and Pilar Remy (Lima: Instituto de Estudios Peruanos, 1992).

Ribeiro, Aileen. *Dress in Eighteenth-Century Europe* (New Haven: Yale University Press, 2002).

Romero, Carlos. "Libro de la visita general del virrey don Francisco de Toledo 1570–1575," *Revista Histórica* VII (1921): 115–216.

————. "Fragmento de una historia de Trujillo," *Revista Histórica* VIII: i–ii (1925), 87–118.

Rostworowski de Diez Canseco, María. "Succession, Cooptation to Kingship, and Royal Incest Among the Inca," *Southwestern Journal of Anthropology* 16:4 (1960), 417–27.

————. *Curacas y sucesiones. Costa norte* (Lima, n.p., 1961).

————. "Algunos comentarios hechos a las ordenanzas del Doctor Cuenca," *Historia y cultura* 9 (1975).

————. *Señoríos indígenas de Lima y Canta* (Lima, Instituto de Estudios Peruanos, 1978).

————. *Doña Francisca Pizarro, una ilustre mestiza, 1534–1598* (Lima, Instituto de Estudios Peruanos, 1989).

————. *Costa peruana prehispánica* (Lima, Instituto de Estudios Peruanos, 1989).

————. "La tasa ordenada por el Licenciado Pedro de la Gasca (1549)," in *Ensayos de historia andina: Elites, etnías, recursos* (Lima, Institute de Estudios Peruanos, 1993).

————. *Ensayos de historia andina: Elites, etnías, recursos.* (Lima, Insituto de Estudios Peruanos, 1993).

————. "La mujer en el Perú prehispánico," Documento de Trabajo No. 72 (Instituto de Estudios Peruanos, 1995).

Rowe, John Howland. "Inca Culture at the Time of the Spanish Conquest," in *Handbook of South American Indians*, vol. 2, ed. Julian Steward (Washington, DC, Smithsonian Institution, 1946).

Sabean, David, *Power in the Blood: Popular Culture and Village Discourse in Early Modern Germany* (New York, Cambridge University Press, 1984).

Saignes, Thierry. *Caciques, Tribute and Migration in the Southern Andes. Indian Society and the* 17th Century Colonial Order (Audiencia de Charcas). (London, Institute of Latin American Studies, 1985).

———. "Indian Migration and Social Change in Seventeenth-Century Charcas," in *Ethnicity, Markets and Migration in the Andes: At the Crossroads of History and Anthropology,* ed. Brooke Larson and Olivia Harris (Durham, Duke University Press, 1995).

Salinas y Córdova, Fray Buenaventura. *Memorial de las historias del nuevo mundo Peru* (Lima, Universidad Mayor de San Marcos, 1957).

Salles-Reese, Verónica. "Las divergencias semióticas y el proceso de mestizaje en el Perú colonial," *Colonial Latin American Review* 5:1 (1996), 55–72.

Salomon, Frank. *Native Lords of Quito in the Age of the Incas: The Political Economy of North Andean Chiefdoms* (Cambridge, Cambridge University Press, 1986).

———. "Indian Women of Early Colonial Quito as Seen Through their Testaments," *Americas* XLIV:3 (January 1988), 325–41.

——— and George Urioste, eds. *The Huarochirí Manuscript* (Austin, University of Texas, 1991).

Santa Cruz Pachacuti Yamqui Salcamayga, Joan de. *Relación de antiguedades deste reyno del Pirú,* ed. Pierre Duviols y César Itier (Cusco, Institut Français d'Etudes Andines y Centro de Estudios Regionales Andinos "Bartolomé de Las Casas," 1993).

Santillán, Hernando de. "Relación del orígen y gobierno de los Incas," in *Biblioteca de Autores Españoles,* tomo 209, ed. Francisco Esteva Barba (Madrid, Atlas, 1968).

Sarabia Viejo, María Justina, ed. *Francisco de Toledo. Disposiciones gubernativas para el virreinato del Perú* (Sevilla, Escuela de Estudios Hispano-Americanos, 1986).

Sarmiento de Gamboa, Pedro. *Histórica Indica* in *Don Francisco de Toledo,* ed. Roberto Levillier (Buenos Aires, Espasa-Calpe S.A., 1942).

Schroeder, Susan, Stephanie Wood, and Robert Haskett, eds., *Indian Women of Early Mexico* (Norman, University of Oklahoma Press, 1997).

Schwartz, Stuart. "Spaniards, *Pardos* and the Missing Mestizos: Identities and Racial Categories in the Early Hispanic Caribbean," *New West Indian Guide* 71:1–2 (1997), 5–19.

———. "Colonial Identities and the *Sociedad de Castas,*" *Colonial Latin American Review* 4:1 (1995), 185–201.

Seed, Patricia. *To Love, Honor and Obey in Colonial Mexico* (Stanford, Stanford University Press, 1988)

Shannon, Timothy J. "Dressing for Success on the Mohawk Frontier: Hendrick, William Johnson, and the Indian Fashion," *William and Mary Quarterly* 53:1 (January 1996), 13–42.

Las Siete Partidas, ed. Robert I. Burns, S.J. (Philadelphia, University of Pennsylvania Press, 2001).

Silverblatt, Irene. *Moon, Sun, and Witches* (Princeton, Princeton University Press, 1987).

———. "Becoming Indian in the Central Andes of Seventeenth-Century Peru," in *After Colonialism. Imperial Histories and Colonial Displacements*, ed. Gyan Prakash (Princeton, Princeton University Press, 1995), 279–98.

———. "Lessons of Gender and Ethnohistory in Mesoamerica," *Ethnohistory* 42:4 (1995): 639–50.

Solórzano y Pereyra, Juan de. *Política indiana* (Madrid, Compañía Ibero Americana de Publicación, 1948).

Spalding, Karen. "Kurakas and commerce: A Chapter in the Evolution of Andean Society," *Hispanic American Historical Review* 53:4 (November 1973), 581–99.

———. "Exploitation as an Economic System: The State and the Extraction of Surplus in Colonial Peru," in *The Inca and Aztec States, 1400–1800*, ed. George Collier, Renato Rosaldo, and John Wirth (New York, Academic Press, 1982).

———. *Huarochirí: An Andean Society Under Inca and Spanish Rule* (Stanford, Stanford University Press, 1984).

Stern, Steve J. *Peru's Indian Peoples and the Challenge of Spanish Conquest: Huamanga to 1640* (Madison, University of Wisconsin Press, 1992).

Suárez, Margarita. *Comercio y fraude en el Perú colonial. Las estrategias mercantiles de un banquero* (Lima: Banco Central de Reserva del Perú y Instituto de Estudios Peruanos, 1995).

———. *Desafíos transatlánticos: Mercaderes, banqueros y el estado en el Perú virreinal, 1600–1700* (Lima, Pontificia Universidad Católica del Perú, Instituto Riva-Agüero, 2001).

Terraciano, Kevin. "Native Expressions of Piety in Mixtec Testaments," in Susan Kellogg and Matthew Restall, eds., *Dead Giveaways: Indigenous Testaments of Colonial Mesoamerica and the Andes* (Salt Lake City: University of Utah Press, 1998), 115–40.

Teruel, Ana and Raquel Gil Montero, "Trabajo familiar y producción de textiles en las tierras altas de la provincia de Jujuy: mediados del siglo XIX," *Revista Andina* 14:1 (julio 1996), 197–222.

Torres de Mendoza, Luis. *Colección de documentos inéditos relativos al descubrimiento, conquista y organización de las antiguas posesiones españolas de América y Oceanía*, (Madrid, n.p., 1867).

Trelles Aréstegui, Efraín. *Lucas Martínez Vegazo: Funcionamiento de una encomienda peruana inicial* (Lima, Pontificia Universidad Católica, 1991)

Twinam, Ann. *Public Lives, Private Secrets: Gender, Honor, Sexuality, and Illegitimacy in Colonial Spanish America* (Stanford, Stanford University Press, 1999).

van Deusen, Nancy. *Between the Sacred and the Worldly* (Stanford, Stanford University Press, 2001).

Vanstan, Ina. "Did Inca Weavers Use an Upright Loom?," In *The Junius B. Bird Pre-Columbian Textile Conference*, ed. A. P. Rowe, E. Benson, and A. Schaffer (Washington, DC, The Textile Museum, 1979).

Varón Gabai, Rafael. *Curacas y encomenderos: Acomodamiento nativo en Huaraz, siglos XVI–XVII* (Lima, Villanueva, 1980).

Vergara Ormeño, Teresa. "Migración y trabajo femenino a principios del siglo XVII: el caso de las indias de Lima," *Histórica* XXI:1 (1997), 135–57.

Villanueva, Margaret. "From Calpixqui to Corregidor: Appropriation of Women's Cotton Textile Production in Early Colonial Mexico," *Latin American Perspectives* 12:1 (Winter 1985), 17–40.

Wachtel, Nathan. *The Vision of the Vanquished: The Spanish Conquest of Peru through Indian Eyes,* 1530–1570 (New York, Barnes and Noble Books, 1977).

Wightman, Ann. *Indigenous Migration and Social Change, The Forasteros of Cuzco,* 1570–1720 (Durham, Duke University Press, 1990).

Williams, Raymond. *Marxism and Literature* (Oxford, Oxford University Press, 1977).

Young, Robert. *Colonial Desire: Hybridity, In Theory, Culture and Race* (London, Routledge, 1995).

Zárate, Agustín de. *Historia del descrubrimiento y conquista del Perú* (Lima, Pontificia Universidad Católica del Perú, 1995).

Zevallos Quiñones, Jorge. "La ropa tributo de las encomiendas trujillanas en el siglo XVI," *Historia y cultura* 7 (1973), 10727.

———. *Los cacicazgos de Lambayeque* (Trujillo, Gráfica Cuatro, 1989).

———. *Los cacicazgos de Trujillo* (Trujillo, Fundación Alfredo Pinillos Goicochea, 1992).

———. *Los fundadores y primeros pobladores de Trujillo del Perú* (Trujillo, Fundación Alfredo Pinillos Goicochea, 1996).

Zulawski, Ann. "Social Differentiation, Gender, and Ethnicity: Urban Indian Women in Colonial Bolivia, 1640–1755," *Latin American Research Review* XXV:2 (1990), 93–114.

———. *They Eat from Their Labor: Work and Social Change in Colonial Bolivia* (Pittsburgh, University of Pittsburgh Press, 1995).

Index

Carua Sacsa, María, 112
Carua Sisue, Madalena, 143
Cassanosan, Diego, 97–98
Castañeda, Juan, 116
Castañeda Bustamante, Juan de, 68–69
castas. *See* ethnicity, castas
Castro, Alonso de, 82
Castro, Juan de, 84
Castro, Lic. Antonio de, 108
Catacaos, 158, 163
Catholic Church, 168, 176, 189, 191, 220n49;
    conversion, 7, 10, 11, 52, 65, 187, 188, 190,
    192, 210n3, 217n68; and credit, 3, 6–7;
    policy on divorce, 197n4; and wills, 61,
    62, 95–96, 97, 103, 105, 110–11, 112, 113,
    114–15, 190. *See also* clergy; cofradías;
    convents; religion
cattle raising, 30
Cayn, María, 86
Centeno, Juana, 90
Centeno, Leonor, 90
Chachapoyas, 18, 77–78, 141
Chacón, Luis, 49
Chacón de Lara, Juan, 58
Chamo Chumbi, Carlos, 90
Chañana Cury Coca, 162
Chancay, 18
Chan Chan, 13
Chani, Francisca, 84
chaplaincy/capellanía, 110, 111, 113,
    114, 181
Charcas, 41, 64
Charney, Paul, 213n63
Chérrepe, 63
Chicama, 42, 82
chicha production and sale, 1, 62, 72–74,
    77, 91, 140, 143, 144, 149–51, 207n38;
    role of slaves in, 89, 154
Chiclayo, 55–56, 108, 151
Chilca, Ysavel, 153
Chilean Indian slaves, 209n82
Chimbay, Catalina, 66
Chimbo, Juana, 96, 210n5
Chimú, 77
Chimú kingdom, 13, 163, 164, 177, 219n14
China: cloth from, 1, 50
Chincha, 180, 208n61
Chinmis, Juan, 54
Chucuito, 27, 32, 33, 35, 37, 51, 52, 55

Chumbi, Catalina, 63, 77
Chumbi, Juana, 116–17
Chumbi, Lucía, 108
Chumbi, Quico, 168
Chumbi, Xancol, 168
Chumbi Guaman, María, 176–78
Chunbe, Francisca, 103
Chuqui, María, 118–19
Cieza de León, Pedro de, 163
Ciguatán, 161
Cinto, 45–46
cities: and creolization, 21–22; design of,
    15, 199n31; indigenous migration to,
    11–13, 15–16, 17, 19, 21–22, 31, 44, 58, 62,
    70, 80, 84, 123, 135, 140, 146, 151, 188–90,
    193, 199n37; indios criollos in, 21–22,
    147–48, 151, 190, 191, 217n68; links to
    rural areas, 5, 29, 58, 67–68, 73, 77–78,
    80, 84, 95–96, 132, 144, 149, 179, 188, 191,
    207n27; as multiethnic, 8, 12–13, 15–17,
    81–82; occupations in, 70–76; plazas in,
    12, 15, 70, 75, 81, 89, 91, 145; traza of, 81,
    82, 86
ciudadanos, 17, 200n44
clergy, 15, 17, 24, 134, 138; chaplaincy, 110,
    111, 113, 114, 181; and indigenous cloth
    production, 30–31, 37–38, 45, 52, 56, 57;
    Jesuits, 84, 95, 116, 117, 151, 179; and
    real estate, 84; and wills, 23, 100, 114,
    117, 120, 213n62
cloth, types of: awasca, 35, 37, 70, 133,
    145, 146; bayeta, 1, 133, 147, 152; black
    satin/veinticuatreño paño, 130; bro-
    cade, 124, 205n78; cotton, 2, 29, 35, 38,
    43, 46, 49, 51, 54, 57, 64, 74, 91, 125, 131,
    137, 139, 141, 143, 144–45, 151, 152, 153;
    cumbi/cumbe, 33, 37, 57, 70, 91, 123,
    131, 132, 133, 137, 141, 142, 143, 144,
    145, 146, 147, 152, 155; damask, 1, 136,
    139, 143, 145, 146, 149, 205n78; grana,
    153; jersey, 147, 152; linen, 124, 137,
    139, 141, 145; paño, 64, 89, 130, 133,
    136, 138, 139, 141, 142, 143, 146, 147,
    149, 152, 153, 155; perpetuán, 150, 152;
    raso, 150; ropa de la tierra, 2, 29, 43–50,
    59, 138, 147, 151–52, 152, 217n83; ruán,
    64, 70, 124, 130, 136, 138, 139, 141, 142,
    145, 146, 147, 149, 150, 155, 205n78;
    satin, 151; serge

mercedes, 80–81

merchants, 9, 15, 17, 24, 30–31, 66–67, 89; in cloth, 27, 29, 42, 45, 47–49, 50, 51, 51–52, 54, 56, 58, 59, 125, 202n8; and encomienda system, 42, 44, 45, 47–49, 50, 56, 57; relations with caciques, 136, 139; Spaniards among, 10, 33, 37, 70, 74, 108, 136, 202n8; in Trujillo, 42, 49, 90

mercury, 11

Mesocoñera, Diego, 158

mestizos: clothing of, 2, 121–22, 134, 138, 152–55, 156, 184; Crown policy regarding, 106; Garcilaso de la Vega, 42, 136, 137; identity of, 105–9, 121–22, 132–33, 134–35, 138, 152–55, 156, 184, 192, 193, 201n57, 214n2, 215n37; Francisca Pizarro, 199n36, 220n42; in Trujillo, 16, 18, 67, 68, 74

Mexia, Jordana, 173–74

Mexico/New Spain, 11, 50, 80, 104, 136, 139, 150, 179, 197n6, 199n33; Mexico City, 8, 212nn33,39; Oaxaca, 206n4; women weavers in, 203n29

midwifery, 25, 74

migration, indigenous, 11–13, 31, 80, 123, 135, 188–90, 193, 199n37; and domestic service, 17, 24, 63–70, 93, 146; to evade tribute, 44, 58; by mitayos, 13, 15, 16, 63, 78, 188; Trujillo vs. Lima regarding, 13, 15–16, 19, 62, 84, 92–93, 140; women vs. men regarding, 17, 62, 63, 76

Mincha, María Josepha, 178

mining, 11, 24, 28, 30, 31, 43, 49, 52, 58, 59, 75

Miranda, Pedro de, 73, 102

mita: in encomienda system, 11, 13, 16, 28, 31, 43, 49, 63, 78, 87, 151, 169, 175, 178, 198n27, 209n84; in Inca Empire, 11, 28, 43, 44, 187, 198n27

Mixtec-language, 206n4

Moche culture, 33, 35

Mochumi, 178

Monacuyo, Hernando, 84

Monsalve, Miguel de, 64

Montenegro, Lucía de, 205n88

Montenegro, Ysabel de, 66

Montero, Raquel Gil, 222n4

Montesinos, Fernando, 39

Montiel, Alonso de, 63

Mora, Alonso de, 179

Mora, Florencia de, 46, 68, 173

Mora, Juan de, 42

Mora, Pedro de, 136, 215n37

Mora Caxahuamán, María de, 179

Motape River, 164

mulattos. *See* ethnicity, mulattos

Nahua Indians, 80, 212nn41,43; Nahuatl, 104, 165

naming patterns, 108–9, 119

Nariqualá, cacicazgo of, 158–61, 176, 185

"natural" children, 104, 105, 182–83

Nieva, Conde de, 43, 169–70

Nieves, María de las, 106

Niles, Susan, 214n8

Niño Jesús, 117

notaries, 99, 103, 134, 141, 191; and contracts, 46, 49; and sales of property, 98; and wills, 1, 4–5, 9, 19, 22, 23, 61–62, 100, 110, 114, 120, 153

Nuestra Señora de Copacabana, 117

nuns, 6–7, 16

O, María de la, 105–6

obrajes, 37, 50, 138, 141, 147, 152, 154, 155

Oja Guaman, Pedro, 177

Oliva y de los Santos, María de la, 108

Ordem, Lic. Cristóbol, 79

Ortíz, Alonso, 65

Ortíz, Fernando, 20

Osorno, Luisa de, 84

Osorno, Melchior de, 47, 205n85

Otusco, 180

Oviedo y Valdés, Gonzalo Fernández: *Corónica de las Yndias y la conquista del Peru*, 161

Pachacamac, 13, 150

Pacho, Ysabel, 51, 205n85

Pácora, 46

Padilla, Ysabel de, 75

Palomino, Ysabel, 173

Panas Payco, Juan, 88

Panpa Guanca, Diego, 144

parcialidades, 37

Parry, J. H., 130

rural communities, 115, 217n68; links to
cities, 5, 29, 58, 67–68, 73, 77–78, 80, 84,
95–96, 132, 144, 149, 179, 188, 191,
207n27; migration from, 11–13, 15–16,
19, 24, 29, 31, 44, 55, 58, 62, 70, 80, 84,
92–93, 123, 135, 140, 151, 188–90, 193,
199n37; women in, 4, 25, 27–28, 54–55,
58, 202n9
Ruray, Francisca, 182, 183, 184

Sacsa Nurma, Catalina, 149
Saignes, Thierry, 207n27
Salinas y Córdova, Buenaventura de, 70,
200n38
Salles Reese, Verónica, 213n47
Saña, 49, 58–59, 82, 108
San Antonio de Padua, 114
Sánchez, Francisco, 114
Sánchez Cortés, Francisco, 102
San Juan de Coyata, 181
San Pedro de Lloco, 45, 53, 54
San Pedro de Mama, 71
Santa, 88, 113
Santa Cruz Pachachuti Yamqui
Salcamaygua, Joan de, 162
Santa Eulalia, 73
Santa María de la Parilla, 205n78
Santiago de Huamán, 176
Santiago de Miraflores de Saña, 17
Santillán, Hernando de, 166
Santísimo Sacramento, 114
Sarmiento de Gamboa, Pedro, 162
Schroeder, Susan, 197n6
shoemakers, 16
silver, 11, 15, 46, 58, 133; tribute paid in,
44, 45, 53, 54–55, 217n83
Silverblatt, Irene, 96, 197n7, 214n5; *Moon,
Sun, and Witches*, 4, 5, 218n12
silversmiths, 16, 19, 30, 142
slaves. *See* Africans, enslaved
social classes: and clothing, 21, 38, 39–42,
94, 122, 124, 128, 132–34, 135, 136–38,
154–57; as fluid, 2, 3, 9, 59, 123, 186, 187;
social mobility, 3, 5, 7, 62, 66–68, 69–70,
74, 78, 81–82, 86–87, 92–94, 124–25, 145,
154; social status/calidad, 105, 108, 123,
124–25, 128, 135, 136–37, 155–56; vecinos, 13, 15, 16, 17, 18, 82, 86, 94, 131,
159, 191, 200nn41,44
Socola, Isabel, 159

Solano, Juan, 85
solares, 15, 88; indigenous ownership of,
16, 18, 66, 67, 81, 82–83, 85, 86, 94, 98,
114, 117, 135, 143, 151–52, 171, 190, 191
Solórzano y Pereyra, Juan de, 174–75
Spalding, Karen, 29, 43, 51, 205n84
Spanish Crown: crusades of, 93; Ferdinand II, 124–25, 130; Philip II, 124, 199;
policies on cities, 13, 199n33; policies on
clothing, 41, 124–25, 130, 138; policies
on cofradías, 116; policies on credit, 136;
policies on ethnicity, 106, 191, 192;
policies on illegitimate children, 105;
policies on marriage, 13, 106; policies on
silver and gold, 11; policies on tribute,
9, 37–38, 44–45, 50–51, 53, 57, 87, 134–35,
202n10; policies regarding cacicazgos,
169–71, 174–78, 188; policies regarding
encomenderos, 12, 44–45, 138, 172–73,
174; policies regarding land ownership,
80–81; policy on indigenous nobility,
221n57; Two Republics policy, 9–13,
169–71
Spanish language, 21, 96, 135, 148, 191
Spanish law: regarding cacicazgo succession, 174–76, 181–85, 190; regarding
children born outside of wedlock,
183–85; regarding clothing, 124–25, 154;
regarding credit, 136, 215n37; regarding
encomiendas, 173–74, 220n43; indigenous use of, 3, 7, 11, 20, 24, 48, 51, 65,
68–69, 96, 118–19, 158–61, 166, 168, 174,
180–85, 189, 190, 210n5; juicio de residencia, 53, 55–56; juzgado de bienes de
difuntos, 97; Laws of Burgos, 138; *Leyes
de Toro*, 98; regarding marriage, 3;
regarding men, 32–33, 94, 98–99, 104,
189–90; New Laws of 1542, 220n43;
Nuevo recopilación de las leyes de Castillas,
98; *Política indiana*, 174–76; regarding
primogeniture (mayorazgo), 172–73,
175; regarding property, 72, 80–81,
83–84, 87, 88, 93, 94, 97–105, 172–73, 175;
pruebas de hidalguía, 176; pruebas de
limpieza de sangre, 176; *Recopilación de
leyes de los Reynos de las Indias*, 97; relationship to use and custom (uso y
costumbre), 158–59, 160, 169–71, 176,
182, 185; relationship to wills, 95–98,
99–103, 111, 115; *Siete Partidas*, 98, 124;